Private Work
and
Public Causes

Private Work and Public Causes

A Personal Record 1881-1978

by

Sir George Schuster

K.C.S.I., K.C.M.G., C.B.E., M.C.

with a Foreword by
Right Rev. Launcelot Fleming, K.C.V.O., D.D.

1979
COWBRIDGE
D. BROWN AND SONS

First Published November, 1979

© Sir George Schuster

ISBN 0 905928 03 2

Designed and printed in Wales by
D. Brown & Sons Limited, Cowbridge and Bridgend
Glamorgan

Contents

		Page
	List of Illustrations	ix
	Foreword by Bishop Launcelot Fleming	xi
	Author's Preface and Acknowledgements	xv
I	MY EARLY LIFE, 1881-1914	1

My family's German background — schooldays at
Charterhouse — 'Greats' at Oxford — Aristotle's conception
of happiness — country sports — the Chambers of R. J.
Parker — entry into business — marriage to Gwendolen Parker
— Liberal Parliamentary candidate.

| II | THE FIRST WORLD WAR | 12 |

The Oxford Yeomanry — Winston Churchill joins the regiment
— staff work with Alan Brooke — we settle in Oxfordshire —
the invitation from North Russia.

| III | NORTH RUSSIA, 1919 | 16 |

The origins of the Allied Intervention — arrival at Murmansk
— problems of administration and finance — the White
Russian Authorities — currency difficulties — the Governor —
the polyglot forces — the Serbs — the Finns — planned
Bolshevik uprising — growing disillusionment — training
Russian troops — continuing difficulties — the Karelian
regiment — preparations for withdrawal — discussions with
Russian Officers — the final offensive and evacuation.

| IV | RETURN TO CIVIL LIFE, 1919-1922 | 35 |

Training as a schoolteacher — the economic survey of the
'Succession States' — the Finance Committee of the League of
Nations — on the fringes of the Labour Party — appointment
to the Sudan as Financial Secretary.

| V | THE SUDAN, 1922-27 | 39 |

The Anglo-Egyptian Condominium — the 1924 crisis —
Zaghlul in Egypt — discussions with Ramsay MacDonald —
the assassination of the Governor-General — Allenby's
ultimatum — the Egyptian evacuation from the Sudan — the
financial consequences — my work as Financial Secretary —
The Gezira Irrigation Scheme — negotiations with the Sudan
Plantations Syndicate — relations with King Fuad and Sir
George Lloyd — the character of the Sudan Political Service —
disagreement with Sir Geoffrey Archer over relations with the
Mahdi — Archer's resignation — accumulating tasks.

Contents

		Page
VI	THE HILTON-YOUNG COMMISSION, 1928	61

The establishment of the Commission — my preliminary
thoughts — arrival at Entebbe — Sir Edward Grigg — my view
of the Commission's tasks — visits to Kikuyu reserves —
discussions with settler leaders — Tanganyika and Sir Donald
Cameron — confrontation with settlers — differences of
opinion among the Commission's members — Oldham changes
his views — Nyasaland and Northern Rhodesia — settler rule
in Southern Rhodesia — discussions in South Africa — need
for a coordinated race relations policy for Colonial Africa —
our Majority Report and the Chairman's Minority Report.

VII   ADVISING ON COLONIAL FINANCIAL   83
AND ECONOMIC POLICY

The East African Loans Committee — the call for a coordinated development policy — the Zambesi Bridge —
discussions with Leo Amery — Treasury meanness.

VIII   INDIA, 1928-1934   90

Not Whitehall's servant — interview with Birkenhead —
dispute over capitation payments — the rupee ratio — Lord
Irwin — the responsibilities of the Finance Member — Motilal
Nehru and my first Budget — bomb incident of 1929 — Public
Safety legislation — the Dominion Status declaration —
confrontation with Birkenhead — dispute over cotton duties —
Civil Disobedience campaign 1930 — the decision to arrest
Gandhi — preparations for the Round Table Conference — my
approach to MacDonald — the Irwin-Gandhi pact —
agreement with Gandhi on salt duties — 1931 currency crisis —
our threat to resign and the Cabinet's appeal — the Emergency
Budget — visits of Gandhi and J. Nehru — Lord Willingdon as
Viceroy — the Ottawa Conference — the Reserve Bank Bill —
retrenchment during the depression.

IX   BUSINESS AND POLITICS, 1934-1945   126

Work for Allied Suppliers — the Shop Assistant's Union —
visits to the U.S.A. — 'Welfare States' vs 'Power States' —
Walsall By-Election in the aftermath of Munich — the contrast
between Chamberlain and Churchill — collaboration with
Keynes on post-war planning — the fall of Chamberlain — the
Home Guard — tank and aircraft production — letter from
Nehru — the war-time House of Commons — defeat in 1945
Election.

X   HUMAN RELATIONS IN INDUSTRY, 1945-52   140

The Cotton Industry Working Party — management
recruitment and training — The Committee for Industrial
Productivity — The Human Factors Panel — The Medical
Research Council — management's failure to co-operate —
Beckley Lecture on 'Christianity and Human Relations in
Industry' — the example of Stafford Cripps.

Page

XI   A VARIETY OF TASKS, 1950-1963   150

   (i)   The Oxford Regional Hospital Board : the administration — the common spirit of service — bureaucratic growth in recent years.

   (ii) Malta and Dom Mintoff : 1950 visit — a broker between Mintoff and Lennox Boyd — 1956 visit — continuing contacts.

   (iii) India Again : 1953 visit — the priorities for development — Nehru in government.

   (iv) Oxfordshire County Council : progressive initiatives and budgetary control.

   (v) Voluntary Service Overseas : reorganisation — my work as Hon. Treasurer.

XII   THE ATLANTIC COLLEGE   167

Kurt Hahn's aims — financial crisis — securing government and private support — the educational experiment — Lord Mountbatten and international development — achievement under two Headmasters — the College in 1978 — my own thankfulness.

Index   180

Illustrations

		Frontispiece
		Page
1.	One of my many sketches of my father	3
2.	One of the decorated envelopes I sent my mother	6
3.	Report of our wedding in *The Queen*	9
4.	Electioneering in North Cumberland	11
5.	A wartime portrait	14
6.	The author with General Maynard and colleagues	19
7/8.	Some means of winter transport	21
9.	Murmansk after the thaw	24
10.	White Finnish deserters under escort	29
11.	Polyglot lunch party with the Lake Flotilla	30
12.	One of the vulnerable railway bridges	33
13.	Tenants bagging cotton in the Gezira	48
14.	The Sennar Dam across the Blue Nile (1925)	51
15.	The Kassala Railway built in the 1920s	51
16.	With Nubians in the Southern Sudan	53
17.	The Government of the Sudan in 1926	56
18.	My family with trophies in our Khartoum garden	59
19.	(a) Sir Edward Hilton Young	64
	(b) Leo Amery	64
20.	On my East African journey	88
21.	The Viceroy, Lord Irwin, and his Council at Simla, 19:	94
22.	In court dress	98
23.	Relaxing at our camp at Naldera	101
24.	On the North West Frontier	103
25.	Contemporary sketch of Gandhi from my notepad	111
26.	In an official rickshaw at Simla	113
27.	Lady Schuster and Mr Gandhi at tea	116
28.	Lord and Lady Willingdon in 1933	118
29.	With Henry Strakosch on *SS Bremen* crossing to the Ottawa Conference, 1932	120

30. 'The Reserve Bank Special'   123
31. Election Meeting in Walsall, November 1938   130
32. Arrival at the House of Commons with my mother and my
     wife   132
33. One of many factory visits in the 1940s   145
34. With the Minister of Health, Enoch Powell, at Nether
     Worton, May 1961   152
35. Presenting trophies at the Paraplegic Olympics   154
36. With Dom Mintoff in Malta, 1956   158
37. With Moraji Desai, then Chief Minister of Bombay State, in
     India in 1953   161
38. Meeting of the Heythrop Hounds at Nether Worton   163
39. Laying the foundation stone of the Schuster Science Building   172
40. In discussion with staff and students, 1973   175
41. 90th Birthday Party at St. Donat's, 1971   177
42. At St. Donat's in the 1970s   179
43. Diamond Wedding   184

Maps

North Russia in 1919   17
East and Central Africa in 1928   68

Foreword

by BISHOP LAUNCELOT FLEMING, K.C.V.O., D.D.

YOU HAVE only to meet George Schuster to realise that you are in the presence of a man with an exceptional and penetrating personality. In his book he is characteristically modest and reticent about himself, as indeed he is about his wife Gwen, who has been his constant and devoted support throughout their long married life. Given a little reflection, however, the reader will soon appreciate that no man could have had such a strong and effective influence over so wide a variety of fields, or been the close and trusted friend of so many leading figures during his long life, without unusual personal qualities—and this indeed is the case. Through all the years the evidence suggests that, to a remarkable degree, he combined extraordinary charm and generosity with outstanding clarity of mind and sense of purpose, and was always ready with a warm response to idealism and sincerity in others.

As he himself confesses, he had too independent a temperament to find satisfaction as a party politician, but those responsible for the administration of projects, large and small, always placed great faith in his judgment. In the currency crisis of 1931 the Viceroy of India and his entire Council were ready to resign with him in defiance of the British Government. In the mid 1960's this octogenarian through his personality and sheer force of argument carried such conviction that he enabled the survival and the long term prosperity of the Atlantic College.

What many must find remarkable about this story is, in the first place, the length of George Schuster's working life—there can be few alive today who had graduated and were already engaged in professional life before the outbreak of the First World War—and secondly, the great variety of fields in which he got involved. What is it that has enabled him to be so fruitfully active over so long a period? This must partly be due to his strong physique and good health, linked to the serenity of his home life. I have already mentioned the support which he has been given throughout his life by his wife Gwen. Indeed, he accepted many of his special tasks only on the condition that she should accompany him. Daughter of the first Lord Parker of Waddington, Gwen Schuster is herself a charming, intelligent and undaunted personality, a delightful companion and a gracious hostess. They acquired Nether Worton House, an attractive Manor in North Oxfordshire, as long ago as 1919 and still live there. Gwen Schuster made this into a lovely home. She was also an intrepid motorist and must have driven her husband many thousands of miles in their formidable Bentley—at considerable speed, with plenty of incident, but happily without accident. Fortunately Sir George's nerves are made of firmer stuff than many of those who were offered lifts in their car.

Another factor contributing to the fruitfulness of George Schuster's work in so wide a range of activity is the constancy of his thought for the public interest and, in decades of rapid change throughout the world, his concern for the future—to which must be added the pungency of his thought, so effectively combined with a practical outlook. Though gifted with the ability to take a long view, he has always been swift in indicating the immediate priorities. The freshness and independence of his judgement have always given his advice a special value.

Through all the variety of tasks which he undertook, some threads can be discerned.

First I would name his humane liberal values and the emphasis he placed on the social implications of the Christian Gospel. This can be illustrated by the character of his Beckley Lecture on 'Christianity and Human Relations in Industry', excerpts from which he has quoted in this book, and by his friendship with William Temple, Stafford Cripps and Kurt Hahn.

Then, secondly, throughout his working life he has shown a readiness to respond to developing political aspirations, as witness: his links with the Labour party from 1919 onwards, although in no way a party political socialist himself; his conciliatory response to Indian nationalism and the good relationship he had with the Nehrus, father and son, and with Mahatma Gandhi; his readiness to appreciate the strengths of Dom Mintoff whose confidence and friendship he won, without being blind to his later weaknesses; and his lead during the last few years in getting the United World College Movement to respond positively and imaginatively to the challenge of the Third World.

I would also regard far-sightedness as a further thread in Sir George's outlook. There was an instance of this quite early in his life in his appreciation, at the time, of the likely consequences of the anti-Bolshevik intervention in Russia. Some years later in 1939 he was already planning with Maynard Keynes how to avoid a repetition of the post 1919 tragedy of economic collapse. But perhaps the most significant instances of the need he saw for a long term vision were in regard to colonial and industrial development. Already in the 1920s he was calling for a co-ordinated programme of government grants and loans for economic development in the colonial world. He clearly saw the need for a long term plan by which the peoples of the colonial territories could progressively grow in economic, social and political responsibility—and it was this vision which led him on the Hilton Young Commission to resist a further spread of white settler control in East and Central Africa. He took an equally significant lead in the industrial field in stressing the need for better human relations based on a sense of fulfilment and community for all involved in an enterprise. His Human Factors Panel of the Committee on Industrial Productivity provided a series of Reports, the value of which was recognised by, among others, Left-Wing members of the Labour Party. On all these issues his own words written at the time still have a remarkable relevance today.

Yet another thread in George Schuster's life and work was his sense of public service. There was always present in his mind a very strong sense of Trusteeship in matters affecting the British Empire. Sir George Schuster never stopped working and using his own talents in the service of others. It was particularly appropriate therefore that he should have been so closely associated with Voluntary Service Overseas and Atlantic College which seek to cultivate and harness such a sense of service in the young.

Linked with his sense of public service was his sense of community, the importance of which he mentions several times in this book, particularly in connection with the comradeship he found in the Oxfordshire Yeomanry, the Sudan Service, the Oxford Regional Hospital Board and the Atlantic College.

These then, as I see it, are some of the threads which are most evident in Sir George Schuster's life: his humane liberal values, his readiness to respond to developing political aspirations, his far-sightedness, his sense of public service and his sense of community; and these are among the factors which have enabled him to make an instinctive appeal to the young.

I had the good fortune to be present at the dinner at St. Donat's Castle to mark the retirement of Sir George Schuster from the Chairmanship of the Governing Body of the United World College of the Atlantic. Reference is made to this occasion in the last chapter of this book. It is rather out of the ordinary for anyone in his 94th year to be retiring from the Chairmanship of any institution, let alone an International College of 16-19 year old students. After dinner the Headmaster, Governors, staff and students were held spellbound by Sir George's speech, delivered without a note in a clear strong voice. It was a deeply moving exposition of the faith and vision he saw in the process of fulfilment in this, the first of the United World Colleges to be founded. He saw the world as the heritage of all its peoples, he saw its future as dependent on the attitudes, ideals and leadership of the younger generation, he saw these factors being realised in this College for which he had worked with such vigour and imagination. His speech, simple and straightforward in its wording, was an expression of so much of the faith and purpose that had guided his own life. Although 94 years of age, what he said and the way in which he said it had a freshness about it which clearly appealed to the more youthful members of his audience—albeit he spoke with the wisdom and authority of an elder statesman. At the end of that speech the applause was more in the nature of an ovation. It was a striking tribute of affection, respect and gratitude to the author of this book.

April 1979   *Launcelot Fleming*

Author's Preface and Acknowledgements

THE RABBI ZUSYA once remarked 'In the coming world they will not ask me 'Why were you not Moses?' They will ask me 'Why were you not Zusya?' Looking back over my long life I can truly say that in every line of activity which chance has opened to me, I have tried 'to be George Schuster'—to concentrate on this activity as an end in itself. I have taken each chance or challenge as it came. I have never envisaged any sort of plan for a career. To compare my minor background role with that of a major public figure, I have never had thoughts like those of Harold Macmillan who has recorded how in his early boyhood, after studying British political history, he thought of the office of Prime Minister as the greatest prize to be won in life and asked himself 'Why shouldn't I have a go at that?'

I will record one other introductory thought. I might have called this book 'The Life's Work of an Amateur' using the last word in its double sense. I have had no training as a 'professional' for any job which I have undertaken. It has been my belief that the essential need for one who is responsible for the general direction of an enterprise is the capacity for logical thought. I have had a profound belief in the educational value of the school of 'Greats' at Oxford and in my own experience I have found that the legal training required for being called to the Bar has added value to my Oxford education. My use of the word 'amateur' has had a second connotation. I have in a special way loved my work in all the main activities of my life. It is fair to say that I have loved it because, as I shall explain later, I see the sense of work well done as the essential element in the foundation for true happiness in this world.

In telling the story of my very long and varied life it was difficult to decide what to include and what to omit. This book essentially describes my involvement in public affairs and is not intended to be a record of my family life.

I HAVE TO acknowledge debts of gratitude to many friends who have helped me in the production of this book, but there is one debt the significance of which overshadows all the rest. Without the interest, sympathy and devoted hard work of my friend, Colin Reid, a valued senior member of the teaching staff of Atlantic College, the book could not have been produced at all. I was already in my 96th year when I set myself to the task of writing it. I then found that I had many memories, some files of correspondence with my wife recording the accomplishment of tasks in the rare periods when I was separated from her, and three large packing cases of papers and records which had been hastily evacuated from London just before our house there was destroyed by a German air raid in 1941. I then had the supreme good fortune of finding in Colin Reid a helper who, as an historian, was interested in my records and was happy to devote his spare time to going through papers, selecting important passages and providing me with a pattern for the arrangement of each chapter. My personal need for such help increased when, after a year's work my eyesight failed and I found myself unable to read any papers. As a result of Colin Reid's friendship, interest and intelligent work the whole exercise of producing this book has been an experience of stimulating value. As one sign of my appreciation I have made him my literary executor and left him custody of all my papers.

Apart from this very special debt I must record that I owe much to the encouragement and advice of other friends. I am specially grateful to Launcelot Fleming not only for having agreed to write a foreword to the book but also for his interest and encouragement as he has read through the chapters of my draft.

I have received much help also from individual friends who have worked with me in the series of adventures of my life. Amongst these the first to mention is George Bredin, a former member of the Sudan Political Service. His friendship and help have had a very special value for me since they have reminded me of what I look back upon as one of the two most rewarding episodes of my life—my work in the Sudan and my work for the Atlantic College. It has been an inspiring experience to be brought back again into the comradeship of the Sudan Political Service.

Passing on to other episodes I have had practical help from friends and fellow workers on the Oxford Regional Hospital Board—Tony Oddie, George Watts and Charles Poole; with my chapter on the Oxfordshire County Council from Gerald Burkitt who was Clerk to the Council during my years of membership; and with my chapter on Atlantic College from David Sutcliffe and Michael Schweitzer.

Taking account of the limitations of my personal capacities the completion and typing of the draft has been a specially difficult task which could not have been accomplished without the unfailing help of my supremely efficient personal secretary, Mary Cadman.

In conclusion I must add an acknowledgement of gratitude which is of overriding importance. A special source of inspiration to me in completing my task has been the interest shown by the whole body of those concerned with the operation of the Atlantic College: members of the Governing Body, teaching staff, students and ex-students—an interest which has now found practical expression in a form which has given me deep satisfaction. The closing passage of this note of acknowledgements must be to record my profound gratitude to the Chairman and Governing Body of the Atlantic College for their generous offer to undertake the responsibility for the final printing and publication of this book.

Nether Worton, December 1978   *George Schuster*

CHAPTER I

My Early Life, 1881-1914

I WAS BORN in a house in Hampstead on 25th April 1881. My family had first settled in England in 1808 in order to get away from Germany under Napoleon, but my father's branch had stayed on in Frankfurt to manage the family business of merchant bankers. This branch came finally to settle in England in 1866 in order to escape from Frankfurt after its occupation by the Prussians. At this date my father, Ernest, the eldest of the family, was sixteen. His two younger brothers were Felix and Arthur. Together the three brothers were a notable family. My father himself became a distinguished K.C. specialising in International Law. Felix was one of the leading figures in the City in his time and played a great part in the series of banking amalgamations which led to the formation of the 'Big Five'. He also acted as financial adviser to Mr. Asquith when the Liberal Government came into power in 1905, his services being recognised with a baronetcy. Arthur took up Science, working first at Manchester University, and then as Fellow and Secretary of the Royal Society.

My father's family was of Jewish race but had adopted the Christian religious faith under the influence of his mother who, herself Jewish, had become one of the most devout believers in Christianity whom I have ever known. My mother's family were entirely German without any Jewish connections. Her father, Sir Hermann Weber, became a leading medical consultant in London.

My family background had therefore a distinctive German colouring—not a very good setting for my early years since the prevailing feeling in England at the time was very definitely hostile to Germans. This background had two effects on me. On the one hand I embarked upon my schooldays with a sort of inferiority complex. On the other hand it helped to give me a special appreciation of English character and English ways of life backed by a deep love for the English countryside. These feelings have, throughout my life, had a dominant influence on my outlook. I still retain my faith in this country in spite of the depressing conditions affecting us as I write these words in 1978.

The memory of my early days includes pictures of Christmas family gatherings at the homes of two grandfathers and of a great grandmother who was born in 1799. (I got to know her very well since she lived till I was 13.)

1

I also have a vivid memory of my nurse, the daughter of a Norfolk miller, who cherished a picture of John Bright whom she venerated as the one 'really good man' in public life. Other early memories include drives in the carriage and pair of my medical grandfather on one of which, along the gated road through the fields below Harrow, we chanced at one gateway to meet and exchange words with Mr. Gladstone driving with his wife. He was a familiar character for us in our nursery days, since, at our meals, we were constantly reminded of his practice of chewing every mouthful 24 times, which accounted for his vigour as the 'Grand Old Man'.

At the age of ten I went to a preparatory school—at Stoke House, Stoke Poges (then in rural countryside), adjacent to the church and churchyard which were the setting for Gray's Elegy. My elder brother was already there and owing to our German name I found myself with the nickname of Sausage Minor. Since I had no skill at games to give me any counter-balancing distinction this reinforced my inferiority complex. Looking back, however, I can record that I took all this as it came and I cannot regard these early school years as an unhappy time. Pictures which stand out in my memory are of close boyhood friendships, of walks after Sunday services, and of the Queen's Staghounds running over our playing field with the huntsman jumping the boundary fence.

In 1894 I got a scholarship at Charterhouse. My five years there were a colourless period for my story. Social status in the school depended entirely on skill at football or cricket in which I ranked very low. On the educational side these five years ought to have been much more valuable. As a Scholar I entered halfway up in the range of school classes and I was promoted after only one term in each class until I reached the 'Under-Sixth' and came under the Headmaster, Haig Brown. He was a 'dry as dust grammarian' who made us in the sixth form spend time in learning Hebrew. My general impression is that in my five years at Charterhouse I got practically no true education. There was at that time only one master, T. E. Page, who had an inspiring enthusiasm, mainly concentrated on the Odes of Horace.

Among my contemporaries at Charterhouse the most notable figure was William Beveridge who had specialised in Mathematics but came back to the Classical side in his final term, and, in T. E. Page's words, proved to be the best of us all. He was in those early years an engaging individual enjoying the nickname of 'the Beagle Pup', because of his rather bandy legs.

I must have had some spirit of rebellious adventure in those drab days because on one Wednesday half-holiday afternoon, I got leave for myself and a friend to go bicycling on a bird-nesting expedition and we took the chance to get to Epsom downs to see the Derby—won that year by the Duke of Westminster's 'Flying Fox'.

The happiest memories of my years at Charterhouse are of holidays when I could enjoy my love for the countryside, especially wild places, and make first beginnings in country sports. There was one period during which we took our autumn holidays in Switzerland and I became fascinated with the

W. Usham

September
· 04

1. One of my many
sketches of my
father

mountains and first experiences in mountaineering. This period came to a tragic end. We always arranged to stay together with the Hopkinson family whose father was a Professor at Manchester University. He with two daughters and a son of my own age were brilliant climbers and always went without guides. One day they were all killed. We could not face Switzerland after that.

My years at Charterhouse had given me the kind of knowledge tested in ordinary Classical examination papers and in 1899 I got a Classical Exhibition at New College, Oxford. That marked the beginning of an entirely new phase in my life.

The record of my years at Oxford is of key importance for my whole life story. It was in these years that I first became intellectually and socially

3

alive. When I found myself established in my own rooms at New College, I felt a new sense of freedom, partly in the release from a rigid timetable for each day's activities—but still more in the escape from a society in which social status depended entirely on skill at football and cricket. The chance to make new friends among a wide group instead of being limited to one's own age group in a small house community was of great significance for me.

This change on the social side began at once. On the educational side, however, my first two years at Oxford were spent in reading for 'Classical Honour Mods.' and this meant continuing on the lines of what had been my Charterhouse curriculum. My natural aptitude should have enabled me to get First Class Honours; but I was stale and only got a Second.

The real change for me came when I started reading Philosophy for 'Greats'. It was the practice at New College in my time to put each student of Philosophy under a separate tutor for Moral Philosophy and for Metaphysics (Hastings Rashdall for the former and H. W. P. Joseph for the latter). There was also a convention that in each year Rashdall should be given the responsibility for one student in both divisions. And in my years I was the student chosen for this. This was in fact fortunate for me because Rashdall's line of thought was much more intelligible to me than that of Joseph. Rashdall was very useful to me. He cleared my mind on many issues in a way which was helpful for answering questions set in examination papers. My evenings in his rooms, when I read him my weekly essay on some theme set by him, were always stimulating. He used to sit in a deep armchair before the fire with his feet up on the mantelpiece, and occasionally some parts of an essay made him roar with laughter.

Although I owe a great deal to Rashdall, I feel I owe much more to W. H. Hadow for his lectures on Aristotle given by him in a room at his own College of Worcester. One lecture in particular gave me a revelation which has been a decisive influence on my creed of life. In my memory I still see a vivid picture of Hadow, then a very young man, striding up and down the lecture room with his gown flying behind him. In this lecture he was dealing with Aristotle's conception of happiness (*eudaimonia*) in human life (*Ethics* 1-7) which he saw as active work (*energeia*) done with a quality of excellence (*arete*), and if a man has a capacity for 'excellence' in more than one form of work then in that kind of work for which he has the best capacity.* Hadow's exposition made me see in a flash what should be the main purpose of my life—to do jobs of work for which my capacities were suited and to do every job in which I was engaged just as well as it could be done—according to a standard of excellence. I have always seen special significance in this conception of 'excellence' (*arete*)—a conception which, as my friend and New College contemporary Richard Livingstone wrote, 'runs like a gold thread through the achievement of Greece'. Only a small fraction of human beings can hold posts of direct social importance, and

* *Energeia kat' areten—ei de pleious hai aretai kata ten aristen.*

4

even those have many minor tasks to perform. The determination to do every task just as well as it possibly can be done (i.e. according to a standard of excellence) can make even the humblest task of true value, not only to the individual who does it but also to the society of which he is a member.

What I have written is a true record of the immediate impact on me of Hadow's lecture. Later, however, as my subsequent story will make clear, I came to recognise that Aristotle's ideas were too cold, self-centred and intellectual and that to give true meaning to my life my conduct must be founded on a religious and, for me Christian, faith, and that as a guide to my practical action I must rely on Christ's ethical teaching, in particular His interpretation of the second of the two great Commandments.

In due course I got a First Class in 'Greats', sharing the distinction among my New College contemporaries with Richard Livingstone and Walter Moberley.

Turning to my social life at Oxford, I made new friends among a very wide circle, and it is sad to reflect that almost all my most valued friends of this period were killed in the war of 1914-18. Among those who survived I think chiefly of Geoffrey Lawrence who became the first Lord Oaksey, and with whom I kept in touch until his own death when we were both over 90. Among those who were killed I think specially of Robert Gregory. I and two other New College friends stayed with him at his home in Ireland (Coole Park, Co. Galway) during the weeks between the written examination for 'Greats' and the final viva voce interviews. His mother, Lady Gregory, was one of the founders of the Abbey Theatre in Dublin, and W. B. Yeats and A. E. Russell were staying with her when we were there. We had fascinating evenings when they together read over drafts for Abbey Theatre plays, including one of Lady Gregory's own plays *The Workhouse Ward*.

I had always been fond of riding and had some skill in handling difficult horses. In my last years at Oxford I was able to get some fox-hunting and I have happy memories of days with the Heythrop and South Oxfordshire hounds. These brought me into contact with a new set of friends, particularly the contemporaries of my younger brother Alfred who came up to New College two years after me. Notable among these new friends were Seddon and Fred Cripps, sons of Alfred Cripps (later Lord Parmoor). During my last year at Oxford and the following years Fred Cripps arranged to take the Oxford University Draghounds to Parmoor for the Christmas vac. and we had some exciting runs through the beech woods on the Chiltern Hills. For several years after that I used regularly to stay for weekends at Parmoor and my friendship with that family meant much to me. Stafford Cripps, however, was very much younger than his two elder brothers, and I cannot recollect ever having seen him in these early years.

Looking back over my life I see that my love of country sports and my pleasure in friendships with sporting characters has been of great significance for me. It has not in any way reduced my intellectual and social interests or the value which I have found in friendships with people who

2. One of the decorated envelopes I sent my mother

have no 'sporting' interests, or possibly even despise them. I hope that I can say truly in the words of Terence: *Homo sum nihil humanum a me alienum puto*.

To complete my picture of my years at Oxford I must add one finishing touch. Those years marked the end of the long chapter of Victorian peace and stability. We did not realise this at the time and the impression which stands out in my memory is that this was, in a sense, a dull period, making no demands on, and offering no scope for, a spirit of adventure. I must have wanted adventure, since I felt a strong urge to go out as a volunteer in the South African war. Family pressure stopped that, but I remember looking with envy at a New College friend when he got into uniform for training at Cowley Barracks.

After passing my final Schools I felt very reluctant to leave Oxford. On reflection, however, I was forced to the conclusion that I had not the qualities to make me excel in an academic career. I turned to the Bar as the only alternative suitable for me. It was, at that time, still unusual for an Oxford graduate of high academic qualifications to go into 'business' of any kind.

I started reading for the Bar at the end of 1903. I found great educational value in these studies and indeed in my whole experience at the Bar. The legal training made me appreciate the need to get an understanding of the essential points in any problem and to test the accuracy and relevance of evidence. This experience helped me greatly in tackling the wide range of practical tasks for which I became responsible in the later chapters of my life.

After 'eating my dinners' and passing the necessary examinations, I was called to the Bar in Lincoln's Inn and spent a year as a pupil in the Chambers of a leading conveyancing barrister. Then in 1905 I was accepted as a pupil in the Chambers of R. J. Parker who later, as a Lord of Appeal and the first Lord Parker of Waddington, established a name as one of the great lawyers in English history. Parker had a most interesting practice and working for him was inspiring. He had the generous qualities of a great man and lacked pettiness of any kind. If I drafted an Opinion on one of his cases which he thought right in substance, he would accept it without altering a word.

That year (1905-6) stands out in my memory as a happy period. It gave me happiness according to Aristotle's conception as an exercise of faculties for which I had the capacity for excellence. I had time on weekends and in vacations for my sporting activities. I was also able to widen my social contacts, helped greatly by weekends with the Parker family at their country home. That was a time in which we still lived in an atmosphere of Victorian peace. We did not think of international dangers, with threats of war, though we were concerned about internal social problems. I, with some friends, formed a small group called the Agenda Club for discussing such questions.

In addition to my work on Parker's cases, I got a few briefs of my own which I handled successfully. These experiences seemed to show that I had good prospects for a career at the Bar, but I could not feel complete confidence about this. I felt doubts about my own practical capacities and I had seen too many examples of briefless barristers. Then, in the autumn of 1906, two things happened. The first was that Parker was appointed as a High Court Judge, so that I would be unable to continue working in his Chambers. The second was that I was offered an appointment in business with a substantial starting salary and prospects of a really large income.

After deep reflection I decided to accept the business offer. This had come to me through my father, who, having started life as a partner in a family firm of merchant bankers, had at the age of 40 been called to the Bar and practised mainly as an adviser on cases involving questions of international law. In the course of his legal work he had been consulted by a large international organisation concerned with metal trading, supported by

7

manufacturing, metallurgical and mining interests. The central directing authority for this organisation was the Metallgesellschaft in Frankfurt, while in the U.K. its instrument was the metal trading company of Henry R. Merton & Co. and in the U.S.A. The American Metal Company. The Merton family in Frankfurt took the lead in deciding general policy and they had recently felt it necessary to make changes in the U.K. organisation. They formed a separate company in London to take over all existing holdings and to be responsible for deciding about new investments. They wanted to appoint a Chairman and Managing Director for this new Company and this was the appointment which was offered to me. The proposed Board of Directors was to include some men of high standing in the City, for example the stockbroker Alfred Wagg who later became one of my life-long friends.

I accepted this offer, spent three months over Christmas in Frankfurt learning about the business, and then found myself established in an office in Cornhill. My first need was to find a colleague to work with me, and for this I managed to get Arthur Villiers who, though two years my junior, had been one of my friends in my last year at Oxford, and who remained a most important personal friend for the whole of the rest of my career. My work became wide ranging, including directorships of a large manufacturing company in South Wales, tin mining ventures in Cornwall, companies in Paris and in Spain, all involving the development of new processes in metallurgy and the treatment of complex ores.

All this was in many ways interesting, and it certainly enlarged my personal experience; but I was at bottom profoundly unhappy. I was not in sympathy with the kind of people with whom I had to work, and I had not really got the capacity for money-making success in the kind of business operations with which we were concerned. At this point I can note when in a later chapter in my life I became engaged in activities in the City on my return from India, I found myself associated with a totally different kind of business character with whom I was in complete sympathy.

I looked back with regret to the work and companionship which I had enjoyed in my first start at the Bar, and my only relief came in keeping up my contacts with R. J. Parker and his family. This led to the great blessing of my life. In September 1907 Parker's second daughter Gwendolen agreed to marry me. Her companionship has had a decisive influence on my personal life. She has given me self-confidence and courage to face all the problems of my later career.

It is worth recording how this happened, since such a record may illustrate the social conventions of 70 years ago. I had invited Parker and his daughter to dine with me and then go on to see *The Pirates of Penzance*. After this was over, Parker saw us off together in a hansom cab to drive to his flat in Buckingham Gate. I decided to take this chance to make my proposal; but I did not screw up my courage to do so until we were passing Buckingham Palace with only about 300 yards to go to the flat. Gwen was

Dec. 19, 1908. ## THE QUEEN

SCHUSTER—PARKER.

Many well-known people in the legal world gathered on Saturday afternoon last in St. Peter's Church, Eaton-square, to witness the wedding of Miss Gwendolen Parker, second daughter of Mr Justice Parker and Lady Parker, of Browsholme Lodge, Haslemere, and 3, Buckingham-gate, S.W., with Mr George E. Schuster, son of Mr and Mrs Schuster, of 12, Harrington-gardens, S.W. The bridal procession was a very pretty one, headed by the bride, who was escorted by her father; her lovely gown of richly tinted ivory Bengal satin was made *en princesse*, and draped in classical folds to the left side of the waist, where it was secured by a large buckle, which held in place a cascade falling over a petticoat of fine old lace. The Court train, slung

[Photograph by H. Bullingham, 21, Harrington-road, South Kensington, S.W.

MISS GWENDOLEN PARKER (MRS SCHUSTER).

from both shoulders, was of rich ivory brocade lined with crêpe de Chine, and a charming tulle veil, embroidered at the hem with silver bugles, was arranged in a somewhat original manner over a wreath of orange blossoms. Master Hubert Parker, the youngest brother of the bride, made a fascinating little page in his cream satin suit and blue sash, whilst the little cloak which fell from his shoulders was lined with blue satin. Two very small maidens were in picture dresses of cream satin with blue sashes and forget-me-not wreaths upon their heads, whilst the trio of elder maids were in gowns of deep ivory Bengal satin with draped Empire bodices and big black satin hats trimmed with feathers and lined with blue velvet. The fully choral service was admirably rendered, the officiating clergy being the Rev. the Hon. Charles Byron (cousin of the bride), the Rev. H. E. Shaw Stewart, and the Rev. Guy Vernon Smith. Mr Alfred Schuster was best man to his brother. A very large reception was held at Buckingham-gate by Lady Parker, and amidst general congratulations the bride and bridegroom departed for their honeymoon, Mrs George Schuster wearing a soft blue satin gown relieved with old lace trimmings, hat *en suite*, and beautiful Russian sables.

9

not ready to say 'yes' and, in my confusion, I forgot to pay the fare for the hansom cab, so that Parker was left to settle this some hours later.

Our engagement was finally settled as we sat on the grass beside our horses at the top of the Cheviot Hills. Parker had rented Roddam Hall in Northumberland for the grouse shooting and I was staying there as one of his guests. We were married on December 12th 1908 at St. Peter's, Eaton Square and the page at the wedding was Gwen's much younger brother, Hubert Parker, then a boy of six who later, as Lord Chief Justice, became the second Lord Parker of Waddington. Our honeymoon in Corsica gave us a first experience in facing problems together, because after an adventurous trek on foot and muleback from Ajaccio to Calvi on the north coast, it ended with my getting an attack of what, when we finally got to Nice, was diagnosed as a modified form of smallpox.

When we settled down as a married couple in London I began to look for a new field of work. Before my marriage I had come to the definite conclusion that my post in the Merton organisation would not give me satisfying life's work. My thoughts had turned to the possibility of a political career. My father had agreed with me in this and undertaken to give me financial support. As a first start I stood as a Liberal candidate for Chelsea in a Local Government election. This was only a trial run since Chelsea was an impregnable Conservative seat, but it brought me into touch with political circles which eventually led in 1911 to my being adopted as Liberal candidate for the Parliamentary constituency of North Cumberland.

This gave great new interest to my life. I still continued my work in the City; but all my holiday periods were spent in North Cumberland working together with my wife. To be a Liberal candidate in those days was to be a social outcast in so-called 'upper class' circles. But North Cumberland was a special area in having some leading families which were by tradition Liberal, such as the Howards, the Lawsons of Isel and the Chances of Carlisle. The constituency covered a large area ranging from the wide open spaces of the Border country and running down to the shores of the Solway Firth and the sea town of Silloth, including the coal mining district of Aspatria. The hill farmers—statesmen as they were called—were fine people. Working on a large scale map my wife and I visited every statesman in the constituency. We also had many social evening meetings throughout the constituency and I made friends with the Conservative candidate Christopher Lowther, the son of the 'Speaker' at that time. My prospects of success were considered quite good and I must have been regarded as a promising young recruit at Liberal Party Headquarters, justifying Cabinet Ministers coming to speak at local meetings for me.

And then the war came: on August 4th 1914—the actual day when John Simon had planned to come to speak at a large meeting in Carlisle for me. That meant the end of my North Cumberland adventure. As a man with a German name I had to resign immediately. Public opinion at the time was bitterly hostile to anyone with any hint of a German connection; even

4. Electioneering in North Cumberland

having a German governess in the family was regarded as a cause for suspicion.

For me the war meant much more than merely resigning as a Parliamentary candidate for North Cumberland. Arthur Villiers and I decided that we must immediately resign from our posts in the German controlled Merton organisation. He, as an officer of the Oxford Yeomanry, had been called up to join his Regiment. I also felt that I must undertake military service and I was fortunate in getting, with Arthur's support, a commission in the Oxford Yeomanry. I found the atmosphere of August 1914 inspiring and I shared Rupert Brooke's thoughts when he wrote *Now, God be thank'd Who has match'd us with His hour*. That sonnet has been widely ridiculed as over-sentimental. I can only say that for me it rang true.

CHAPTER II

The First World War

THE OXFORD YEOMANRY (Queen's Own Oxfordshire Hussars) played a distinctive part in the war because Winston Churchill was second-in-command. As First Lord of the Admiralty he had organised a special naval division which was sent out to Antwerp in an attempt to stop the encircling movement of the invading German army, and the Oxford Yeomanry was sent to Dunkirk in September 1914 to be on the spot to serve as the divisional cavalry to the naval division.

There have been many books about the war years in France and here I can only give a brief record of my personal story. I had felt a challenge to play an active part in the war and to do this in whatever way my capacities would be most useful. I did not feel that a useful part could only be played in front line fighting. I was already in my 34th year when the war started and was married with two children. My younger brother had been killed in November 1914 at the first battle of Ypres.

I was posted initially to the Reserve Regiment which was billeted at Christ Church College, Oxford, and eventually moved to the east coast, when I became Adjutant. In May 1915 I was posted to France to join the First Regiment with which I served for the next year. This period included the futile endeavour with the Second Cavalry Division to break through the 'G' in Gap after the battle of Loos, and then some weeks in the trenches when the whole Cavalry Corps was used as an Infantry Division to man the trenches just north of Loos after the failure of that effort to break through. During these weeks I was in control of the snipers and raiding parties for the Brigade, so that I got some experience of fighting in the front-line.

One incident during my time with the Cavalry is worth recording. After our period in the trenches I had been attached as intelligence officer to the Headquarters of the 4th Cavalry Brigade. Following his resignation from the Government after Gallipoli, Winston Churchill came out to France to join the Oxford Yeomanry as his own Regiment. I have a vivid picture of his arrival, modest and almost nervous in his manner, dressed in a new uniform covered with strange medal ribbons and wearing bright yellow polo boots with long swan-necked spurs. After his talks with us he went on to stay the night at the Headquarters of the Henley Squadron commanded by Val Fleming and kept them all up for a whole night giving them his detailed account of what had happened at Gallipoli. After that evening with his own

12

Squadron he went straight off to see the Commander-in-Chief at St. Omer and got command of an Infantry Battalion. He, of course, wanted to play a more active part than would have been possible as an officer of a Cavalry Regiment and we all had some feeling of relief because if he had stayed with us he would certainly have tried to win the war with the Oxford Yeomanry, which would have meant the end of us.

In May 1916, on my return from a short leave in England, I found that without any reference to me I had been posted to a Staff appointment with the Artillery for the 6th Infantry Division then holding a sector of the Ypres Salient. A series of Staff appointments followed, leading eventually to that of Chief Administrative Staff Officer (with the rank of Major) to the Major General R.A. at First Army Headquarters. This gave me really interesting and valuable work. When my colleague on the operational side, Ernest Lewin, was sent for a staff training course in England his place was filled by Alan Brooke who, as a young major, was then Chief Artillery Staff Officer, Canadian Corps. This gave me a chance to work for two months at the same desk with him, during which time he was mainly concerned with working out plans for the first Army attack on the Vimy Ridge, to be led by the Canadian Corps. Working with 'Brookie' was an inspiring experience. His mind worked with lightning speed and his thoughts were concentrated on getting effective action based on an accurate appreciation of available resources. This left me with the lasting impression that a really first class soldier was the best kind of colleague to have when faced with the responsibility of settling practical plans for dealing with a difficult problem in any field. This impression was confirmed in later experiences in my life when I had the opportunity to work with really fine soldiers such as Philip Chetwode and Gerald Templar.

My work at First Army Headquarters became specially important in the course of 1917 and in the first months of 1918 with the German breakthrough on the Fifth Army Front at the southern end of the British line. There were anxious moments and to us in our junior positions the ending of the war seemed a long way off.

As I write these words in 1978 it is also worth recording that I was able to maintain personal contacts with the Oxford Yeomanry as they were moved about to different parts of the Front and that the spirit of comradeship established in the 1914-18 war has been retained until today and has meant very much to all its members. For me it has led to friendships of great value in my life—with Arthur Villiers above all, but also with friends like Tommy Hutchinson (later Bursar of Christ Church, Oxford), Charlie Nicholl and Gerald Wellesley.

My connection with the Oxford Yeomanry had in another way a significant influence on my life. I have already referred to my love of the English countryside and, after the upheaval of the war, I was even more determined to give to my two sons what I myself had never enjoyed, the stable background of a country home where they could feel that they truly belonged.

13

5. A wartime portrait

With many friends in Oxfordshire it was in this county that we now sought to make our home and in the years following 1918 we established ourselves at Nether Worton which ever since has been a main foundation of our lives.

In the autumn of 1918 it was recommended for me to attend a Staff Training Course at Cambridge for which I left First Army Headquarters in France at the beginning of October without any thought that the war might end long before the completion of the course. When the Armistice actually came I was ordered to remain in England pending demobilisation and was employed in a Government project under the Ministry of Education for the resettlement of officers in civil employ. This was for me an unhappy time. I had a general feeling that I had not fully responded to the war's challenge for national service.

Then suddenly a new opportunity came in the form of an urgent telegram from the Headquarters of the British Forces at Murmansk in North Russia asking for me to be appointed as Chief Administrative Officer (AA and QMG) with the rank of Lieutenant Colonel. The request for my services had been made by Colonel Lewin, my former colleague on the Artillery Staff at First Army Headquarters in France, who had been posted to North Russia as Chief Operational Staff Officer (GSO 1) for the Murmansk Forces.

After a period of agonising reflection I decided to accept this offer—a fateful decision as in essence it involved for the moment giving second place to my family responsibilities as a husband and father. I can only record now that I felt it to be a challenge with which fate had confronted me and to which I must respond. Whether right or wrong, the decision had been taken, and as I look back over the memories of my life I see as one of its blackest moments my parting with my wife as we stood alone at about mid-night on a Thames quay. Then I was rowed out to embark as the first passenger on the *S.S. Umtali*, a small coastal trading steamer from South Africa due to start at dawn for the voyage to Murmansk.

CHAPTER III

North Russia, 1919

IN THE SUMMER OF 1918 a small allied force under the command of Major-General C. Maynard had been sent to North Russia to prevent the Germans, then established in Finland with an army of 55,000 men, from pushing north in the name of the 'White Finn' government to set up submarine bases in the ice-free ports of Murmansk and Petchenga. At first the Bolsheviks, whose own invasion of Finland had now been overturned and who were fearful of German intentions in the area despite the peace of Brest-Litovsk (March 1918), had been ready to accept a British presence in North Russia. By June, however, it seemed clear that the Bolshevik peace with the Germans was going to hold and Lenin took steps to try to oust the allies from Murmansk. In July 1918, the British government established another small force under the command of General Ironside at Archangel with the aim of lending support to a White Russian government in favour of reopening the Eastern Front against Germany. By the time of the armistice in the west in November 1918 Maynard had consolidated his control over the Murmansk-Petrograd railway as far south as the southern shores of the White Sea and was heavily committed to the anti-Bolshevik government in the area. With the collapse of Germany the Bolsheviks were 'the only enemy we have left'. As I set out for North Russia in early 1919, Winston Churchill, now Secretary of State for War, was still pressing his case to step up foreign intervention against the Bolsheviks.

The voyage out on the *S.S. Umtali* was long, rough and very cold. After calling at several coastal ports and picking up eight Naval Transport Officers and one Colonel going out to take command of the Scottish Battalion at Archangel, we had to go north almost to Spitzbergen before turning in to reach Murmansk. The foredeck got covered in ice and we spent some perilous hours helping to clear this off.

Throughout my time in North Russia my letters to my wife took the form of a diary, extracts from which I have used to form the basis of my account.

> '25th February: Then at about four we came round a bend and saw the great town of Murmansk before us! The first thing that we could see was the crowd of shipping. After all these days on the lonely sea it looked a very big crowd indeed and standing out among all the smaller craft lay one of our battleships (a pre-dreadnought battleship—the

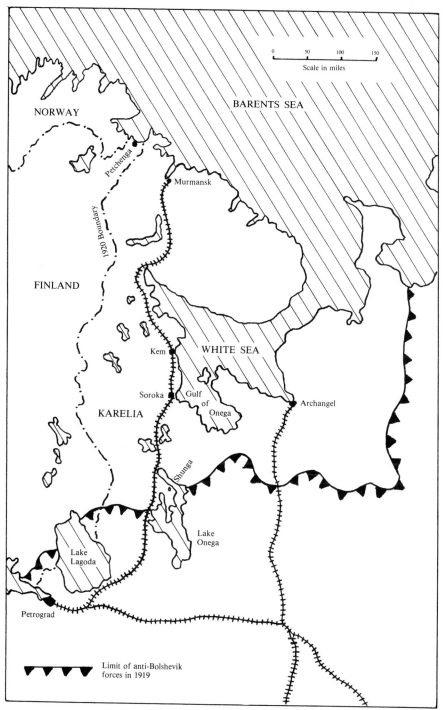

Scale in miles

BARENTS SEA

NORWAY

Petchenga

Murmansk

1920 Boundary

FINLAND

Kem

WHITE SEA

Soroka

Gulf
of
Onega

Archangel

KARELIA

Shunga

Lake
Onega

Lake
Lagoda

Petrograd

Limit of anti-Bolshevik
forces in 1919

North Russia in 1919

17

Glory) and an old Russian cruiser. As we got nearer we could see the town consisting of quite a number of new looking timber huts and houses—certainly very much bigger than I had anticipated.'

I was met at the quay by my old friend Ernest Lewin, the Chief of Staff (GSO 1) who took me up to the headquarters where I had my first meeting with General Maynard and sat long into the night discussing the overall situation. These talks at Headquarters were always entertaining, chiefly because Sir Ernest Shackleton was with us at the time and told us innumerable stories of his own adventurous life.

'26th February: I spent the morning jawing hard with Lewin— looking through various papers and finally getting bewildered. There is a lot of administrative work to be done . . . endless little demobilization questions, all the ordinary questions of establishment promotion. Then there is a most fearfully confused labour situation for the port, the building work, for guards, etc. etc. and all sorts of committees half-started which have not yet functioned—such as a labour bureau for civilian labour—a claims commission, a finance commission and so on. In addition every unit which we have got seems to be on the move in various directions and there are numberless questions about horse, dog and reindeer transport—frictions with the Italians on working parties—mobilisation of the Russian army—accommodation for all sorts of odd people in odd places, reorganisation of the port and erection of labour-saving machinery, construction of a light railway round the town of Murmansk in anticipation of the spring when all the roads become impassable, sanitation of Murmansk which will be an awful problem when the thaw begins, water supply for the town which has been built, mushroom-like, with no regard for this sort of thing, canoes and motor boats for the spring, hospital accommodation for the large number of scurvy cases which are developing among the civilians in the south and a thousand and one other matters. Lewin's idea with everything is to get it going on a basis so that the Russians can carry on by themselves, and he says they have now got a very good man as Governor of the province who is also to be Commander-in-Chief of the local forces.'

Financial and currency problems were constantly at the forefront. For the White Russians, as for the Bolsheviks, economic factors were vital to their survival in power.

'27th February: The position here is ridiculous. We accept payment in old Russian rouble notes at a fixed exchange rate of 48 to the £, whereas they are really practically valueless. In South Russia they are being printed as fast as the presses can turn them out and even here when a man really wants to buy anything he will pay ridiculous sums in roubles. There was a case of 150 roubles being paid for a lemon!'

6. The author (far right) with General Maynard (far left), Colonel Lewin (second left) and colleagues

'6th March: I am trying hard to do everything possible to get a properly run municipal show, but at present there is no municipal organisation at all as the town is entirely an artificial growth created as a government enterprise entirely for war purposes. In Russia it is quite normal for the employer to provide all services (water, electric light, fuel, housing, etc.) for his employees free of charge and this is what has been done here with the government as employer. Consequently the town has no revenue of any kind and as the government undertaking was entirely the very unremunerative one of war there is nothing but expenditure.'

'7th March: I had an interesting conversation with the Governor, Ermeloff, and the Russian Chief of Staff, Colonel Kostandi. We have heard lately that a number of very senior officers of the old Russian army have been taking high commands in the Bolshevik army. Kostandi thinks that a number of these men accepted these offices with a view to gradually influencing public feeling in the direction of something like the old regime. A number have resigned again because they found this hopeless and as to the balance he fears they may gradually adopt the views of the other side. However, a recently captured routine order impressed him very much as it referred to several

old disciplinary regulations which applied in the old regime and it looks
as if the Bolsheviks were finding this type of discipline necessary. The
Governor said his latest information was that in various districts now
there were peasant risings against the Bolsheviks mainly because they
can't get any food . . . Of course they are now in their worst time for
food and by July ought to be better off but people here don't think that
they can support the population because their means of distribution are
so bad. The way I am coming to look at the thing now is that by helping
the people in districts like this to get a good government we are forcing
the Bolsheviks on their side to organise themselves properly. In a year
or two they ought to have a fairly stable government and, it is to be
hoped, a more moderate one, and then it might be possible to make
terms with them and leave the people here without fear of massacres.'

I shall continue to illustrate my story with these pictures from contemporary letters, but at this point I must record some comments about particular problems and personalities and also explain the general purpose
decided on for our whole operation.

First, as regards the currency problem which afforded an interesting confirmation of the truth of 'Gresham's Law' that bad currency drives out
good: some time before my arrival General Maynard, greatly concerned
about finding satisfactory means of payment for work done by the Russians
for us, had paid an emergency visit to London asking first for a special
allocation of gold. This had been refused, but eventually the British
Government had agreed that Barclays Bank should be authorised to issue a
series of North Russian Rouble notes convertible into sterling at a fixed rate
of exchange. These notes had then been used by General Maynard for some
time. I found on my arrival that those issues had completely disappeared
and that in fact payments for services rendered, especially for running the
railways, were still being made in ordinary Russian Rouble notes. All the
old trouble had recurred. I suggested a simple solution, that all those working for the British Forces (which in fact included practically all ablebodied
Russian personnel) should be authorised to purchase necessaries at our
Naval and Military canteens by payment in ordinary Russian Rouble notes
at a fixed rate of exchange. This arrangement worked quite well and no
more North Russian Rouble notes were issued. It was, of course, impossible
to trace into whose banking accounts those which had been issued had
found their way.

I must next say something about personalities. Mr. Ermeloff, the Governor and Commander-in-Chief, was a small man of great courage and high
principles. I formed a great admiration for him and for his wife, an extremely interesting and cultured woman. When the time came for us to tell
our Russian friends that all British Forces were to be finally withdrawn it
was the almost certain fate of people like these two that caused us the
greatest distress. Mr. Ermeloff had an engaging sense of humour and I

7. & 8. Above and below: Winter transport

recall at one of our many convivial gatherings, at which gin had to take the place of vodka, the ending of his personal speech (as interpreted to me at the time): 'There are all kinds of dogs—big dogs and little dogs. I am only a little dog but one thing I can promise you: I will never bite an Englishman.' Colonel Kostandi on the other hand was the type of so-called White Russian which I particularly disliked. He was autocratic, surrounded himself with luxury in one of the old Royal railway coaches and, having trained at a German Staff College, was very efficient in preparing paper plans without regard to what was possible in the form of practical action.

The general plan settled at these and other preliminary meetings was that we should help the Russians to develop and equip a Russian force on the scale of a single Infantry Division and that this force, supplemented with Russian irregular forces combined with the British and other available units, should press forward as far as possible along the railway line towards Petrograd. Through the vast uninhabited tundra, frozen in winter and impassably swampy in the summer, the fighting front was limited to this single track railway line as far south as the shores of Lake Onega.

At this point it is necessary to summarise what were the available forces. The allied troops were a most polyglot collection: British, Canadians,

French and Italians were later joined by invaluable railway companies of American troops, the intervention forces never totalling more than 10,000 men. In addition to these allied troops General Maynard had been relying on three other important contingents. The first of these was an Infantry Battalion of Serbs, second a Finnish Legion, and third a Karelian Regiment.

The Serbian Batallion provided invaluable support:

> '4th April: The Commander of our Serbian Regiment came into lunch. This is indeed a warrior who has been fighting hard since 1912. His tales of fighting range over war with the Bulgarians, and punitive expeditions against the Albanians before the Great War began, the days against the Austrians in 1914 when they made such a brilliant victory (little talked of at the time) and took 80,000 prisoners. Then in their terrible retreat at the end of 1916 he found himself with his regiment forced to cross the Albanian frontier into the very village where he had been sent on a punitive expedition some years before. Then the journey to Odessa with an infantry battalion in May 1917 and his wonderful journey from the south to the north of Russia during the revolution when during the course of three months they got into Siberia, then out again and finally ended up in this area where they have been fighting for us ever since. It really is an incredible tale of adventure and they are all still full of fighting spirit. He told us how as they passed through Russia the crowds used to shout out at the officers "Take off your epaulettes. Down with the officers, etc.!" Then they would talk to his men and ask why they tolerated such distinction and why they were not really democratic and did not do away with the officer class who were only out for their own ends. But the men replied "Our officers will not take off their epaulettes because we will not let them. They are our officers and their task is to help us get back to our country. When we have got back to our country they will take off their epaulettes and go to their own homes." '

The Finnish Legion confronted us with a very special problem. When the first British contingent went to Murmansk in the summer of 1918, they found that there had been established in the area a Finnish Legion composed of about 500 Red Finns who had got out of Finland in order to escape from the White Finns who were collaborating with the Germans. This Legion had provided valuable support for the British forces in the initial period, but after the Armistice and the confirmation of the Treaty of Brest-Litovsk the British forces had found that the only enemy with which they were confronted was the Russian Bolshevik Government with whom the members of the Red Finnish Legion were naturally in sympathy.

The presence of these Finnish troops was therefore an embarrassment and Colonel Lewin paid a special visit to Helsinki in order to get approval from the Finnish Government for their repatriation. The Finnish Government agreed to the repatriation of the general body, but adamantly refused readmission for the two Commanders, in particular General Lehtimaki. While these discussions were proceeding our Intelligence Service got evidence of a plot at Finnish Legion Headquarters to invite a number of British officers to join in Easter celebrations and then to assassinate them. In Lewin's absence it was my duty to report this to London and I sat up all night encoding a secret message. To my great surprise, two days later I found that the exact contents of my secret message were reproduced in the daily Reuter Telegram of news from Britain. We interpreted this as a sign that Churchill had been anxious to get publicity for the news as affording justification for sending further British troops to North Russia. As nothing came of the reported plot our discussions with the two Finnish Generals continued and eventually it was agreed that, as their return to Finland had been refused by the Finnish Government, they should be allowed to make their own way south to join the Bolshevik forces. An amusing incident was that Lehtimaki then paid me a personal visit and asked me to give him a recommendation to the Russian Commander. This I accordingly did on one of our normal staff forms recommending the Brigade Commander for the command of a division. Strengthened with this recommendation Lehtimaki made his own way south and we heard no more from him.

The spring of 1919 was occupied with efforts to create administrative machinery and to train a Russian force as agreed at our March meeting. The general atmosphere was not favourable as there were elements of disagreement among the Russian population and also some discontent among the allied forces.

> '12th March: A busy morning over papers and interviews chiefly about claims. Got rather an excited message on the telephone this afternoon from French HQ to say that a crowd of 400 men were parading outside waving red flags with Bolshevik inscriptions and singing Bolshevik songs but not showing any violence. Rang up our chief interpreter and asked if he could give any explanation and got reply that it was the 2nd anniversary of the revolution. So that was fairly alright but I had quite an excited moment as all the rest of the staff were out. In the end I warned the base commandant to have parties handy at the various barracks in case of any disorder. Later the procession passed us—a most mournful affair—all the men trudging along with heads down in the snow singing Russian words to the Marseillaise. No trouble resulted though some were a bit drunk.'

A week later, however, we obtained foreknowledge of a planned Bolshevik rising in the town. The insurgents calculated on finding many sympathisers among allied troops, including British, and they thought some of these would side with them openly. I was asked by the General to draft him a speech with which to brief our own officers. The Allied troops were prepared, the ring-leaders arrested and the plot forestalled. There remained,

9. Murmansk after the thaw

however, many Bolshevik sympathisers within the local community. Action to deal with this embarrassment is recorded in the following letters:

'11th April: They are taking down the line and distributing an edition of the *Murmansk Gazette* which contains a new proclamation issued at Archangel. This is to the effect that everyone who sympathises with the Bolsheviks is given until 20th April to declare himself. If he does that he will be taken down the line, given three days' rations and allowed to go over but any Bolshevik sympathiser who does not avail himself of the chance will receive no mercy if he is discovered afterwards.

'10th May: Had lunch with Meiklejohn who had just returned from conducting the first party of the big lot of Bolshevik sympathisers whom we have been sending over the line. He had taken them to the furthest point on the railway line and then got out and marched with them a distance of 20 miles to our outposts. He said it was marvellous how they managed the march as there were many women carrying small babies and also some small children walking. The whole thing is rather a hateful business as one feels certain they will have much misery where they are going and also a miserable time getting there. But they insist on going and think they will somehow be able to get back to their own homes. It makes one think much of this whole business. You say in one of your last letters that the attitude of the *New Statesman* articles irritates you. I think in a great many ways they are incorrect and exaggerate their point of view but I cannot help feeling that there is a large element of truth in the line that they take, for example in their last article in the number of April 26; that is to say, although they hate the rule of Lenin and Trotsky they are nevertheless more strongly influenced by their dislike of foreign intervention. The picture that one liked to conjure up of all the patriotic Russians flocking to us and welcoming us as deliverers is unfortunately not a correct one and one cannot say that in general the British are at all popular with any class of Russians. I think one can feel most honestly, at any rate as regards our staff here, we are genuinely out to help the Russians to make a good show and are not in the least playing our own game (whether that is true of the British policy as manipulated by British politicians, I cannot say). In spite of that there is practically no class here from which we get any cordial cooperation. There is of course the exceptional character like Bennigsen who, being inspired by high ideals himself, is capable of giving credit to others for them and such a man as he does, I think, gratefully accept British help and friendship—though even with his type the fact that they should be in need of foreign help is painful to their national pride . . . Many of this type whose national pride may be stronger than their hatred of Lenin and Trotsky may in this way be kept against us on the other side.'

In the midst of the pessimistic picture given in the letters which I have quoted, I find one gleam of encouragement in a letter of May 26th recording an inspection of one of the units training for the new Russian Army.

'26th May: At Soroka we inspected the Russian training battalion, about 1,300 men altogether. After the parade they started the most beautiful chorus singing. A very simple refrain to the tune of their slow march but with the parts really well sung and exactly in harmony with the whole atmosphere. As each platoon passed near us the chorus burst out loudly and got familiar till it was drowned by the next lot coming and then the last passed and the last notes died away leaving our group standing alone on the dusty, peaty track. It was just like the closing of an act in an opera which had inspired me greatly—and I wonder if they felt the same inspiration from it. If only one could feel that they were really fighting for a great cause and that the overthrow of Bolshevism would mean the creation of a good regime and not the establishment of a crowd of office hunters and reactionaries. Looking at my companions and knowing their lives and ideas of morals and of work I fear I felt more than doubtful . . . We also have in the Russian army in front a dashing lot of irregular adventurers called "partisan troops" under a Colonel Krugliakoff. These we have no responsibility for and they look after themselves entirely. They have already worked half-way down the Eastern shores of Lake Onega. Their plan of working is that they have a large number of officers and they raise say 200 men in one district then advance with them for some days and then they raise more men in the new district as they go along and send them back with the men. They are now asking us for rifles as the peasants in a certain district, having killed the 'Red' commissars, have come in to say they want to fight for us. I have already sent out 200 rifles to them . . . I have just been reading a very interesting article on Bolshevism in the *Round Table* for March that you sent me. Reading it again one feels doubtful whether our intervention is really going to help the right cause. However much one hates the methods of the Bolsheviks and disagrees with their objects one does feel that among them are at least some who are fighting for an ideal and not for personal aims. I should feel so much happier if on our side there were more such spirits.'

I look back on my memories of that day as having given me a picture of what a well-disciplined unit of the old Russian Army could have been.

At the end of May we moved our Headquarters from Murmansk to Kem on the White Sea and concentrated on plans for pushing on towards Petrograd.

'28th May: I had a very interesting talk with the Governor-General, at first on purely business matters but I went on to question him about his ideas on the future of this country. He thinks it very probable that the Bolsheviks will collapse about August but that if the collapse does not come then it will be a much longer business as by then they will be quite well off for food again. He argues that the Bolsheviks represent a minority in the country which is ruthlessly enforcing its ideals on the majority but he thinks they have so terrified the peasants that it is only some great stimulus such as the shortage of food (which may cause internal trouble among the Bolshevik leaders also) which could cause them to rise generally all over the country. Of course the near approach of anti-Bolshevik troops might have a similar effect and that accounts for the risings south of us now. I went on to speak about the re-establishment of normal life afterwards and to ask him whether he did not think it would be necessary to work for a definite religious revival. He said no, he did not think it necessary—the people who were fighting Bolshevism already regarded it in some sense as a holy war and there were in Kolchak's Siberian army some regiments definitely enrolled as fighting for religion. Here in the country that we are advancing over the Bolsheviks nail up all the churches and have made the priests take to ordinary work; but when they have gone (as in the case of places occupied by Col. Krugliakoff's "partisan" troops who are working wide on our left flank) the first thing the villagers do is to reopen the church and have a thanksgiving service and to get their priests back again . . . The country peasants must always be rather out of sympathy with the essential teaching of Bolshevism. What they wanted was to own their own land, not to wage war against the whole institution of private property. It is indeed rather a queer combination in Russia.

I believe that what the Bolsheviks (or the best of them) are fighting for as an ideal, namely the destruction of capitalism, is something that must inevitably come, but in that they are before their time. The world is not educated up to it and the stage of development which the organisation of life in civilised countries has reached is not ripe for such a sudden change and other processes of development must be gone through first. They are trying to enforce this change in Russia on a population which is 200 years behind the ordinary civilised European country in development. What the Russian people wanted was political reform and political freedom and they must live under that a generation and more before they are ready for the economic revolution.

21st June: (Kem) The government here are now in considerable financial difficulties. We have stopped making advances to them and the Archangel government are supposed to finance them. They, however, take little interest in this side and have not given this province a kopek since the British advances stopped. The result is that the railway wages have not been paid since March and the men are now threatening a strike. The loco repair shop here have already come out. I get frantic wires from Murmansk but I cannot do anything nor do I wish to do so as I want to force the Archangel government into solving their own difficulty.'

In July, while continuing our further push towards Petrograd it became necessary to clear up the position as regards the Karelian Regiment as shown in the following letter:

'5th July: The Karelian regiment has long been a problem. Briefly its history is that in the early days when the White Finns and Germans were expected to come across the frontier from Finland and our chief job was to stop them, the Karelians sent a deputation to General Maynard and asked if they might be enrolled and fight under him. As a result a somewhat ragged and irregular regiment was formed which did however some very good work in August 1918 and cleared the Northern parts of Karelia of White Finns. They were left in being under a handful of British officers and their numbers grew on paper to about 3,700-4,000 in the Kem district, the rest scattered at frontier posts and about the country. No one could really check their numbers as the area is vast and the country is very difficult to travel over. Their predominating colour was undoubtedly 'red' not 'white' and they had many friends and relatives on the Bolshevik side. Still, they·were quite happy to remain under us quietly drawing pay and good rations and doing nothing for it except the few who were working and providing train guards, etc. They were guaranteed against fighting anywhere outside their own country. That sort of thing couldn't go on indefinitely. Either they had all to fight and work under us or they must be dismissed from our regiment and left free for the Russian army mobilisation.

So when we first came down we started to re-classify them into a volunteer battalion who would be ready to go and fight the Bolsheviks on the southern front, a Pioneer company also 'fighting troops', a garrison guard company, a labour battalion and a frontier guard company. To get this news out all over the country took a long time as just at that season all the snow tracks were gone and the rivers and lakes were not yet open for navigation. However, to start with all went well and of the troops who were accessible a very large proportion came into the fighting battalion. The men from up country came in with disappointing slowness and in the meanwhile all sorts of influences got to work against us both up country and among the men already enrolled. These were chiefly Bolshevik agitators who worked up a very clever propaganda in an easy field. Trouble came from most unexpected quarters—such for example as a Russian-speaking sailor from one of the American navy ships who got in among the men one afternoon and worked on their feelings against us. Various incidents of insubordination occurred and then deserting began. The time given for enlisting had also run out with only about 1,350 in all the units instead of the numerical strength of 3,700. One day last week 70 deserted in a body and went up country. The general then decided to parade the fighting units and tell them he was sick of this nonsense and it had got to stop. He gave them a chance to decide within 24 hours whether they would withdraw altogether—in which case if mobilisable they would become liable to mobilisation in the Russian Army and stop getting pay and rations from us—or change over to the labour battalion in which case their pay would be reduced. I had expected quite an exciting and dramatic show when the general came to make his speech but the reality was rather far from my imagination. In the first place the men were paraded without arms; in the second place we had the parade quite close to the barracks where we had got a company of Serbs got up in case there was trouble; in the third place it was a wild and windy day with squalls of rain so that any effect of oratory on the part of the general was lost; and lastly speaking through an interpreter when each sentence is read and then repeated in another language is most unimpressive. But perhaps the chief factor against a dramatic effect is the character of the Karelians themselves. They are so very immobile and expressionless and they stood there looking like dull animals while the general cursed them at secondhand through his interpreter. The speech was a good one of its kind but I fear my faculty of seeing both sides of a question and perhaps also my liberal sympathies made me feel rather strongly the men's point of view. To talk of loyalty to the Russians and to ourselves leaves me, I fear, rather cold. These men have no vivid cause of enmity against the Bolsheviks among whom are many of their own friends. The Bolsheviks would never worry about marching an army up into their country which is far too poor, too remote and impassable and too sparsely populated to interest them. On the other hand they have no special reason to trust or wish to fight for the present Russian government here. They have always felt a grievance against the Russians who have never done anything to help them and treat with contempt their national aspirations. The White Finns on their own border are far more their enemies and these are the people on whose side they are now asked to go and fight the Bolsheviks. True they have accepted our food and pay for many months without doing anything for it but if we were fools enough to give it on these terms I don't see how one can blame them much for taking what they could get, seeing there was no other source from which they could get a living in these times. We also had on parade General Marouchevsky, the Russian C-in-C from Archangel. He followed the general with a speech in Russian. He is a tiny little man with a fat neck which bulges over his collar and which seemed to bulge still more as he got excited. He worked himself up to a violent peroration, shaking his fist and almost bursting with indignation, and all around him stood the rows of men stolid and almost expressionless. Then it was over and we returned to await the result of the men's decision. In the end next day it came out—almost 300 of the Fighting Battalion out of 700 volunteered to remain, 80 to join the Labour Battalion and the remainder voted to be discharged, while in the Pioneer Company only 11 out of 250 remained and the balance went off. Practically all those who voted for discharge were outside the Russian age limit for mobilisation and so out of a strength that has figured on paper for all the last months as 3,700 fighting men we raise a fighting unit of 311.'

I can take this record of what happened to the Karelian Regiment as marking the end of one stage in my story, since in July we got the news that

10. White Finnish deserters under escort

the British Government had decided to withdraw all British and allied troops from Russia and to send out a North Russian relief force under the command of General Rawlinson to supervise the evacuation. For us at Murmansk the practical result was the arrival of General Jackson to take over command of the Murmansk forces in place of General Maynard who, in any case, had to return to England for physical reasons. (For me General Jackson's arrival was a welcome event, since we got on very well together, and he in fact became one of the great friends of my life, with whom I renewed my contacts during my years of service in India, and later in 1939 at the beginning of the Second World War.)

At this point also we had to inform all the Russian personnel about the British Government's decision and to work out plans for a vigorous offensive movement to distract attention from the allied withdrawal. Our final offensive push would carry us far southwards along the shores of Lake Onega, and for this purpose it was necessary to have command of the lake itself. When we had reached the northern shores of Lake Onega we found quite an important number of motor boats of various sizes and were able to create a new naval contingent manned by a number of first-class officers who had been members of Ernest Shackleton's polar exploration teams. They had several engagements with Russian units from the southern shores of the Lake and in fact established complete command of its northern waters.

11. Polyglot lunch party with the Lake Flotilla

'20th July: At Shunga we had a parade of the old Lake Flotilla personnel who have had a rather adventurous career. They were a scratch lot
of men got together from all units, a scratch lot of boats, old boats
which we had found lying about in all sorts of places and with great
difficulty gradually got overhauled and running. In spite of all
difficulties they have really done good work and more by bluff than by
anything else have kept the Bolsheviks from coming up to worry us at
the north end of the lake so that we have been able to get our supplies
out to the various detachments without difficulty . . . Then we went on
to the RAF seaplane detachment and then inspected the Horse
Transport School where we are trying to teach the Russians to handle
mules and learn about vehicles and harness.'

The last months in North Russia were a period of great activity for me,
mainly concerned with administrative measures to support our final
offensive action and subsequent withdrawal.

'21st July: At Maselga we met the Russian General Skobeltsin and pro-
ceeded to inspect his training battalion. These made a very good show
on parade but of course the question with them all is—will they fight?
and what will they do when we are gone? Also from my point of view
the great trouble is that I cannot get them to produce the necessary personnel for ASC and Ordnance work. They *cannot* or *will* not get it into
their own heads that they will have to stand on their own legs very soon
for administrative as well as for fighting work. They say yes, they quite
understand that our government doesn't want to join any more in the
fighting now that the peace is signed but surely it will have no difficulty
in sending enough administrative personnel out here to run their side of
the business, and they persist in refusing to do anything, to force our
hands to remain.'

In spite of this lack of businesslike response from the Russian units, we
had to continue our efforts to make a decisively effective push forward
before our final withdrawal, and at this stage we got valuable help from individual British officers who had come out to North Russia in association
with General Rawlinson's relief forces. One of these was Major Brocas
Burrows of the 5th Dragoon Guards, who had been a prisoner during the
main years of the war in France and taken those years to learn Russian and
who saw a final chance of fighting adventures. He was an inspired leader of
Russian contingents and I was able to keep in touch with him by flying over
the forward country and taking a chance of landing on one of the many
lakes in the hope of finding him.

I had to interrupt this process in August for a visit to Archangel in order
to discuss the evacuation programme, and while there I was invited by my
friend Colonel Archipoff, the Russian Chief of Staff at Murmansk, to a
private lunch with a group of senior officers at the Club of the Knights of St.

George. There, among friends, I spoke very frankly of my mixed feelings about our impending withdrawal.

'16th August: (Archangel) I must confess that under the influence of a very unusual quantity of strong spirit I found myself talking with extra-ordinary eloquence in French. I told them in brief that I was against foreign intervention and that I felt that the fact of foreign intervention had all along been a great unifying force on the Bolshevik side and that when all foreign troops were withdrawn it would in many ways weaken the Bolshevik cause and motive. But on the other hand I felt that we had come here during the German war for our own objects and that in doing so we had induced many to commit themselves to our side and had incurred obligations. That therefore although I felt very clearly that we ought to go, yet the time of our going must be arranged so that we did not let down people who had relied on us and that at present I felt that we might be doing that. On the other hand that they must reckon with public opinion on our side and also that they must realise that a very great deal of blame rested on their own shoulders because they had not made the strongest possible effort to strengthen themselves during the time that we were there to help them. That at Archangel especially there had been much too much intrigue, too much search for amusement and personal aggrandisement by the leaders and indeed by all officers. I found that they agreed with practically every word I said. I told Archipoff that I could say what I did without embar-rassment to him as he was one of the few who ever since he had been here had put his back into it. And that is true of him and I think it is true of the other officers whom I met there today. I think they were all workers and stout fighting officers with no nonsense about them. They all pressed me with the question: did we and did our politicians at home realise that by deserting Russia now we were opening the doors to German influence? I said we realised it only too well but that they must appreciate that the policy in all countries today was really being dic-tated by labour and that the eyes of the Labour parties throughout the world were fixed, not on questions of international aggrandisement and whether Germany increased her power or not, but on the social and economic questions and the relations between capital and labour. Those were the subjects with which the attention of the world was to be filled during the coming years at any rate and the old diplomacy to that extent belonged to a past age.'

The final offensive was an astonishing success, mainly due to the leader-ship of Major Brocas Burrows. It is clear, however, that his success would not have been possible unless the Bolshevik Army Units in this area had been very badly organised and extremely inefficient as a fighting force. Major Burrows had been able with a small contingent of Russian troops to land on the western shore of Lake Onega and make his way to a railway

12. One of the vulnerable railway bridges

station where he found two trains in working order. He blocked the line by staging a collision between two engines and then with his own small force of about 70 waited for the arrival from the north of a train with Russian troops over 300 strong. He had managed to get this force to surrender and hand over their arms. To give a full account of how all this happened and how it all ended would involve writing at length, which is not necessary for my present story. For that, it is sufficient to say that this final episode provided exactly the conditions which we had hoped to create for our own final withdrawal on which we could now concentrate all our attention.

A withdrawal was successfully accomplished, but it was a very risky business. It involved evacuating troops northwards over a single railway line several hundred miles to Murmansk which crossed no less than 500 wooden bridges, any one of which could easily have been destroyed. The whole process was, however, accomplished without any serious accident and, by the beginning of October all the allied forces had been evacuated from Murmansk. For me it was a time of much anxiety and many petty irritations, not the least of which was caused by the meanness of the French contingent. This contingent had, as part of their normal rations, been receiving French wine in wooden casks and the French Commander refused to embark unless we could provide space for including all the empty French wine casks. As we were desperately short of shipping space this was an extremely embarrassing demand, but in the end I had to give way.

Finally, on October 9th, General Jackson, Colonel Lewin and I were left alone and we embarked as the only passengers on the last transport to leave Murmansk. I myself had one walk alone through Murmansk before going aboard and saw the shape of things to come by encountering a line of skirmishing troops working their way across the area of the stores and the scattered wooden buildings of the town. I was very glad to find myself back again on board.

CHAPTER IV

Return to Civil Life, 1919-1922

ON MY RETURN to England at the end of October 1919 I was engaged for several weeks in detailed work at the War Office winding up the Murmansk operation. I then had to face the question 'What shall I do?' I had no position of any kind to which I could return. My future was wide open. Looking round contemporary conditions I asked myself what were the outstanding needs of the country and in what field my services might most usefully be employed. My tasks in the war years and my contacts with the troops had left me with the impression that there was a great need for constructive social policy and I felt a sympathetic understanding for the ideals of some of the Labour Party leaders.

My general conclusion was that one of the greatest needs of the country was an improvement in the national system of education and I was strongly attracted by one feature in the educational plans proposed by our Minister of Education, H. A. L. Fisher. This was the proposal for the creation of Continuation Schools which would provide opportunities for further education for young industrial entrants whose employers would allow them time off for part-time education. I noted that the Education Department of Birmingham University was planning a course for the training of Continuation School teachers and I sent in an application. As a result I spent about three months in residence in Birmingham as a member of the first course. This was in many ways an interesting experience, enabling me to make a wide range of contacts in circles with which I had previously had no connection. I did not, however, find it entirely satisfying and in the end this whole development came to nothing, because the Fisher Plan for the establishing of Continuation Schools had to be abandoned because the Government decided that the necessary funds could not be provided.

It so happened that just at this time a new approach to me was made by one of my friends in the City. A group of Merchant Bankers and Acceptance Houses had been engaged in discussing practical measures for reviving economic enterprise in what were then called the 'Succession States', i.e. Austria, Czechoslovakia and Hungary, which had formerly been united in the Austro-Hungarian Empire. The City group had formed a syndicate called the Anglo-Danubian Syndicate and it decided to send out a representative to study local conditions and make proposals for practical action. I was asked to undertake this task. This opened up for me a wide new field of opportunity. I saw it as a challenge to which I must respond.

35

The most active firm in the Syndicate was Frederick Huth & Co. (of Tokenhouse Yard); but Rothschilds were also greatly interested and I had many discussions at their historical old office in New Court. The Syndicate's venture did not lead to any practical results which are worth recording; but my impressions of conditions in the three 'Succession States' have some historical significance.

Austria in its diminished form had been left like a head without a body, since all the industrial enterprise of the old Empire had been located in what was now the separate country of Czechoslovakia. Vienna, with its great palaces and its world-famous Opera House, its Chamber of Commerce and other headquarter organisations, had no foundation for economic life. The dominating problem was shortage of food. The only people who were assured of quite adequate supplies were those few who had their own agricultural and forest estates. It was tragic to see all others, including those of the highest intellectual capacity, dominated by their concern about food—how to get their next meal. The Government was unable to cope with the problem and I have a picture of the typical minister as a small man baffled by his problems and seated in the corner of some vast room of one of the old Viennese palatial residences.

In Czechoslovakia the position was totally different. That territory had been the workshop of the old Austro-Hungarian Empire. All its factories, some of international importance, were located there and had resumed activity after the war. The country therefore enjoyed economic prosperity, but I got an unfavourable impression of the attitude at that time of many of the leading politicians. The veteran Masaryk impressed me as the one really great and far-sighted statesman. In particular I remember the bitter hostility of their policy for dealing with the large minority of Sudeten Germans in the new state. I specially note this because later it had some effect on my view of Hitler's policy for extending German control over Czechoslovakia.

When I went on to Hungary I found myself again in completely different conditions: there were serious dangers of Red Communist risings inspired from Russia and at the time of my visit one under the leadership of Bela Kuhn had to be dealt with. At the same time, with Admiral Horthy at the head of the Government and the leading figures in social life still retaining their belief in the old aristocracy, the whole atmosphere seemed to me completely unstable and unrealistic. I felt no sympathy for what I regarded as the snobbish 'aristocratic' ideas of the educated social classes. My personal visit to Admiral Horthy in his great palace south of the Danube lives in my memory. I was conducted to see him through long passages with military guards stationed at many points clad in mediaeval crimson uniforms and holding long pikes. Admiral Horthy's general appreciation of the situation in Europe was that all troubles and all disturbances were due to the influence of Jews. So far as concerned economic viability, however, the new state of Hungary could have provided the necessary basis, but the frontiers had been drawn without taking account of detailed local conditions and in certain cases left factories on one side of a frontier with their sources of labour supply and raw materials on the other.

My broad impression about the whole area of the 'Succession States' was that the division into separate governments and the drawing of the frontiers between them had been settled in Paris without any proper consideration of local conditions, thus creating a situation which would inevitably lead to trouble in the future. This impression affected my views about Hitler's aspirations when he became the leader in Germany.

Although my report for the Anglo-Danubian Syndicate did not contain any effective proposals for helping the revival of economic activity in the 'Succession States' it was regarded by the members of the Syndicate as a valuable and realistic document and eventually led to my being offered a salaried post with Frederick Huth & Co. which gave me a financial basis for acquiring a house in London.

During my work in that position I was also asked to attend meetings of the Finance Committee of the League of Nations at Geneva, chiefly those concerned with the floating of reconstruction loans for Austria and Hungary. The Finance Committee was at the same time also examining ways for helping economic revival by assisting private businesses and eventually approved a scheme for enabling individual undertakings to get supplies of raw materials on loan supported by guarantees from the Governments of their countries, to be repaid by the sale of finished products. This scheme had been originally proposed by Mr. Ter Meulen, a partner in the Dutch banking firm of Hope Brothers, and had, much to his surprise, been fully approved by the Finance Committee of the League of Nations. Having approved this scheme the Finance Committee decided to appoint an Organiser of International Credits (Sir Drummond Drummond Fraser) and I was offered a well paid post as Chief Secretary to the Organiser. This meant retiring from my post with Frederick Huth, though I still maintained close contacts with them.

I established a convenient office in London and was in constant touch with Geneva which led to the formation of many friendships with leading League personalities such as Nansen and Philip Noel-Baker. One amusing personal experience was that Nansen had expressed a great desire to have a day's fox-hunting in England and I had to arrange to get him a horse and take him out for a day with the Heythrop Hounds. We happened to have a very bad day in pouring rain and I still retain a vivid picture of Nansen galloping about at top speed on every possible occasion, regardless of what hounds were doing.

During the years of my work for Frederick Huth & Co. and for the Finance Committee of the League of Nations I continued to take an active interest in the general economic position in Britain. I maintained close friendships with certain members of the Labour Party, notably Arthur Greenwood and J. J. Mallen, and I was appointed a member of the Economic Research Organisation of the Party. I also took a leading part in organising discussions among a wide group which led to a series of conferences arranged by John Astor at Hever Castle. In these discussions I established a close friendship with Seebohm Rowntree and the group produced a broad appreciation of the British economic position under the title of *The Third Winter of Unemployment* (London 1922).

In the meanwhile my general interest in economic conditions had led to another important appointment. As a significant feature in its plans to stimulate economic recovery the Government had decided that it would guarantee the service of loans raised by private industrial companies for capital expenditure on measures which would help to provide employment. To give effect to this policy, legislation was approved in the form of the Trade Facilities Act (1922). One provision of this Act was that a small Committee should be appointed to scrutinise and approve all applications for guaranteed loans. The Government decided to appoint Sir Robert Kindersley (Lord Kindersley) and Sir William Plender (later Lord Plender) and also consulted the Labour Party about the appointment of a third member. I can record that the Senior Treasury Officers who were concerned with this matter were surprised and greatly relieved when they found my name on the list of individuals proposed by the Labour Party. I was duly appointed as the third member of the Trade Facilities Act Advisory Committee and as the junior member who would have time available to give detailed attention to the study of individual applications. This provided me with a valuable form of activity and enabled me to establish a wide range of personal friendships and connections throughout the British financial and industrial world.

This was my position when I received the opportunity of a new adventure—a request from the Foreign Office that I should accept the appointment for five years as Financial Secretary in the Sudan. I and my wife were then faced with a very difficult choice involving much reflection. In finally deciding to accept the challenge I was greatly influenced by Sir James Currie, one of the original members of the Sudan Government, who after his retirement from the Sudan had become the general director of the Empire Cotton Growing Corporation and whom I can regard as one of the main friends in my life.

CHAPTER V

The Sudan, 1922-27

I LOOK BACK on my years in the Sudan as the most rewarding experience of my work in positions of government responsibility. For me it was a personal success story; and it also gave me the chance to take part for five years in what I regard as one of the finest chapters in the history of the 'British Empire'.

As a background to my personal account I must give an outline sketch of the constitutional position of the Sudan. From 1820 the responsibility for the administration of this vast area of a million square miles had rested on the Government of Egypt and the record of these years, taken as a whole, is one of the blackest stories of maladministration in human history—a record of corruption by Government officials, of slave trading, of local wars and complete civil disorder. In 1884 the British Government (which in 1882 had undertaken responsibility for the tutelage of the Government of Egypt) was forced to the conclusion that Egypt's only course in her own interest was to abandon the Sudan (except the Red Sea ports) and got the Egyptian Government to agree that General Gordon should be sent to carry out the process of evacuation. There was some confusion as to General Gordon's interpretation of his task, but it is only necessary to record the tragic results—his failure to effect the evacuation, his own assassination in Khartoum, and the relapse of the Sudan into worse disorder under the Mahdi.

For the next years conditions in Egypt made it impossible to organise any effective action but in 1896 the British Government decided (partly as a result of the Mahdi's raids on Upper Egypt, but still more because of Egypt's dependence on the waters of the Nile) that plans must be made for the re-conquest of the Sudan—plans which were accomplished under Lord Kitchener and led to final success at the Battle of Omdurman in 1898.

The re-conquest of the Sudan having been achieved, the British Government was faced with the problem of how to provide for its future administration. We could not allow it to fall back into maladministration under Egypt—yet, for many reasons, we could not undertake its government as a British responsibility. There were international reasons (particularly possible trouble with the French) and also the fact that, although the re-conquest was due to British leadership and the participation of British troops, the main part of the army had been Egyptian and the main part of the cost had been met by the Egyptian Government. Lord Cromer, the British Commissioner in Egypt, devised the solution—that the Sudan should be made a condominium under the joint authority of Egypt and Great Britain, flying the flag of both countries together, and administrated by the Khedive of Egypt but nominated by the Queen of England. It was further provided that the Governor-General of the Sudan should also be Commander-in-Chief or Sirdar of the Egyptian Army, the greater part of which was to be stationed in the Sudan.

The working out of the government under this arrangement proved notably successful; and the credit for that belongs largely to Lord Cromer, who saw that everything depended on (a) the quality of the officials to be responsible for administration and (b) the education of the Sudanese population.

In the autumn of 1921 I was asked by the Foreign Office to accept the appointment for five years (1922-27) as Financial Secretary to the Sudan and Member of the Governor-General's Council. The request came from the Foreign Office because, as a result of the constitutional arrangements described above, the responsibility for the Sudan was in the hands of the Foreign and not the Colonial Office. (A very fortunate arrangement for me because the Foreign Office had no machinery for controlling overseas territories and therefore left me completely free to do my job.)

The reason for my appointment was that the Sudan Government had got into financial difficulties. At the end of 1919 the British Government had guaranteed a Sudan loan of £6,000,000 mainly to finance the completion of the extensive Gezira Irrigation Project, work on which had been started before the 1914 war. The canalisation had been entrusted to the Egyptian Irrigation Department (directed by British irrigation experts) and it was found in 1921 that, with the money nearly all spent, less than half the work had been completed. This had given the British Government a rude shock and led to a complete re-shaping of the plan by giving the completion of the canalisation work on contract to Pearsons, after calling for competitive tenders. The additional finance was provided by a further Sudan loan guaranteed by the British Government under the Trade Facilities Act.

The new plan worked out well. The works necessary for the operation of the Gezira project were completed by the due date in 1925, and, as explained in a later part of my story, became a main factor in the economic development of the Sudan. Satisfactory progress was also made in other parts of the Government's financial and economic responsibilities and so for two years all went well for my work on the economic front.

On the political front, however, signs of trouble began in 1924. After the 1914-18 War a move towards a system of parliamentary democracy in Egypt had been inevitable. The British protectorate was terminated in 1922 and a General Election in January 1924 had resulted in the return of Zaghlul, the leader of the extreme nationalist Egyptian party—the WAFD, with a 90 per cent majority in Parliament.

Zaghlul was violently anti-British and he started to make a series of public speeches on the theme that the British were usurpers in the Sudan and that no patriotic Egyptian could sleep quietly in his bed as long as a single Englishman remained there. At the same time anti-British agitators were sent in and encouraged from Egypt. To appreciate the significance of all this it must be realised that the whole of the armed forces in the Sudan, except for one British battalion, were provided by the Egyptian Army. These forces consisted partly of Egyptian units (three infantry battalions and three batteries of artillery) and partly of locally recruited Arab and Sudanese units (infantry and camel corps). In these units the three senior officers were British regular army officers seconded for 10 years service with the Egyptian army, while half the junior officers were Egyptian and half Sudanese. The whole Egyptian army was still, as in Kitchener's time, under a British Commander-in-Chief, the Sirdar—who was also Governor General of the Sudan. He himself, together with all the British officers, was thus in the service of the King of Egypt while all the non-British regimental officers (Sudanese as well as Egyptians) had, in taking their commissions, sworn an oath of allegiance to the King of Egypt.

Clearly, therefore, it was a highly dangerous situation to have the Prime Minister of Egypt, a country which in agreement with Britain had adopted a constitution of parliamentary democracy, preaching that it was the duty of every patriotic Egyptian to join in driving out all Englishmen from the Sudan.

In telling the story of what then happened I may sound rather egotistical, because I must tell it in a personal way; but it so happened that, having been sent out by the British Foreign Office, I had inevitably a rather special position of authority and also, as one coming fresh from outside, I was inclined to take an independent view. At any rate I did take the initiative in the course which was followed. In the first place it seemed to me as clear as daylight that a situation in which all the armed forces of the Sudan owed their allegiance to the King of Egypt could not safely continue. Therefore it was necessary to work out a plan for two purposes; *first* to evacuate the Egyptian units and eliminate the Egyptian officers from the Sudanese units and *secondly* to reconstitute a Sudan Defence Force under the control of the Sudan Government. The detailed preparations were made by the Chief Staff Officer to the Sirdar, a man of first class ability and great courage in the person of General Huddleston, who had won a great reputation as Commander of the Camel Corps in the First World War and who was to become Governor-General in the Second World War.

My next step was to get the Governor-General to allow me to go back to London in the summer of 1924 to put up our case and play our hand with the British Government. I look back on that as the most interesting experience of my life. In 1924, the first Labour Government was in office, though with only a minority in Parliament. Ramsay MacDonald was both Prime Minister and Foreign Secretary and he, at that time, according to my experience, was a really fine man—well informed, interested, and ready to take quick decisions.

My main official discussions were of course with the Foreign Office, but beyond this I felt that somehow or other I must get our case understood by the rank and file of the Labour Party. For this purpose I first went to see old George Lansbury who was Chairman of the Labour side of the Empire Parliamentary Association. Lansbury was a lovable, if unpractical, idealist and he listened to me with great sympathy. I had of course to expect that the natural inclination of Labour Party members at that time would be to take an anti-Imperalist view and therefore to have some sympathy with a democratic Egyptian party trying to throw off British Imperial control. So I had to get across an understanding of what Egyptian control of the Sudan had in the past meant. George Lansbury arranged for me to address a large group of Labour members and I got some of their leading personalities—notably Tom Johnston—to read some accounts of Egyptian maladministration after 1820.

To have obtained support from the Labour rank and file was most satisfactory, while at the same time I had got a most sympathetic hearing from the officials of the Foreign Office and, most important of all, from Ramsay MacDonald himself at personal interviews. In spite of his immense burden of work as both Prime Minister and Foreign Secretary he was always accessible and ready to appreciate the problem.

During the summer of 1924 serious outbreaks of violence, inspired by Egyptian agitators, occurred in the Sudan at the railway workshops at Atbara and at, Port Sudan. Then in September Zaghlul came to London to see Ramsay MacDonald. He came with great hopes, because Ramsay himself in the days when he was a rebel against the British Government had spent time in Egypt and fraternised with Zaghlul as a fellow rebel. So Zaghlul thought he would have an easy task in getting support from his old friend for his claims on the Sudan. He got a rude shock—Ramsay the Prime Minister was a very different man from Ramsay the rebel. Zaghlul with his claims made him extremely angry. "That old fellah", as he called him, must be put in his place.

So Zaghlul went back to Egypt at the end of September having completely failed in his mission. He was a violent man and clearly would not accept the situation quietly. We had many discussions about future action at the Foreign Office leading to a special meeting on October 6th with Ramsay MacDonald in his small private study at No. 10 Downing Street. This meeting remains vividly in my memory. There were present Ramsay MacDonald, Lord Allenby (High Commissioner in Egypt), Sir Lee Stack (Governor-General of the Sudan), Sir William Tyrell of the Foreign Office and myself. Sir Lee Stack was a charming man with strong feelings of loyalty to and friendship for all the Egyptian officials and officers with whom he had worked for many years, and he had a temperamental dislike for violent action. Ramsay, who was always specially friendly to me, allowed me to express my views. I said, "You have sent Zaghlul back with a flea in his ear. He is bound to make violent trouble. I cannot predict exactly what form it will take, but it is certain that it will mean bloodshed." I therefore urged strongly that immediate action should be taken and that this must include getting the Egyptian army out of the Sudan (for which we had all our plans ready).

Ramsay MacDonald said "You say there will be bloodshed; but you are asking me to take the initiative in a line of action which may well start it. I can't do that. It is against my character and I'll tell you why. I'm a bad sailor and when I have to make a voyage and the sea is likely to be rough I find a sheltered corner, wrap myself up in a rug and keep as quiet as I can. Then all my friends say to me 'What a fool you are Mac. You ought to walk about and get it over'. But my reply is, 'If I once start being sick, I don't know when it may stop. I'd rather keep quiet on the chance that I can get through!' And that's how I feel about what you are asking me to do" "Anyhow" he added "after another day I shall no longer be Prime Minister". (In saying this he had in mind the debate in Parliament on the "Campbell Case" fixed for October 8th, which did in fact result in a heavy defeat for the Labour Government followed by the dissolution of Parliament on October 9th.)

But this was not Ramsay's last word. He went on to say that he fully recognised the dangers of trouble ahead and the need to be ready to fight Zaghlul and that, although he could not now take responsibility for starting trouble by firing the first shot himself, he would "load a pistol' for Lord Allenby by sending him a despatch containing a strong statement about British policy affecting the Sudan. The despatch was duly sent on October 7th 1924 and published in a White Paper (Cmd. 2269).

During the weeks which followed until the General Election of October 29th (which resulted in a large majority for the Conservative Party) we remained in constant touch with the Foreign Office and had some further meetings with Ramsay MacDonald. I continued to emphasise my warning of danger ahead and the need for definite action about the Egyptian Army in the Sudan. I note from my records that I tried to get J. H. Thomas who was then Colonial Secretary to emphasise the need to Ramsay MacDonald.

The Foreign Office officials however took the view that we ought to be very satisfied with having got Ramsay MacDonald to send his despatch of October 7th and that with the General Election pending it was impossible to expect him to do anything more.

After our final meeting before Sir Lee Stack's return to the Sudan I have a vivid recollection of urging him to go straight back to Khartoum and not to stay, as he usually did, for several weeks in Cairo. He did not heed my advice. I myself had meant to travel back with him, but at the last moment I was delayed by some important business negotiations for the Sudan Government in London. So I left two weeks later and, as I got on to the boat at Trieste for the crossing to Alexandria, I was handed a telegram saying that Sir Lee Stack had been shot in Cairo and, though still alive, was unlikely to survive. So my foreboding of bloodshed was fulfilled, though in a form very different from any action which might have been contemplated by Zaghlul. He had in fact failed to control the anti-British agitation which he had started and the result proved disastrous for him.

When I arrived in Cairo many things had happened.* Lee Stack himself had died on November 19th and Lord Allenby had sent a proposed form of ultimatum for approval to the Foreign Office; but no reply had come for several days. Allenby had information that Zaghlul's Government might resign at any moment. As that would mean that he would be left without any Government to which to present an ultimatum he decided on November 22nd that he could wait no longer. He called out the whole regiment of the 16/5th Lancers (then stationed in Cairo) to act as an escort and drove down to the Egyptian Parliament. As he was leaving the Residency one of his officials rushed in to say that a long telegram from the Foreign Office had just arrived and was being deciphered, but Allenby said, "I can't wait now. I have got what I want in my pocket".

Unfortunately Allenby's ultimatum included a demand that the Sudan should have an unlimited right to divert Nile water for the Gezira irrigation project, instead of for the limited area of 300,000 acres which had been formally agreed with the Egyptian Government. This was a condition which the British Government could not support. They cabled that it must be withdrawn and at the same time the Foreign Secretary (Austen Chamberlain who had just succeeded Ramsay MacDonald) informed Allenby that he was immediately sending out to Cairo a senior diplomatic official, Neville Henderson, to be Allenby's chief adviser. It is not part of my story to comment on this, but I have often thought that if Ramsay Macdonald had still been Prime Minister and Foreign Secretary things might have been handled differently.

I arrived in Cairo in the midst of the confusion caused by all this, and I was ordered by the Foreign Office to stay there until the position was cleared up. The Foreign Office seemed very anxious at the time to give Allenby plenty of advice, for a message was also sent to old Asquith, who happened to be in Cairo at the time, asking him to be at hand. He, as a wise old man, promptly decide to get out of Cairo on a hastily planned visit to Palestine.

The offending clause about the Nile Waters was quickly withdrawn but what mattered to us in the Sudan was that the clause demanding the evacuation of the Egyptian Army units and the Egyptian officers of the Sudanese units was confirmed. As soon as that was clear it was only necessary to send General Huddleston a telegram of one word: 'Evacuate'. All our plans for this complicated operation had been worked out, but would it be possible to

---

* The story of the events in Cairo is fully told by Lord Wavell in his book *Allenby in Egypt* (1941). My memory of what happened agrees exactly with his account; though I do not attempt to go into such detail I can perhaps add a touch of local colour because I was actually present in the days which followed.

get the Egyptian units to go and to persuade the Egyptian officers to leave the Sudanese units?

There was trouble in two places about getting the Egyptian officers to leave the Sudanese units, and serious difficulties in getting some of the Egyptian units to entrain. We had to get the Egyptian Minister for War to fly down to influence them. The one serious and tragic incident was caused by Egyptian officers having misled some men of one of the Sudanese battalions stationed at Khartoum. This resulted in a mutiny which led to casualties on both sides and to the final destruction by shelling of the building in which the mutineers took refuge.

After the military evacuation, sporadic outbreaks of disorder still continued in the Sudan as a result of the work of Egyptian agitators. The Legal Secretary, Sir Wasey Sterry, was Acting Governor-General at Khartoum and he kept sending me telegrams asking for further drastic action. Though we had got rid of the Egyptian Army personnel, the status of the Condominium still remained, so that the two flags, the Union Jack and green flag of Egypt, still flew side by side on all Government buildings. 'We shall never have peace and security as long as the green flag flies' had become the catchword at Khartoum, and Sterry finally sent me a telegram to be put before Allenby describing the current situation and demanding a termination of the Condominium. Allenby read it, flung it down in fury and turned to me saying 'Sterry is a die-hard. I am not a die-hard. Tell him that he has got to carry on and that if there is a riot and they stone him to death we shall find another man with a thicker skin to put in his place'. I myself agreed with Allenby. I did not pass on his brutal words to Sterry, but I felt sure of two things: first that the local fears were exaggerated and that the trouble would calm down, secondly that there was not the remotest chance of getting the British Government to denounce the Condominium. In the event my view on both these points proved right.

I got down to Khartoum soon after this last exchange with Allenby. As a first task I had to tackle the financial situation. The Egyptian Government had hitherto borne the cost of all the troops in the Sudan except our one British battalion. We had now kicked them out and organised a Sudan Defence force. This left us with a substantially smaller garrison than that provided by the Egyptian Army, but its annual cost would be £750,000 and our Sudan Government revenues could not possibly provide this sum. It seemed to us obvious that, since the whole process had been approved by the British Government, they would accept the financial consequences. When, however, we put in an application for a special grant, we were met with a flat refusal by the Treasury and told that we must apply to the Egyptian Government for the money. That, at the time, seemed to us a humiliating course. But it had to be followed. I was fortunate in having as my representative in Cairo a very wise and experienced Syrian, Shoucair Pasha, who had worked with the British and Egyptians since Kitchener's time. I had to tell him that he must make an application to the Egyptian

Government. Such an application could only be based on the ground that it would be in their own interest to give us a grant as a recognition of their continuing claim for a share in the responsibility for maintaining security and order in the Sudan. Shoucair Pasha was immediately successful and we got the necessary annual grant of £750,000 from Egypt.

Looking back today, I can appreciate that the British Government's decision was right and should be seen as part of a consistent and correct policy. The guiding lines of this policy have been to recognise Egypt's vital interest in the Sudan (mainly because of her dependence on Nile waters), and to work according to the principles of the Condominium while it lasted; but, looking beyond that, to help to create conditions in which the people of the Sudan would themselves be responsible for the administration of their country and for deciding in what way recognition should be given to the legitimate interests of Egypt.

A further reflection is concerned with the way in which things actually worked out in 1924. It was in fact a miraculous stroke of good fortune for us that Zaghlul's plans for a well-organised anti-British movement in the Sudan were upset by the murder of Sir Lee Stack. This put Zaghlul wrong in the eyes of the world and gave us a justification for immediate action before he had had time fully to organise his contemplated plan for spreading anti-British movements in the Sudan. In particular, if he had had sufficient time to bring political influence to bear on the Egyptian troops in the Sudan and on the Egyptian officers in the Sudanese units, it might have proved impossible for us to secure their orderly withdrawal.

My account of the political crisis of 1924 has been a necessary part of my personal story; but, although that crisis involved considerable diversion of effort for me, its results did not affect the significance of my normal task as Financial Secretary. The political disturbance had no appreciable effect on the general economic life of the country, while the general financial position of the Government was not affected because the grant from the Egyptian Government covered the cost of the new Sudan Defence Force.

My essential tasks in the Sudan were on the one hand to work for efficiency and economy in the Government services, and on the other hand to develop sources of revenue for a country in which the possibilities of tax revenue were limited because there was no substantial volume of private business enterprise earning taxable profits.

Looking back I see myself as having been influenced by two general purposes which deserve special mention.

The first was to make all members of the Government recognise that they were involved in a joint responsibility for ensuring the financial viability of the Government. In many of the positions of financial responsibility which I have held during my long life I have had to fight against the idea that 'finance' is a mystery which only the financial expert can understand and that the 'finance member' of a directing body must have the responsibility for handling financial issues in the light of his special 'expertise'. (In the

Sudan I had an impression that my predecessor had encouraged this idea.) It was my special effort in the Sudan to make all heads of departments understand the financial position as a whole and to get general agreement on financial allocations based on an accepted order of priorities.

A second important purpose for me was to ensure technical efficency in all fields of work in which practical experience was needed, and for this purpose to get outside advice and cooperation where this was appropriate and available. There is a special need for this in the case of a small government establishment such as was possible for the Sudan. As one illustration of this, I got Sir Felix Pole, then General Manager of the Great Western Railway, to visit the Sudan and study our railway position. He produced a valuable report and, as a result of his visit, the Sudan railway service was adopted as a special protégé of the Great Western Railway.

The other line of my work which illustrates the value of outside experience and which for its own sake deserves special mention was that connected with the Gezira Irrigation Project. That project has been, and still is, a dominating factor in the economic life of the Sudan. It has attracted world-wide attention and the story of its working and development has been fully told by Sir Arthur Gaitskell.* From the first days of the establishment of the new Government of the Sudan in 1898, it had been realised that the most effective way to improve the economic position of the country would be to take advantage of the possibility for increasing agricultural production by use of the Nile waters for irrigation. A unique opportunity existed for this kind of development by the diversion of water from the Blue Nile to irrigate the vast area of flat land lying between the Blue and White Niles. Plans for this purpose had been made before the 1914 war, and active work for the construction of a dam and irrigation channels had been started after 1918. The first stage, settled in agreement with Egypt, had been for the irrigation of 300,000 acres, of which, in a three year rotation, one third was to be used for cotton, one third for the production of grain crops and one third left fallow.

In settling practical arrangements for the working of this plan the policy of the Sudan Government was influenced by two main considerations, first, that the arrangements must be such as to promote the interest of the native population and, secondly, that successful working would involve a wide range of business operations requiring practical experience which the Sudan Government itself could not provide.

The area to be irrigated had previously been used by the local population for the production of such crops as an inadequate and uncertain rainfall made possible. The basic purpose of the Government was to settle the ownership of land with those who had previously cultivated it and, for this purpose, a detailed survey was undertaken. The final plan divided the land in the area to be irrigated into individual holdings of 30 acres with each

* *Gezira* by Sir Arthur Gaitskell (1959).

native owner settled as nearly as possible on land which he had previously cultivated.

Having provided in this way for a recognition of the interests of the native population, the operation of the project was planned as a threefold partnership between the Government, a Syndicate and the native owners. The cost of major works and the main canals was to be financed by the Government. The Syndicate was to be responsible (under Government control) for minor canalisation and for the business management of the enterprise (financing the tenants, ginning and marketing the cotton crop, etc.). The tenants were to receive a rental for the land and supply the necessary labour. The gross profits from the resultant cotton crop were to be divided between the native tenants, the Syndicate and the Government in the proportions of 40, 25 and 35 per cent respectively. All crops other than cotton grown in the process of rotation were to go tax-free to the native tenants. Under this arrangement it is fair to claim that the interests of the natives were given very full recognition. Their ownership of the land was secured, they were to receive a rental for it, they were to get the full proceeds of all crops other than cotton and a substantial share in the net profits realised from the handling of the cotton crop. The most significant feature of the whole plan, as I saw it, was that the native cultivators were put into the position of partners in a joint venture, rather than wage-earning employees under an independent commercial business organisation. Looking back from the perspective of the 1970s it gives me some satisfaction that later commentators were to acknowledge that in subsequent years these arrangements served as an important precedent for major peasant-based agricultural development projects throughout the Third World.

13. Tenants bagging cotton in the Gezira

It remains to explain the circumstances in which the Sudan Government came to appoint the Sudan Plantation Syndicate as the organisation to undertake the business management of the Gezira project. An important figure in all the discussions which led to this was Sir James Currie, who had been the first Director of Education in the Sudan on the establishment of the Condominium after 1898. Currie's heart was in the Sudan, but it also happened that after the 1914 war, as Chairman of the Empire Cotton Growing Corporation, he became a leading figure in our national plan for increasing the production of cotton from countries under British control so as to reduce the dependence of our textile industry on cotton from the U.S.A. Currie, in consultation with Arthur Asquith, who had been a member of the Sudan Political Service before the war, was largely responsible for getting together the group which formed the Sudan Plantation Syndicate and for initiating the discussions with the Sudan Government which led to the appointment of the Syndicate as the business managers of the Gezira project.

Looking back on the relations between the Sudan Government and the Sudan Plantation Syndicate, I think it fair to claim that the working of the Gezira project provided a notable example of how collaboration between a Government and a private profit-making business enterprise can be managed in such a way as to promote the public interest. This was largely due to the personalities of those holding leading responsibilities on the Syndicate's side. The active directors with whom I had close personal contacts were Sir Frederick Eckstein, the Chairman, Lord Lovat and Arthur Asquith. These were men with whom it was possible to have realistic discussions with complete frankness on both sides and without personal acrimony. At the same time the managerial staff of the Syndicate (under Alexander McIntyre in my time) were of first-class quality and worked in friendly cooperation with government officials. While the personal quality of the leaders on the Syndicate's side helped to make true cooperation in the public interest possible, that could not have been fully achieved without vigilance and business efficiency on the government side. The Syndicate quite legitimately was concerned primarily with the interests of its shareholders and had to fight to obtain a reasonable return for them on their investment. It was the Government's responsibility to secure the public interest. I cannot claim any share in having settled the terms of the original agreement with the Syndicate; but I had to play an active part in handling negotiations started in 1926 when the Government was able to consider an extension of the whole project and for a number of reasons decided to work this in collaboration with the Syndicate. A full account of the negotiations which then followed is contained in Sir Arthur Gaitskell's book.

For the purpose of my personal story I need only record the practical result which was that the division of the profits from the Cotton Group was revised in favour of the Sudan Government. The share of the native tenants remained unchanged at 40 per cent, but the Government's share was increased from 35 to 40 per cent and the Syndicate's reduced from 25 to 20 per cent. The negotiations were difficult and in the end the Sudan Government had to take a tough line, but it is satisfactory to note that in a letter from Sir Frederick Eckstein to me he included the following statement:

> 'I desire to acknowledge the generous spirit in which you have conducted a settlement of the difficulties which have arisen and to assure you that everything possible will be done by my colleagues and myself to reciprocate this spirit.'

I will end my reference to the Gezira project on a personal note. Arthur Asquith ('Oc') was a leading figure. With regular annual visits to the Sudan he was able to play an active part in the direction of the Syndicate's work. Beyond this he had a notable influence on its relations with the Government because he was so greatly admired and respected by all the Government officers. He had, before 1914, been one of the best young members of the Sudan Political Service, and during the war he had an outstanding record—five times wounded, three immediate awards of the DSO and rising from Second Lieutenant to the command of a Brigade. 'Oc' was one of the great friends of my life. He used to stay with me at my house in Khartoum and on one occasion his father, the ex-Prime Minister, stayed with him. The old man was wonderful company and they were a remarkable pair. I have vivid recollections of them spending hours talking together walking up and down my long verandah looking out over the Nile—part of my picture of what life in the Sudan meant.

I have written at length about the Gezira Project because that was such an important factor in the field of my financial responsibilities, but in working out general plans for economic development it was necessary to study a wide range of projects—projects for railway extensions, for improvements at Port Sudan, and for cotton growing in other areas. This broad field of my work made it necessary for me to travel widely and gave me the opportunity to learn something about the country and to make personal friendships with a wide range of District Officers.

My work, however, was not confined to the Sudan. There was much business that required discussion in Cairo and in London, where the Sudan maintained an active office. Business in Cairo involved discussions with the Egyptian Government and also with the British High Commissioner. We had to recognise that Egypt was an equal partner in the Condominium and therefore must be kept informed about the administration of the Sudan. Contacts with the Egyptian Government involved tiresome formalities as well as business discussions. For the former it was considered right for me always to ask for an audience with the King of Egypt—in my time King Fuad. On these occasions I had to put on a frock coat and a red tarbush—worth recalling as an illustration of the times. Talking to King Fuad was disconcerting because his remarks were constantly interrupted by a 'bark'—the result of having been shot through the throat in his early life as a private individual in Italy. He was a shrewd man who asked intelligent questions, but I never had any difficulty in dealing with these.

14. The Sennar Dam across the Blue Nile (1925)

15. The Kassala Railway built in 1920's

My contacts with the High Commissioner were of much greater importance. In my account of the political crisis in 1924 I have already referred to my relations with Lord Allenby who had not in normal times concerned himself closely with details about the Sudan administration. Lord Lloyd, who as Sir George Lloyd had succeeded Allenby, was a very different man. He regarded himself as having a definite responsibility for Sudan affairs, and my relations with him were very intimate. He became in fact a close personal friend, giving me support in all that I was trying to do, and I look back on him in my memory with deep affection. He was a dynamic character who created difficulties for himself because he always wanted to be the central figure on the stage in scenes of dramatic action. As High Commissioner in Cairo he could only be such a figure at a time of political crisis. As a result, he did in effect try to create critical situations—a practice which eventually got him into trouble with the Foreign Office. Jumping forward fifteen years, I have a vivid memory of being called to see him one night (in the middle of an air-raid) in 1940 in his room in Whitehall as Colonial Secretary and of his saying to me bitterly that it had taken a world war to get him back out of obscurity into a position of national responsibility.

My annual visits to London also took much of my time. These were essential since there was regular Sudan business which had to be handled in London and for which the Foreign Office had no machinery comparable to that of the Crown Agents for the Colonies under the Colonial Office. During my regular annual visits to London I also got involved in advisory work for the Colonial Office to which I shall refer later.

In my long life I have worked as a member of many different communities. I, as an 'outsider' working for the central government, had a special opportunity to see the distinctive character of the Sudan Political Service, of which I am proud to have been made an honorary member.

The character of the Sudan community was set by the Political Service and the quality of that Service was in effect determined by Lord Cromer's initial decision that its members should be chosen by 'selection' (rather than examination) 'from the English Universities of young men endowed with good health, high character and fair abilities'. (These were Lord Cromer's words, but for those who eventually formed the Political Service the assessment of 'fair abilities' is grossly inadequate.) As a result the Sudan Political Service became the finest service of its kind in the world.

I felt this strongly at the time and, in speaking at the farewell party given to me in 1927 by members of the Sudan Political Service, I quoted with complete conviction Santayana's words: 'The Englishman carries his English weather in his heart wherever he goes, and it becomes a cool spot in the desert, a steady and sane oracle among all the deliriums of mankind. Never since the heroic days of Greece has the world had such a sweet, just, boyish master. It will be a black day for the human race when scientific blackguards, conspirators, churls and fanatics manage to supplant him.'

Writing today I must of course recognise that all was not perfect and that in the course of the years there have been many criticisms, some based on genuine grounds, some voiced by political agitators inspired from Egypt; but I still think that my appreciation of the Sudan Service is broadly justified, and in this I am encouraged by what Dame Margery Perham has written about her impressions gained in her visit to the Sudan in 1936:

'In Colonial government and in the process of decolonisation there is no standard pattern. Yet the Sudan Government struck me as having a marked originality. In travelling round the provinces and districts it seemed to me there was a more friendly and constructive relationship between officials and people than I had hitherto encountered.'

Again, after emphasising the importance of the position of District Commissioners, she wrote:

'Nowhere else in Africa, it seemed to me, was the tradition of these Officers so high or the friendliness and even affection towards them of the people so widespread as in the Sudan.'

What then were the distinctive qualities of the Sudan Government? As I saw it, the essential elements were a strong sense of community, devotion to the task, determination to get practical results without bothering about formalities or personal dignity, friendly collaboration between departments,

16. With Nubians in the Southern Sudan

and, not least important, a sense of humour. To sum up, it was a happy community devoted to its work.

I have many memories of the sense of humour. I still think of how my dear friend Robin Bailey, when as Governor of Kassala Province he was discussing with me his annual budget estimates, telegraphed me 'The Legal Secretary wants me to have another judge. I would rather have a motor lorry'. Or again I recall a minute, written by my senior finance officer, commenting on a financial plan submitted by one of our imaginative juniors: 'Alice tried this in Wonderland, but it didn't come off.'

As illustrating the lack of formality or of any craving for outward signs of status (the 'Royal bug') one of my vivid memories is of a special scene. In succession to Lee Stack, the British Government appointed Sir Geoffrey Archer to be our new Governor-General. He, at the time, was Governor of Uganda and so he came to Khartoum on a Sudan Government steamer down the Nile. We, the members of Council, assembled on the quay in front of the Khartoum Palace to meet him, dressed, according to our normal practice, in our working lounge suits. As the steamer drew up to the quayside we were startled by the vision of Archer's towering figure (6′ 7″ tall) clad in a white uniform with decorations and a cocked hat with flying feathers on his head, and supported by his ADC in a similar white uniform. We would not have expected Lee Stack to arrive like this, and Archer on his side may have been shocked by our shabby appearance. This may seem a trivial incident, but in my view it has significance as a sign of the intimate and informal relationship between Government officials and the people of the country.

The District Officers understood and admired the ways of the people. They wished to improve their standards by developments which fitted in with their own ways of life and not by the introduction of external commercial enterprise. The intervention of the Sudan Plantation Syndicate in the Gezira project was accepted because that improved material conditions for the people without disturbing their normal way of life. Beyond that, however, we were reluctant to encourage the development of external commercial enterprises. We could not of course keep the Sudan as an isolated community, and it was, for example, impossible to avoid granting some concessions for mineral exploration but I (and I feel sure all my colleagues would have agreed) used to pray that nothing would be found to justify the establishment of an important mining industry. (In fact to our great relief nothing was found.)

Reflecting on these considerations and, above all, on the fact that in the climatic condition of the Sudan there could be no possibility of establishing a 'White Settler' community making a home in the country and acquiring large tracts of land, I used sometimes to think that we were finding a way for establishing a form of racial cooperation which might prove of lasting value and provide an example throughout Africa. I remember expressing this thought to Sir John Maffey when he had come to us in 1926 as our

Governor-General. He, however, with his India experience, said 'Make no mistake, the time will come when they will want to get us off their backs'. Maffey of course proved right; but I still think that the policy and practice of the Sudan Government had lasting value. When eventually the Sudan became independent in 1956 the people as a whole were ready to accept the *authority* of Government, and the spirit of friendship between the two races has survived, so that there is no centre in black Africa today in which an Englishman will get such a genuine welcome as in Khartoum.

In writing this account I am reminded of a certain incident which is not only of historical interest, but also in itself provides a significant illustration of the special character of the Sudan Service. I refer to the early termination of Sir Geoffrey Archer's appointment as Governor-General. I feel it necessary to deal with this because Archer himself in his story of his life* has given an account of this incident, which, according to my recollection, is most misleading.

The policy of the Sudan Government had always been to work in harmony with the spirit of the Sudanese people. This spirit was directly influenced by the character of the different tribal organisations; but, over this, there was the influence of certain religious leaders. Of these in my time there were two of dominating importance—Sidi El Mirghani (resident in Khartoum) and Said Abderahman El Mahdi, son of the Mahdi, whose central base was Aba Island on the White Nile. The policy of the Sudan Government had been to rely primarily on political collaboration with Mirghani as a religious leader. They maintained friendly personal relations with Abderahman as an individual who was working on extensive cotton growing projects; but, at that time, the possibility of a Mahdist revival had by no means disappeared, and it was the very definite policy of the Sudan Government (as approved by the British Government) to do nothing to strengthen Abderahman's position as a national leader, religious or political.

This was the position when Archer came to the Sudan as Governor-General in January 1925. A few months after his arrival in Khartoum, Archer decided to undertake a tour round the Provinces of the Southern Sudan and took with him Craig, a senior member of the Sudan Political Service. Archer in his book asserts that before leaving Khartoum he had fully discussed his idea that he would take the occasion of his journey up the White Nile to pay a personal visit to Abderahman at Aba Island. I can only state definitely that according to my recollection he had no such general discussion, most definitely not with me personally as stated in his book. The picture in my memory is that when we in Khartoum got the report of what actually happened on this visit it came to us as a staggering shock. Archer in full uniform had landed in state and presented a gold watch to Abderahman. No ceremony of this kind had ever before taken place in the

* Sir Geoffrey Archer *Personal and Historical Memoirs of an East-African Administrator* (London 1963).

55

17. The Government of the Sudan in 1926 with the author to the right of the Governor-General, Sir Geoffrey Archer

Sudan and the decision to pay such a special honour to one of the main religious leaders involved, as we saw it, an issue of major political importance which ought to have had full discussion by the Governor General in Council. The fact that the honour had been paid to the main religious leader whose possible influence was still regarded with apprehension by the authorities responsible for Sudan Government policy intensified our shock; but the basic point was that the decision had been taken personally by Archer without any previous discussion in Council. This was totally inconsistent with the tradition built up in the Sudan Government.

On receipt of the news we, members of the Council, met to discuss what action, if any, should be taken. There was unanimous agreement that it was our duty as responsible members of the Government to refer the whole issue to higher authority and that for the purpose Sir Wasey Sterry, the senior member of the Council, should send a report to the High Commissioner in Cairo, Sir George Lloyd, as the authoritative representative of the British Government.

Archer's statement in his book that Sterry was influenced by feelings of personal grievance is totally unjustified. We none of us had any personal feelings in the matter. We all felt strongly on the two main issues; first, that Archer had acted contrary to the spirit of the Constitution by taking the decision without consultation with his Council, and secondly that the decision itself had been dangerously wrong. I myself felt most strongly on the first issue; but the general opinion in the Sudan Political Service was more concerned about the second.

I need not give a detailed account of what then happened. It fell to me to explain the position to Archer on his return a few weeks later to Khartoum. He took the whole matter quite calmly and my impression was that, after his meeting with Sir George Lloyd in Cairo, he really saw that he was out of place in the Sudan. At any rate, after this meeting he decided to tender his resignation.

Looking back over my time in the Sudan, I see this as a period of many worries, intense interest and hard work, made happy by the feeling of working in a community of friends who appreciated the value of my contribution. As evidence of this appreciation I end this part of my story with two quotations. The first is from a letter written to me in 1927 by Douglas Newbold who was then in his early years as a District Officer and whose later career showed him to be one of the greatest of all members of the Sudan Political Service. This is what he wrote:

> 'I heard some weeks ago that you were going to leave the Sudan this year. I hope it is not true. If it is true I am sure the many DCs will share my regret. A lot of things have happened since you came to the Sudan and it is very sad to think that just as we have come to understand the things you want and are doing, and to appreciate the value of your help to the political people, you are going to leave us.'

My second quotation is from what my old friend 'MacMic', Sir Harold MacMichael, wrote* about what happened after my appointment as Financial Secretary:

> 'A revival then took place under the auspices of Lieut. Colonel Schuster who had succeeded Sir Edgar Bernard as Financial Secretary in 1922. A stringent enquiry was then held into the whole field of the government's business activities, with a view both to retrenchment of expenditure by the cutting down of staff where such was practicable and to placing the management and finances of each of the public utility departments as reorganised upon a business footing. During the next five years, the whole financial system was recast, reserves were built up, credit established on a firm foundation, remunerative schemes of economic development were launched, and a new stimulus imparted to the services of the country.'

In the course of 1927, as the end of my five years' appointment as Financial Secretary to the Sudan Government came in sight, it became necessary to consider future arrangements. I had by that time accumulated responsibilities, in connection with the financial policy of the Colonial Office, which were quite distinct from the direct responsibilities of the Sudan Financial Secretary. It is interesting to consider how this position had arisen. My impression is that the British Treasury and the Governor of the Bank of England had for some time been feeling anxiety about the general direction of financial policy by the Colonial Office so far as that involved raising capital in the London Market to cover the cost of plans for economic development in Colonial territories, especially Africa. In various ways I had established personal contacts with the Treasury and with Montagu Norman as Governor of the Bank of England. One special reason for such contacts was that I had been one of the three original members of the Advisory Committee appointed to scrutinise applications for loans to be guaranteed by the British Government under the Trade Facilities Act. I have, therefore, the impression that it was due to pressure from the Treasury and the Bank of England that in 1926 I was asked by the Colonial Secretary to become Chairman of an Advisory Committee on East African Loans. I became involved in regular meetings at the Colonial Office during my annual visits to London. Then, much more important, in 1927 the Colonial Secretary decided to appoint an Economic and Financial Adviser and asked me to accept this post on the termination of my five year appointment in the Sudan. I agreed to accept this appointment, and a room at the Colonial Office was reserved for me. At the same time it had been decided by the Sudan Government, in agreement with the Foreign Office, that I should retain a connection with the Sudan as Financial Adviser, working from its London Office. I had also been approached to take on some important

* *Anglo-Egyptian Sudan* by Sir Harold MacMichael pp. 197-8.

18. My family with trophies in our Khartoum garden

directorships in London. I had thus secured an opening for a very full new chapter in my career in London when a further request came to me, in October 1927, from the India Office to accept the post of Finance Member of the Viceroy's Council in succession to Sir Basil Blackett who was due to retire at the end of March 1928.

This faced me with a very difficult choice. It meant giving up important posts in London and, far more serious, embarking on another five years' separation from my two schoolboy sons, involving for my wife a difficult division of her own life. My wife and I reflected deeply about the choice, and when I finally decided to accept the Indian post, I think I must have been influenced by the idea that this was a challenge and that Fate had presented me with the opportunity for a new adventure.

It then remained to settle matters with the Colonial Secretary. I had a feeling that the Colonial Office staff were not unwilling to be relieved of a Financial and Economic Adviser, and eventually the Colonial Secretary agreed to release me on condition that the date for my taking up the Indian appointment should be deferred till the end of October 1928 and that in the interval, after leaving the Sudan, I should travel round East and Central Africa in a dual capacity, first as a member of the Hilton Young Commission to study and report on proposals for 'the Closer Union' of certain African Colonies and secondly as Financial and Economic Adviser to the Colonial Office to study and make recommendations on proposals for several economic development projects, notably a bridge over the Zambesi

59

to open up railway connections with Nyasaland. This involved for me a very heavy burden of work to be fitted into the period of about seven months between leaving the Sudan and my necessary departure for India.

So the sad moment came on Christmas Day 1927 for me to see my wife off at Atbara on her return to England and for me to go back to Khartoum to start my journey up the Nile on the way to join the Hilton Young Commission in Uganda.

My journey started in a way which made me realise vividly what my Sudan service with its wide range of work and its personal friendships had meant to me. I travelled on a Sudan Government steamer and had with me as companions my closest friend Peter Clarke, who had for three years been my main support in the Finance Office, and John Hewins, the Government's general economic adviser. We stopped on our way at Wad Medani for a farewell party with the staff of the Sudan Plantation Syndicate and then had some days for companionship and for reflection on my new tasks before leaving the steamer at Rejaf for the overland journey to Uganda. The final picture which remains clearest in my memory is of a sad farewell at Rejaf to my personal servant—Mahommed. I see him vividly as a tall dignified figure in his long white gallabia looking deeply moved at having to say goodbye to me.

After landing at Rejaf my Sudan colleagues and I had an adventurous two-day journey with our motor convoy to my first stopping place in Uganda. To give a picture of my arrival there I quote from one of my letters to my wife:

'We drove up finally to a large and well laid out station with an enormous red brick Church standing on a hill to one side and the official thatched buildings set out round a sort of village green. There seemed to be crowds of strangely clad people about—natives in trousers and Norfolk jackets—an old man almost entirely naked and wearing the latest 'Foreign Office' soft black felt hat, another learned looking old black gentleman in spectacles, police sergeants in red tarbushes, women in all coloured clothing—the whole thing absolutely and entirely different to the Sudan, with its Biblical atmosphere.'

CHAPTER VI

The Hilton Young Commission, 1928

As a BACKGROUND to my personal story I must give some account of the conditions in which the Commission was appointed and which affected the practical nature of its work.

The official title was 'Commission on Closer Union of the Dependencies in Eastern and Central Africa'. The 'Dependencies' to be considered fell into two groups,

1. Uganda, Kenya and Tanganyika
2. Nyasaland, Northern Rhodesia and Southern Rhodesia.

The Commission was in effect forced to concentrate its work on Group 1 because the position in Kenya demanded most urgent attention.

In Kenya, following the extension of the railway to Nairobi in 1899, some thousands of white settlers from Great Britain and the Dominions had established themselves. By the 1920s, under the leadership of Lord Delamere, they were aiming to create a white man's country in the Highlands of Kenya. There was strong local opposition to this, not only among the African natives but also from the large Indian immigrant community.* A vitally important question of British policy was involved. On the one hand the white settlers' demand could be seen as inconsistent with the British Government's policy as stated in the Colonial Office White Paper of 1923 which had reaffirmed 'the trusteeship of the Imperial Government' and declared that 'the interests of the African natives must be paramount'. On the other hand there were signs that Leo Amery, who had been appointed Colonial Secretary in 1924, had different views and that he had an ambitious plan to create a new Dominion out of the East African Dependencies. In Imperial ideas he was a follower of Milner and 'regarded East Africa in the light of South Africa after the Boer War: for effective growth closer union was necessary. In 1919 Amery had urged this as Milner's Undersecretary at the Colonial Office; now in power, he appointed Grigg to bring it about.'** Sir Edward Grigg (Governor of Kenya 1925-31) told the settlers that their request for progress towards self-government had

---

* Population of Kenya in 1926: Europeans 12,529; Arabs 10,574; Asians 30,583; Africans 2,549,300.

** G. Bennett in History of Africa, Vol. II edited by V. Harlow and E. M. Chilver (1965) p. 304.

his 'instinctive sympathy'. Amery's White Paper of 1927 declared that the Imperial Government wished to expand the settler population and associate it more closely with the government of the native peoples, a declaration which has been generally regarded as an attempted revolution in British policy in East Africa.

Reviewing the position today it is fair to say that it was with the intention of securing authoritative independent support for his plan that Amery appointed the Hilton Young Commission, members of which were Sir Edward Hilton Young, a Conservative politician, Sir Reginald Mant, a retired member of the Indian Civil Service, J. H. Oldham, Secretary of the International Missionary Council, and myself.

The Commission (on page 7 of its Report) summarised the principal question for its consideration as follows:

'First, is federation or closer union between the different territories of Eastern and Central Africa to be adopted as a means to secure more effective cooperation between them?
'Secondly, what form of constitution is suitable for those territories in which non-native immigrant communities have become permanently domiciled?'

A vast amount has been written about the Commission's Report and the discussions which followed its publication. I myself played no part in, and had no knowledge of, these later discussions, since I had to leave to take up my appointment in India in mid-October immediately after recording my own signature and before the formal presentation of our Report. The personal story which I can tell is therefore concerned only with how the Commission worked, and how the Report came to be produced. I have been able to rely on a series of letters to my wife in which I kept something like a continuous diary.

From the day when I was asked to join the Commission I thought deeply about the issues involved. I had opportunities for some preliminary discussion during my stay in London in the autumn of 1927 (including correspondence with Sir Frederick Lugard). My first opportunity, however, for quiet reflection and study of papers came during the days of my journey (at the end of December 1927) up the Nile on my way from Khartoum to join the Commission in Uganda.

Looking back now over half a century I can vividly recall the result of my preliminary reflections. I felt a heavy personal responsibility because I was the only member of the Commission who had experience of working in a Government in Africa and because my work had been in the Sudan—a country in which we had to think only of the interests of the native people, a country in which there was no possibility of white settlers making their home and acquiring ownership of large areas of land, and yet a country in which, as Sir John Maffey had warned me, we must look forward to the day when the native people, in spite of what we regarded as our disinterested service, would 'want to get us off their backs'. I felt that I had been called to play a part in reaching decisions which might make history. Above all I felt that any decision taken now about British Government policy in any part of Africa must be taken with a view which was both long and broad. It must be a long view because it must be based on a vision of how the native peoples of Africa were going to think and what they were going to want for themselves when they became more sophisticated and more closely involved in contacts with the 'developed' countries of the world. It must be a broad view in the sense that British policy in any particular area such as the East African territories must be considered as part of a coordinated policy for the whole field of British responsibilities in Africa.

Seen against the background of these ideas I felt that the proposals for closer union and political development which our Commission was now being asked to consider for the East African territories represented short-sighted proposals for dealing with special local problems. In particular I saw them as influenced by the personal ideas of Amery and Grigg, not as part of a carefully considered British Government plan. My general conclusion was that it would be impossible for our Commission to work out a satisfactory plan for the East African territories which would be acceptable to Grigg and the white settlers of Kenya in their present mood and that the East African problem must be seen as part of a wider problem which required a much fuller and more authoritative review than would be possible for our Commission.

I arrived in Uganda on January 13th, two days before the other members of the Commission. This gave me time for enquiries into matters (such as railway extension plans) in my capacity as Economic and Financial Adviser to the Colonial Office. It also gave me a chance for a personal talk with Sir Edward Grigg who had come to Entebbe for a ceremonial gathering on the occasion of the opening of an extension of the Kenya Railway into Uganda.

In my current letter to my wife I gave the following account of my first talk with Grigg in the late evening of January 13th:

'. . . After the guests went at 11.15 Grigg collared hold of me and got down to real business about what he wants in Kenya. I told him that as at present advised I could not agree with most of his arguments. He argued tonight that he did not want an *elected* unofficial majority but an unofficial majority composed of *elected* settlers, representatives, and *nominated* representatives of natives. For the latter he said he had in mind missionaries and ex-government officials settled in the country. I said either these people would not be really independent or the proposal would not satisfy the settlers. (He gave away afterwards that he really meant the natives' representatives to be settlers.) He said "If you don't do it they will follow Ulster's lead and then HMG must cave in." I broke off the argument at 12.20—Grigg at his worst! . . .'

Sir Edward Hilton Young   Leo Amery

Radio Times Hulton Picture Library

This was not only 'Grigg at his worst', but an astonishing revelation of his sympathy with the white settlers in Kenya and his feelings about their power.

The other members of the Commission arrived in Uganda on January 18th and on the following day, after a morning spent in preliminary discussions with the Governor, Sir William Gowers, we all attended a large garden party in the afternoon and the following description gives a picture of the Uganda in which the Commission began its work.

' . . . The garden party you can imagine, though the general impression differed remarkably from Khartoum. Only a fraction of the number of officials and those that were present a much dingier lot on the whole. On the other hand a vastly greater number of unofficials. Two Bishops, an Archdeacon, representatives of various orders of Religious Fathers, European commercial people, numbers of Indians, the native King of Buganda (called the Kabaka) and his Queen, etc. etc. I, with an eye to my new future, was particularly pleasant to the Indians—and indeed I liked those whom I met very much. They were all very interested in me as being designated for the Indian post. (This no doubt accounts for my liking them.)

I was also generally attacked as Chairman of the Schuster Committee (on East African Loans) by all interested in railway extensions, etc. I talked also to the Bishops—particularly to the Roman Catholic—an Irishman called Bishop Campling—a typical Irish priest. I asked him whether he thought that the natives really understood and adopted the *ethics* of the Christian religion. He said yes, really about 50 per cent of his congregation. But later he said in another conversation that they still puzzled him. They had no real moral stability—his best people were capable of sudden lapses, and there was absolutely no public ostracism of a convicted criminal. The criminal felt no sense of shame and when he came out of prison he was accepted as a friend and member of society just as though nothing had happened.

You can visualise the scene, with me among these differently coloured varieties of British subjects, all standing like graven images on a green lawn looking out over the blue sea of Lake Victoria, bougainvillaea on the trees, sago palms, the Union Jack on a great white flagstaff—the black band playing on the tennis court, Bishops in black, in white and purple, or all white, natives, British officials from Gowers to young gentlemen and ladies from Croydon and Tooting, the distinguished looking English politician in Hilton Young—the earnest Oldham—the solid Mant, etc. etc. etc. You will have a typical picture of one small part of the British Empire.'

Looking back after half a century I might add 'What a contrast to Amin's Uganda of recent years!'

After the garden party crowd had left I felt it essential (especially after my preliminary talk with Grigg) that we as members of the Commission should take advantage of our first day in Uganda to have a frank discussion together about our interpretation of our task.

'. . . My theme in starting the conversation was that we must regard our task not merely with a short view, as one of suggesting expedients for removing immediate difficulties, but rather must relate our recommendations to ideas as to the future of the British Empire in Black Africa. Whatever we recommended must be recognised as a step on a road which must lead, according to all the British Government's declarations, eventually to the self-government at least in a large measure of the Black races, and therefore we must take a view as to the form which that self-government should take in order to be

(a)   natural and therefore permanent, in the sense of being capable of development by continuous steps of evolution and not a forced form which would be thrown off by revolution

(b)   in the real interest of the native

(c)   a sound piece of construction in the fabric of the British Empire.

To illustrate my meaning I developed a line of argument—which I put up rather for illustration and criticism than as being my own finally adopted view. My argument was briefly that all evidence and all sympathetic opinion agreed that the native was not ready yet for self-government on a democratic basis on British lines, i.e. for a government the main feature of which was a popular assembly elected by our system of voting. It was very doubtful if such a form of government would ever be suited to African races or be safely built up by gradual evolution stage by stage, as it had been in England, first from popular control of matters of minor local administration and then onwards higher and higher. Nothing could possibly be worse than to bring the native into contact with our system of popular elections, with all its concomitants of agitation, manoeuvre, demagogy and professional politicians. What we wanted was to allow the native to develop naturally on his own lines which really implied an aristocratic form of organisation, with the power of local administration in the hands of chiefs and the general affairs of this to be directed by a council of chiefs. As Africa cannot any longer be isolated, but must come in contact with modern methods of transport and trade, which the native cannot direct, a paternal overseeing control by the British Government is necessary, and the proper exercise of this control, combining with the natives' own ideas, can ensure that the aristocracy as a form of government, to which the native would be submitted, would be a real aristocracy—i.e. a government by the men *best* fitted to be leaders—because the pressure of public opinion from below, combining with the power of the British Government exerted from above, could secure the removal of any chief who was abusing his position. The possibility of quiet development on the above lines is interrupted by the insertion into the native area of a white settlement area such as exists in Kenya. As long as the white man is only there as a disinterested official of a paternal Government, or as a trader seeking economic advantage but not political control, the paternal Government can with good conscience dominate the situation. But when the white settler begins to demand political influence in the paternal Government the native must in course of time demand it too and there remains no good argument for refusing it. While this difficulty is created on the one hand a second and even greater difficulty is being created on the other, if the white settler seeks to exercise his influence through representatives chosen by popular election. That system will become known to the natives who will want to imitate it partly merely because the white settlers do it, and partly because they will want equality of treatment. The result will be a sudden jump towards politics, political agitation and demagogues so that the process of gradual evolution which I had described above will be impossible, i.e. the evolution from the tribal organisation under the control of hereditary chiefs, to the best form of aristocracy with an ever increasing influence on the part of the people in the selection of their chiefs, an evolution which means a slow building up on sound foundations suitable to the native ground from below, instead of the sudden imposition of an alien system from above. If the system for giving political development to native races which I described is right, then it is a disaster that the Kenya settler demand should arise in the midst of a country which *must* always remain a 'black man's country'. It is there, however, and we cannot make it disappear, but the object should be to restrict the influence of the difficulty to as narrow a sphere as possible and to isolate it from the huge area of purely "Black Africa" which surrounds it. I argued that the *Commission* must consider whether the arguments which I had put forward were correct and that involved forming some view as to the present state of the natives and the possible choices of lines for development i.e. "Is it already too late to prevent their politicalisation?" How have they fared under the Uganda System, the Kenya System and the Tanganyika System—all of which are different? If it is not too late to make the choice, then that choice ought to be made before it is too late, and it is a choice really for the British Government to make before any changes as regards the constitution of Kenya or other countries are made, and certainly before any further powers are given to the representatives of the unofficial committees. In making its choice the British Government ought to consider not only East Africa but the whole of the British possessions in Black Africa. The views of Nigeria and the Sudan ought certainly to be considered. If possible too the British policy should be uniform with

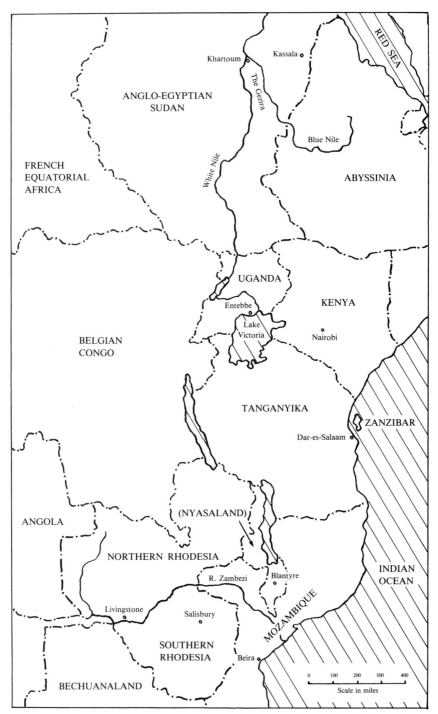

East and Central Africa in 1928

that of the Belgians in the Congo and of the French in their African colonies.

The view taken about the arguments and possibilities outlined above must influence very seriously the scope and direction of the enquiries made by the Commission. If its report is to be of any significance it may influence policy for the whole of the future in Africa.

Oldham agreed with me entirely that enquiries must be on the lines which I had indicated but disagreed with my conclusions. Hilton Young said sadly ''You have certainly brought the native question very near to our enquiries.'' Mant indicated sympathy, and then as the first mosquito had bitten somebody and it was nearly time to change for dinner we moved in . . . '

Looking back today on my statement made in 1928, and taking account of what has actually happened in the intervening half century, it must seem almost childishly unrealistic in its conception of the possible lines for development of African self-government. It is, however, a true record of my thoughts at the time and it was most definitely the right kind of statement for me to make at a first meeting with my colleagues as indicating my appreciation of the significance of our task. It was specially important to make the point that the key problem which we had to consider was not just a local Kenya problem, but one which affected the whole range of British policy in Africa.

We began in Uganda with a long series of meetings with Government officials and delegations representing various interests. The evidence provided at these meetings was important as revealing the wide differences which existed between the conditions in each of the three East African territories.

It was clear, however, that on the main issues to be considered for the three East African territories, our enquiries in Kenya were of central importance. For conducting these enquiries the Commission worked in three different ways: (a) Formal meetings in Nairobi between the whole Commission and delegates representing various interests (b) Tours of selected areas of the country and (c) Social meetings with leading personalities arranged for individual members of the Commission.

My main impression of the formal meetings in Nairobi was that, while an important part of our work, they tended to be tedious and less helpful than they might have been owing to the methods adopted by our Chairman. He planned all the procedure himself without giving us any chance for a preliminary discussion and then took upon himself practically the whole task of putting questions. As I wrote at the time (19.2.28):

' . . . A very depressing day—a dull morning and a tiresome afternoon continuing the examination of Delamere and the unofficial members in which H.Y. skated over all the difficulties and never got to grips with the real problem. At the end he just touched on a ''difficulty'' which he said might be noted, then turned to me and left it to me to deal with it and then when I had spoken and got some answers, wound up the discussion by saying that of course he didn't agree that it was a difficulty—thus putting me in the position of being in a minority on the Commission and being the one who was likely to make trouble. I didn't mind this in itself because I have always been completely frank in talking to the settlers' representatives privately, and, if anything, exaggerated my opposition to their demands, in order to stimulate argument, but I objected to the way H.Y. did it and to the lack of reality in the whole proceedings. In fact writing now after we have left Nairobi I have begun to feel very dissatisfied indeed. H.Y. has been far too clever and shirked difficulties when he ought to have faced them. I believe he is fundamentally wrong in his methods and that these people will suspect cleverness and like blunt and blundering honesty. As someone said to me they "have had plenty of the other thing in Grigg and they are not impressed" . . . '

Our tours in the countryside provided ample evidence of the central importance of the land question (19.2.28):

' . . . We started with a "baraza" of chiefs at Nyeri—an amazing mixture. Half a dozen old chiefs in native garb which meant a cloak of skins and huge ostrich feather erections sticking out behind their heads and back, great earrings, and round brass plates hanging from their necks, with greased faces and bodies and a broad white line painted down the middle of the face from forehead to chin. Mixed up with them were modern young men—much better dressed than I—bright ties and socks, well cut collars and sometimes shorts and very light coloured stockings. They had nothing very interesting to say and only one subject to talk about—their land. They are clearly intensely suspicious of the Government—more so of the settlers—and although the boundaries of the reserves have been gazetted they won't believe that they are not to be altered. They want boundary marks put up and title deeds issued to them. I am bound to confess—having heard Grigg on the subject—that I think there is some ground for their suspicions. His proposal is to vest the land in Trust Boards and then give the Trust Board powers to lease land in native reserves if it is not properly used. This might well be the thin end of the wedge and the natives might find that what had been given them with one hand had been taken away with the other. It is a long story—but I think the Kenya government will have to be very careful if it is to avoid destroying for ever the confidence of these natives in British justice. The contrast to the native attitude in Uganda and the Sudan is most striking and I felt after my day in the Kikuyu reserve—particularly after the second meeting in the afternoon—that here are the makings of a dangerous situation. The native by his contact with white settlers and as workers on their farms has become far more sophisticated than in Uganda or the Sudan, but he has, under Kenya, received far less proper education. Things are moving very fast indeed and there are political associations springing up everywhere—feeble at present but indications of a tendency. We have interviewed two separate "Young Kikuyu Associations" and the manners and sentiments of these associations would be regarded with absolute horror in the Sudan. Until very recently the government has done practically nothing to help the natives towards development in the reserves. Even now very little indeed is being done. Education is going on sporadically and haphazardly through mission activities—without co-ordination or control—very few agricultural officers work in the reserves, etc. etc. Grigg ought to have got down to "putting his own house in order" as soon as he came to the country, and stuck to improving the administrative services. Instead he has tried to make a political splash in England and to glorify his own position by spending £65,000 on a Governor's house in Nairobi—destined ultimately to be the headquarters of his Federal power. By doing this first he has got everybody's heads in the air, whereas they ought to have their noses to the ground and to be getting on with their jobs. By doing the latter he has created a lot of gossip and scandal. I think it a disaster that such a man was sent to Nairobi. The settlers, under Coryndon, were getting into a much more reasonable frame of mind and they *are* people to whom one can talk straight and who will not resent it. But Grigg is always saying "you can't do this and you can't do that because public opinion won't stand for it." He is always trying to reconcile the irreconcilable by political astuteness, and in the end has lost all power and made it almost impossible for any future governor of Kenya really to govern the country. I believe this is a country where frank facing of facts pays and political astuteness does not. They respect the former even if it goes against them. However, I could go on for hours like this—listening to politicians' arguments between H.Y. and Grigg has entirely fed me up.

After staying at Nyeri we started towards Nairobi by another road through the Native Reserve. I had the agricultural officer with me and had some interesting talks with him. He happens to be a very good fellow and is really doing something in his area and there is no doubt that in this fertile thickly populated countryside the native is beginning to produce important quantities for export. We passed an enormous native market on the way. Hundreds of them in to sell their maize, etc. We lunched with a very good D.C. at Fort Hall and then went out to attend a much larger meeting of natives. There must have been 200 of them, partly chiefs and partly representatives of the local associations of young men. We were greeted by the most ghastly rendering of "God Save the King" by about 50 school children and 50 men that one can possibly imagine. I had no notion what they were singing until I saw the D.C. standing at attention and saluting. Then it was difficult to control the desire to laugh.

Then we sat down and had the same tale again and again and again —the land, the land, the land—spoken by both chiefs in skins stinking with mutton fat and flash young men in lounge suits and "club" ties. We got away after an hour and had tea at Mervyn Ridgley's—a delightful house and very attractive people—a long low bungalow— tea under trees on the lawn with a wide stretching view—flowers, old silver teapot, and good china. Mervyn Ridgley coming home hot and fit with a gash on his nose from polo. Other pleasant people there—a complete and sudden switch back to the best settler atmosphere . . . '

Finally as a record of an important personal meeting with the settler leaders I include my account of discussion at a dinner given to me by Delamere and other representatives of the European community.

' . . . An evening with Delamere and Francis Scott cheered me up greatly. They gave us an excellent dinner at the Muthaiji Country Club—which is the settlers' club about 4 miles out of Nairobi, a place which can, I believe, be very gay at times. Conversation was fairly wide of the mark till after dinner and even then shirked the main issues for a long time. At last I butted in and really developed my own ideas about the difficulties of protecting the native interests. I said it was not the question of *negative* protection which I was afraid about, as it might easily be possible to devise safeguards to prevent their being over-taxed or having their land taken away; what really worried me was how to ensure the *positive* "drive" on behalf of native interests. The elected members who had to satisfy their constituents at the next election would be pressing all the time for measures in favour of the settled areas and would see that the best agricultural, veterinary and medical officers etc. etc. were sent there, while there would be no corresponding drive in favour of native interests. Both D. and Francis Scott agreed with me that there was a great deal in this and that we must consider how to meet this point. We discussed it for some time and then sudden-ly D. said "No, it's all 'bunk'! You must trust to the sense of respon-sibility in the white settlers. They are a good lot and will not let the native down". I said that with great respect I could only conclude that what D. said was "all bunk". It would be all very well if he could guarantee immortality for himself and Francis Scott, but looking to the future we must recognise that the normal elected members would act according to their economic interests. D. (referring to my compliment to Francis Scott and himself) said to me "You remind me of the small boy who was up for his viva voce examination for Dartmouth. The old admiral in the chair asked him to name the three greatest British naval commanders. The small boy replied promptly, 'Drake, Nelson and—let me see—what is your name, Sir?'.'' However, he really did see my point and we had a good deal of talk on the same lines and Francis Scott came up to me afterwards obviously anxious to talk futher. They *are* a good pair, particularly Francis Scott . . . '

Looking back today I can record that I left Kenya with feelings of sadness about a lost opportunity. There was so much that was good in the character of the best of the white settlers and so much that was valuable in their practical efficiency that if they had been brought in to confidential discussion with the Governor on how to work out a progressive policy in the interests of the natives of what must always be essentially a black African country, Kenya might have provided a truly progressive solution of the problem of racial relations in Africa, and shown a way for combining collaboration in economic progress with the transfer of political power to the African population.

Our time in Tanganyika was specially interesting for me. I had many matters to examine in my capacity as Financial and Economic Adviser to the Colonial Office, mainly in connection with plans for railway developments. As a result, I did not accompany the other members of the Commission on their visit to Zanzibar and this gave me the opportunity to have long personal talks with the Governor, Sir Donald Cameron, as well as to see a great part of the country. It was a pleasure to talk with Cameron since I found in him a man whose general ideas about the whole problem for future development in Africa closely corresponded with my own. My broad general impression in Tanganyika was that there was a recognition throughout the Government service of the principle of trusteeship, of treating native interests as of paramount importance and of the purpose of bringing on native representatives to undertake responsibility for their own government.

Supplementing this general impression I can add three points:

First, that the general quality of the District Officers, while very uneven, was on the whole better than in Kenya and Uganda and included individuals such as Philip Mitchell who compared with the best of those with whom I had worked in the Sudan.

Secondly, that the effects of the former German administration were still apparent. The Germans had in fact worked to destroy the tribal organisation and establish authoritative German control. I was specially impressed by a visit to the residence of a German District Officer which was built as a fortress and surrounded by defence works.

Thirdly, that the general quality of the white settlers in Tanganyika was lower than in Kenya and that their character and behaviour fully justified Cameron's opposition to any idea of giving white settlers a share in the responsiblity for Government. As I wrote at the time (24.2.28):

' . . . The settlers here are a very truculent lot. Men of no stability, little capital or education, and Croydon stockbrokers' politics. They talked about the Government with the bitterest hostility and also of the natives—all in an ignorant prejudiced way. In evidence before us they supported federation because they were afraid that the Governor of Tanganyika would not apply the agreed system of "dual policy" as it was being applied in Kenya—i.e. complementary development of white and black races. When I came to ask questions I asked whether they could quote actual instances of failure to apply dual policy. The reply was "yes—coffee growing—in Kenya the native quite properly is not allowed to grow coffee. But in Tanganyika he is encouraged to do so. This may be very damaging to the interests of white coffee growers." I said "Surely that is not a failure to apply the dual policy. Your point rather is that a dual policy ought not to be applied to coffee growing." But the speaker couldn't see the point. After lunch we were to have an informal talk with the settlers; but when I got into the room I found that we had been put on a platform and about 60 settlers with some wives were seated in rows in front as for a public meeting. H.Y. invited expressions of opinion and we were then indulged with a series of speeches in favour of federation as a means of escape from Sir Donald Cameron. It was rather unfortunate as a lot of Government officals were there, including Mitchell the provincial Commissioner. In the middle of one violent speech abusing Government officials Mitchell got up and walked out followed by all the other Government officials. As they walked out they were greeted with insulting boos from the back benches. A really disgraceful scene, if it had not been so ridiculous. I thought Mitchell was wrong. He ought to have spoken to Hilton Young, who could have pointed out that as Government officials were present he could not listen to abuse. As it was there was great excitement. H.Y. asked me whether I thought he ought to stop the meeting. I said no, that would be making too much of it, and as we had agreed to hear what they had to say we ought to go on, as others might have reasonable things to say, but I thought he ought to point out that abuse of Government officials was not helpful to us in solving the problems which had been put to us and that we wanted constructive proposals; also that, for any solution for the future, cooperation between officials and settlers was essential. This he did; but the speakers continued in the same strain—until we got a dreary and very common fellow starting on a long tirade against the mandate and the League of Nations and Cameron for trying to be the "blue-eyed boy of the Mandate's Commission". I leaned across to H.Y. and said I thought this was really getting away from anything germane to our enquiry and he stopped the speaker, after which the meeting soon broke up. I got mixed up in an excited group of settlers afterwards, who said they were very sorry for what had happened. I said they need not mind as the meeting has been one of the most instructive bits of spontaneous evidence which had been put before us. They did not quite know what to make of this.

They then said that they were going to write us a public letter to be printed in the East African press apologising for the behaviour. I told them not to be fools and to let the whole matter drop and in the end I think I succeeded. It was indeed very instructive. They are a hopeless crowd, but I also think there is much to blame in the officials' attitude and I think Cameron is a bit of an ass, and might have made things much better if he had tried. Gowers, I feel sure, would have managed to look after native interests without irritating the settlers. However that is a long story . . . '

I can best complete the record of my impressions in Tanganyika by quoting extracts from a letter to my wife of 12th March 1928:

' . . . Last night again (Sunday) we (Cameron and I) had a long talk together after dinner and he spoke at the end about his job here. Said that the lack of companionship was dreadful, one felt like a sort of outcast, and the days at Government House were those of a squirrel in a cage. He said I wouldn't believe what a tremendous pleasure it was for him to have someone like myself to talk to for a few days. Of course I did realise very vividly what it must be to him and I look around and see no-one on the staff of whom he could really make a companion even if it were not for the difficult relations of Governor to subordinates. He said he missed Nigeria terribly when he first went to Tanganyika as he had been there 14 years and had many *real* friends. I did feel for him very much, but I said that after all he was better off than Gowers, for Cameron has his wife with him and also many more people come to Dar-es-Salaam than to Entebbe. He didn't seem very sympathetic about poor Gowers and said that in his Nigerian days he was always known as "the cat that walked alone" . . . '

Finally, Cameron expressed some interesting views about the working of our Commission:

' . . . He talked very fully about H.Y., Mant and Oldham. H.Y. he thinks might have done a "one man show" although he is hopeless as the leader of a team. He realised that he was fencing with C. himself and with us all the time. Mant he regards as a nonentity who takes no interest at all in the whole business and had no idea of doing anything except sucking his pipe. I told him he was wrong there and that Mant would gradually form certain convictions and would not budge from them. Oldham he tells me left England absolutely committed to voting for Federation, and an unofficial majority in Kenya. Cameron told me that he himself had criticised the missionaries in Kenya for their attitude on these matters and their apparent willingness to agree to both points, and their answer had been that they could not do anything

75

else because the organising secretary of their Society (Oldham) had already committed the Society. Cameron refused to believe this, but he tells me that he has, since then, heard from them to the effect that they have got absolute documentary evidence proving that Oldham had committed himself. However Cameron thinks he will go back on that, and as a matter of fact Cameron said to me, "Oldham will in the end follow you exactly"—which is what I had already heard from people whom I had talked to in Kenya. And it all seems to come back to that, that the real responsibility rests on me . . . '

With our departure from Dar-es-Salaam on March 14th on our voyage to Beira we completed our local study of the three East African territories—which was in fact the main problem for which our Commission had been appointed. Our days on the sea voyage therefore provided a good opportunity for joint discussion. It is worth recording that we had in fact had no kind of joint discussions since I made my long statement on the day of our first meeting as a Commission in Uganda on January 15th. Hilton Young throughout had been working alone, seeking no exchange of views with us either in preparing questions for meetings with important witnesses or in reviewing impressions about the views expressed at such meetings. Now on our voyage from Dar-es-Salaam to Beira he presented us with a paper setting out the views which he himself had formed as a result of our investigations.

' . . . (15.3.28) We have had two long morning discussions on the basis of a memorandum written by Hilton Young in which he had worked out certain proposals. It was quite ably done and he had changed his views enormously and came very near to what I have been feeling. But we are a long way short of any real workable solution I fear, and I have been arguing in favour of an intervening probationary period. H.Y. at times gets rather irritated with me and the first morning got very near to losing his temper. I find that in argument the other two, although they may have agreed with me beforehand, tend to drop away. On the other hand they frequently bring forward suggestions which I have made to them privately as their own! It is a great pity that H.Y. and I are so antagonistic and I have really not done anything on my side to encourage it. But his effect always seems to me to be to detach me from the other two and play up to them. I ought not to mind in substance, because, as I said above, he had really in effect come over to my views and has quite given up the line which he was running in Kenya. Curiously enough the line which we are working now is what I had come to on thinking matters over travelling up the Nile. I had written these views to Sir Frederick Lugard and just got an answer from him by a mail which reached me on the boat as I left Dar-es-Salaam. He is himself in agreement. He wrote a very nice letter—but very unhappily at the end poor man, as his wife is terribly ill . . . '

On leaving Tanganyika we had finished our enquiries concerned with what we, at the time, regarded as the most urgent part of our task and on which our report received the greatest public attention. Our investigations in the Central African territories, however, were of considerable importance and in fact brought us into touch with problems which today have much greater urgency and much wider significance than those which we had to consider in the East African Territories. For my personal story therefore it is important to include a record of my impressions of conditions at the time in Nyasaland, Northern and Southern Rhodesia.

I must also refer to a personal incident in Nyasaland which, according to my interpretation, had a considerable effect on our later deliberations and on the way in which our report came to be written. This incident concerns Oldham's attitude. He in fact had a sort of nervous breakdown in Nyasaland which kept him out of action for most of our time there. My interpretation of this was that he had been severely attacked by some of the missionaries in Nyasaland about what they had understood to be his commitment to support some of the political demands of the white settlers in Kenya. This is of course a matter of speculation on my part; but what I can record as a fact is that Oldham's attitude definitely changed after our visit to Nyasaland and that, instead of having reservations about some of my own ideas, he worked in complete harmony with me in all our subsequent discussions and in the drafting of our report. This was a great satisfaction for me, since I had a high regard for Oldham, his wisdom and general philosophy.

Our procedure in the Central African territories differed from that which we had followed in the Eastern group. We had fewer formal meetings and worked more by individual investigations into local conditions. I myself, in my capacity as Financial and Economic Adviser to the Colonial Office, had to spend much time in the study of plans for the Zambesi Bridge as well as some other development projects.

My general impression in Nyasaland and Northern Rhodesia was that in 1928 the Government services concerned with native interests and economic development were lifeless and inadequate, comparing most unfavourably with what I had known in the Sudan. The following illustrates my impressions at the time in Nyasaland: (28.3.28):

' . . . Wednesday was the usual sort of day of interviews. I had a second meeting on financial matters with the Governor and the Treasurer in the afternoon and then went off with the Director of Agriculture in a car first to see some native cultivation and then on to see a research farm being run by the Empire Cotton Growing Corporation. I was pleased with this show and I think the local government is very lucky in getting assistance from outside interests in this way. If it wasn't for the Empire Cotton Growing Corporation which had done all the work on cotton development and for the Imperial Tobacco Company which had done practically all the work on native tobacco growing development, and for the missionaries who have done all the education work in the country, one can only say that nothing of merit would have been achieved at all . . . At 2.30 I started off with one of the Provincial Commissioners for Liwonde—35 miles away on the Shire River—where I was to attend a meeting of a native district council. I had complained that they had arranged nothing which enabled me to form any opinion of the natives and this meeting had been got up to meet my wishes. I got there at 4 and had to inspect a police guard of honour and then meet the chiefs and then attend the Council. The natives are a "mesquin" lot. They look underfed and querulous. The meeting developed into a harangue in *English* to them by the local Resident Commissioners and I learned very little of the natives. But one got the impression that there is no *life* about native administration in this country; and it badly wants more inspiring guidance. There is an extraordinary contrast to the Tanganyika atmosphere. What the government had done here had been originally (40 years ago) to put down deliberately all native chiefs and tribal organisation and then neither to make the native do anything for himself, nor to do anything for him ...'

A week later from Northern Rhodesia I wrote describing our arrival at Government House in Livingstone (4.4.28):

' . . . Sir James Maxwell, who was only appointed three months ago was on the steps to meet us, a benevolent looking old gentleman with long white hair who had started his African career in the Medical Service . . . We adjourned to Maxwell's room for our first interview with him. We then had to listen to this old Scottish doctor expounding his views on the local situation, telling us all sorts of things about the neighbouring countries and their plans for railway construction, etc., which showed that he lived miles up a backwater completely out of touch with the world and had not appreciated that we, having visited these countries, knew much more than he did about them . . . Certainly the British Empire is a wonderful place and it is astounding to find each little Government in each of these detached countries working out, on its own, problems which are common to all, without any knowledge of what its neighbours are doing and without any direction on main lines of policy from the Colonial Office. I had had some talk after lunch with the local director of education and found that they have only *one* native school in the country run by the Government. This is in Barotseland, 21 days' journey from Livingstone, so that the director of education can only visit it once in 3 years. He seemed very depressed at the way in which it was going . . . Maxwell in his way is quite shrewd but it is this backwater atmosphere which is so depressing to find and I have certainly gained the impression that the Governments in

Nyasaland and Northern Rhodesia are too small to stand alone and ought at least to be brought into closer touch with some first class man (who lives in touch with the great world) as a supervising authority . .'

In Nyasaland and Northern Rhodesia there was no question of the establishment of a white settler community with demands for political representation, but I was left with the impression that the vitality and efficiency of the Government might have been greatly improved if more active steps had been taken to bring representatives of private business enterprise into consultation with the Government in an advisory capacity, not only on plans for economic development but also on many issues affecting the interests of the native population. As I have written in my story of the Sudan, that Government had, I believe with great success, taken steps to follow this practice.

Our enquiries in Southern Rhodesia brought us into the field of the basic issue—the problem of how to create satisfactory relations between the white and black races in African territories in which large numbers of white settlers had made their permanent home—the problem which has become the subject of world-wide concern today. As I wrote to my wife after I had visited the impressive native agricultural school established by the Government of Southern Rhodesia at Dombashawa on the edge of the Mashona Reserve:

' . . . It was altogether an interesting experience, seeing a country in the first days of responsible government and dealing with "Ministers" instead of the normal government officials. They may not be very high class people—but, so far, I really think they have done well and there is an air of life and energy about the whole thing which is encouraging. In fact Nyasaland and Southern Rhodesia together have done a good deal to alter my personal outlook—the former as an instance of how bad an official Government can be—and the latter as showing a popularly elected Government as a practical possibility with not a few merits. For the first time I felt some real understanding for the Kenya settlers' point of view. But of course the great questions are "How long will the good features of the S. Rhodesia Government last? Will there not soon be an introduction of political jobbery? and can a member of parliament who owes his seat to the votes of white settlers really be trusted to be not merely—negatively—not unfair to the native, but, positively, keen to push forward his interests?" I am very doubtful about this. The other question is: cannot something be done to give a better and more true form of official government than has existed under the C.O.? I *do* think the Sudan shows that it *is* possible . . . '

Later in the same letter, after reporting a talk with the Governor, Sir John Chancellor, I wrote:

' . . . As regards social companionship he (Chancellor) said "It has been like living 5 years in the servants' hall and not very nice servants at that!" But he himself would be the first to admit that in a way this gives a wrong impression. For there *are* merits about this Southern Rhodesian Government. It is certainly alive and ministers are at present on their mettle about native interests and trying to make a good showing before the world. The question really is what will happen when it has gone a bit further and various parties have been formed, each trying to outbid the other for votes in the elections. Promises will then be made to the white settlers who have all the votes. No "pro-native" party will be formed, while the quality of the Government officials administering native areas is likely to deteriorate, if, as is only too probable, the cry of "Rhodesia for the Rhodesians" is raised and posts are filled, not with English public schoolboys, but local products . . . '

During the course of our Commission's discussions in Southern Rhodesia it became clear that there was a major difference of opinion between our Chairman and the rest of us. Hilton Young, with his thoughts on administrative efficency, was shocked at the artificial way in which the frontiers had been drawn between Southern Rhodesia and the other two territories and made it clear that he wanted to recommend some kind of federal structure which would ensure a unified direction of administrative services.

We, the other three members of the Commission, were concerned mainly with the political implications of any form of closer union between the three territories. I felt that we had to face the reality that Southern Rhodesia, with its large settler population, had been recognised as part of what could be regarded as 'White Africa' and since 1923 had had responsible government under the control of the white settlers. I, however, saw great dangers in this situation and the one thing which I felt with absolute conviction was that at some point a line should be drawn between 'White' and 'Black' Africa and that, whatever might be the right line, it most certainly should not be drawn north of the present frontier of Southern Rhodesia. Looking back on all that has happened since 1928 it is fair to claim that this appreciation was right.

As the final stage in the Commission's work in Africa we spent five days in Cape Town, during which we had discussions with Herzog, then Prime Minister, and many leading figures in the political and business world. Since I wrote no letters from Cape Town I cannot refer to any contemporary record of my impressions; but my memory is clear that I left South Africa with feelings of deep concern and confirmed in the opinion that there was an urgent need for a fundamental review of long term 'native policy' in all the African territories and very specially in the Union of South Africa. This opinion was recorded in our report from which it is relevant at this stage to quote the following passage (p.8):

'The contact between the white and black races in Africa constitutes one of the great problems of the twentieth century. It is a problem the solution of which demands a consistent policy carefully thought out, rather than emergency action designed to meet particular difficulties only. It is not safe to allow policy in Kenya to be framed regardless of what is being done in Tanganyika and Uganda. It should be framed for Eastern Africa as a whole. But more than this, policy for Eastern Africa should be framed with regard to experience in all other territories of Africa. South Africa and Eastern Africa have closely connected interests. They can learn much from each other and do much to help each other, while this inter-connection of interests extends even beyond the limits of the British Empire to all other European Powers who are responsible for the administration of African territories. We received striking evidence of the realisation of this inter-connection during our visit to Cape Town.'

Writing today I can add some further reflections. Among the Smuts papers I note that in a letter of 22.5.28 he wrote to Amery that he was sorry to have been out of Cape Town at the time of Hilton Young's visit 'otherwise I would certainly have expounded my grandiose dreams to him—"Africa from the Equator downwards ought within so many generations to take a high place with Canada and Australia among the great dominions in the Empire". Therefore there is a need for the reservation of sufficent elbow room for our great white civilisation.' This is a most revealing statement and shows that I had been right in my interpretation of Amery's ultimate objective, i.e. the inclusion of Kenya in a great white dominion, since Smuts in his letter clearly thought that he was expressing views with which Amery would be in sympathy. I had many occasions in later years for talks with Smuts which left me with the impression that he himself in his later life realised that he could not see a satisfactory final solution for the basic problem of how to establish satisfactory relations between the white population and the vastly greater black population in Southern Africa. He gave me the impression that he felt that the political structure, in the establishment of which he had played the greatest part, would survive for his lifetime and that he could not look beyond that.

We left Cape Town on April 20th 1928 and during the sea voyage home we had daily meetings to discuss our general conclusions and the form of our report. These discussions showed that Mant, Oldham and I were thinking alike, but that on many points Hilton Young either differed from our views or felt that we wanted to deal with questions which were really outside our terms of reference. He was clearly in a state of nervous tension and in fact, soon after our return to England, he 'went into retreat' leaving for us the message that he found it difficult to collaborate in the process of writing the kind of report which the three of us wanted to produce, to the subject matter and length of which he felt serious objections. (Eventually he was in the unusual position, as Chairman, of submitting Minority Reports on both areas under investigation.)

In these circumstances the only practical course was for the three of us to complete our version for the Commission's report, leaving it to Hilton Young to record his own views in whatever way he might finally decide. Mant and Oldham had already expressed complete agreement with my lines of thought, and since it was essential for me to leave for India in time to take up my post before the end of October I had to take the main responsibility for seeing the work through. Mant was constantly available for discussion and Oldham wrote important parts of the draft.

I was very clear in my mind that the practical purpose of our report should be, not to produce a definite plan for dealing with the problems in the Eastern and Central African territories which our Commission had been asked to examine, but to force the British Government to recognise that these local issues ought to be considered as part of the problem of British policy in Africa and indeed of the much wider problem of the relations between the white and black races in Africa.

If the purpose of our report was to stimulate informed discussion it seemed to me appropriate that it should include statements of the Commission's views on basic issues such as the ownership of land and suggestions for forms of organisational changes such as the appointment of men of wide experience to supervise general policy among groups of territories. Judging by the actual result this purpose was certainly achieved, though the discussions themselves fell below the standard which I had contemplated.

I was completely convinced at the time that the purpose itself was right and, looking back in the conditions of today, my conviction is confirmed. I consulted Sir Warren Fisher, then Head of the Civil Service, about my general idea and I think it worth quoting the following passage from his letter to me of October 8th, 1928:

> ' . . . This section of your report is deeply interesting and stimulating. I read it as your conception of an ordered progression towards an ultimate ideal not realisable all at once or in whole . . . I do feel that it is a real service that some one should have looked ahead and have provoked thought in the direction of development along the lines of a systematic plan instead of proceeding by jerks and spasms without regard to any formulated principles . . . '

This letter, written by one of the greatest civil servants of our time, gave me, and still gives me, deep satisfaction. It provides indeed a suitable end to my personal story, since I had to leave for India immediately after its receipt. I wrote my own signature to the main report but could not take part in the final stage of preparing the documents for publication, or in the subsequent discussions with the Colonial Office.

CHAPTER VII

Advising on Colonial Financial and Economic Policy

IN MY STORY of the five years when I was working as Financial Secretary to the Sudan, I have explained how, during this period, I became involved in advisory work for the Colonial Office, first as Chairman of the East African Loans Committee and later as Financial and Economic Adviser. Further, in my record of my work in 1928 as a member of the Hilton Young Commission, I have referred to certain tasks in which I personally was involved in my capacity as Financial and Economic Adviser to the Colonial Office. As I come to write the full story of my life, I realise that these references are inadequate and that I ought to include a separate chapter on my work as an adviser on colonial economic and financial policy.

Looking back today I can see that I was chiefly concerned with two questions. The first question was whether, on the Colonial Office side (which included the Colonial Office itself as well as the Governments of individual territories), efficient arrangements existed for reviewing needs and working out practicable and far-sighted development plans. The second question was whether British Government financial policy (as determined by the Treasury) was right in insisting that *in all cases* the Colonial territories concerned should from the beginning be liable to provide funds to cover the interest charges on loans raised in Britain for economic development.

The significance of both these questions was most clearly demonstrated in the case of the project for a bridge over the Zambesi to which I shall refer later; but, in the opening stages of my work for the Colonial Office as Chairman of the East African Loans Committee, I was chiefly concerned with the first question.

The East African Loans Committee was appointed in 1925 following the report of the Ormsby Gore Commission which had recommended the provision of a total sum of £10 million (to be raised by British guaranteed loans) to finance projects for economic development in the East African Territories. Our terms of reference were

> 'To advise the Secretary of State for the Colonies upon the various development schemes, including capital expenditure on existing works, that might be paid for out of the £10 million East African Guaranteed Loan with special reference to
>
> (a) their prospects of economic success

(b) their order of urgency
(c) their relation to a coordinated scheme of transport
in East Africa generally.'

In our Committee's first Report (Cmd. 2701 published in 1926) we had to note that our practical recommendations were affected by a restriction which we explained in the following passage:

'It had been decided before the appointment of our Committee, not to adopt the recommendation of the East Africa Commission that interest on loans from the £10 million fund should be met by the Imperial Government for the first five years, but to make the borrowing Governments accept responsibility for interest payments from the outset.'

This restriction (insisted on by the Treasury) meant that our Committee had of necessity to rule out certain projects, for example the proposal for a major extension of the Tanganyika Railways into the South West Highlands. In our first report we recommended the allocation of £4¾ million for a number of railway projects, and called for further investigation of several other projects as a basis for taking properly informed decisions. We concluded our 1926 report with the following significant passage:

'The position in this respect illustrates the difficulties which we have felt in dealing simultaneously with a number of propositions in widely different stages of maturity with a view to settling a complete allocation of a fixed sum of money. It appears to us that the provision of a fixed sum for distribution in this way must have an inevitable tendency to force intending borrowers to put forward immature propositions in order not to miss an opportunity which may not recur, while on the other hand it may result in the fixing of the amounts allotted to each proposition according to what is available, rather than what is required. We venture to express the view that it might prove a sounder method for encouraging development within the Empire to create machinery which would provide for the continuous study of new developments and afford to the various dependencies an assurance that they would have fair chances at all times to raise money for really sound and carefully prepared projects.'

The passage which I have quoted provides a good illustration of the way in which my own mind was working at the time and in particular emphasises my feeling that the methods for studying plans for economic development under the responsibility of the Colonial Office were definitely quite inadequate.

At the same time it can be claimed that our report led to some significant practical results, in particular the passing of the Colonial Development Act of 1929, which provided for an annual sum (£1 million sterling) for Colonial development grants and for the appointment of a Committee to advise on the allocation of this sum. As I see it, the Act of 1929 was satisfactory in so far as it secured improvement in the procedure for selecting economic development projects qualifying for capital expenditure, but in its conception of the scale on which capital expenditure would be justifiable it was totally inadequate.

In 1929 I had already taken up my new post in India but I had already expressed my personal views on this issue when, as directed by the Colonial Secretary, I visited the Colonial territories in East and Central Africa in my dual capacity as a member of the Hilton Young Commission and also as Financial and Economic Adviser to the Colonial Office. In this second capacity I had to study and report on projects for railway extensions in Uganda, Kenya and Tanganyika, but my most important responsibility was to study and advise on the ambitious proposal for a bridge across the Zambesi to replace the existing ferry and to open up railway connections with Nyasaland.

Looking back over my papers it is clear that from the beginning I saw two main needs. The first was to establish the case that, with improved railway communications, Nyasaland could achieve the kind of economic development which would eventually justify the cost of a railway bridge over the Zambesi. The second requirement was to get the British Government to agree that, during the early years of development, the service of a loan to cover the cost of a bridge should not be imposed on the Nyasaland Government.

As a step towards meeting the first need I had in 1926, as Chairman of the East African Loans Committee, recommended that a special Commission under Brigadier-General Hammond should be sent to Nyasaland to review the general economic position. I had strong views about the composition and task of this Commission and I wrote on 15.8.26 to Sir Samuel Wilson at the Colonial Office urging the inclusion:

> ' . . . of an independent economic man so that we could work out a really sound and comprehensive constructive programme for Nyasaland and be armed with strong arguments to use against the Treasury for the necessary financial backing . . . What we were really aiming at was a two-fold object:-
> (a) to take advantage of the occasion of building the bridge to put the whole system of railway communications on to a sound basis and make a good business deal with the other interests;
> (b) to use the occasion to initiate a programme which would really help Nyasaland. We felt that the bridge alone would not "do the trick".'

One of my great difficulties when I was personally faced with the responsibility of making a final recommendation about the bridge was that no really authoritative and comprehensive survey of economic possibilities was available. The Hammond Report did not provide it and, as I have noted in my story about my work on the Hilton Young Commission, I had found that the Nyasaland Government itself had made no attempt to make a comprehensive economic survey or to initiate any effective steps for encouraging economic development. I had seen great possibilities in arranging cooperation between the Government and some of the non-Government agencies that were doing very good work in Nyasaland, such as the Empire Cotton Growing Corporation and the Imperial Tobacco Company. If there is to be criticism of Colonial Office policy, it must be directed not only to headquarters in London but also to the inadequacies of the individual Governments of territories like Nyasaland or Northern Rhodesia.

On 18.3.28 I wrote, as follows, to my wife about my visit to the proposed site of what, at 2¼ miles, would be the longest railway bridge in the world:

' . . . We started at daybreak on Sunday morning and reached the proposed bridge site about noon. It was an interesting place—the one point where the river seems fairly well tied to a definite channel by hills and rising ground on each side—though over the south side it might wander away about 2 miles if not checked. On the south—now about 2 miles from the river—is a Portuguese port called Seria which was established by them in 1500! In those days the river channel must have run by the settlement. The Portuguese have been all these years in this country and done absolutely *nothing* for it, but the local Portuguese official says that 'the flower of Portugal' is buried at Seria. The river journey itself was not interesting—just this huge wide river meandering about through reedy swamps with rocky mountains in the far distance—drenching rain—some flights of spur-winged geese—but otherwise not a sign of life . . .

. . . It is a great thing how it has fallen to my fate to decide important points about building railways all over Africa—the Sudan—Kenya—Uganda—Tanganyika—and now this bridge. In all these places I have had to settle questions affecting millions. And really in all cases the whole responsiblity for deciding has fallen on me. Of course it is very interesting and this Zambesi bridge question particularly so. I have not made up my mind yet—but on what I say £2½ millions of expenditure depends—huge orders for manufacturers at home—hundreds of people employed out here and the whole future of Nyasaland. And on this question I really have no one whose judgement is worth anything to help me (as I have realised bitterly after arriving in Nyasaland) . . . '

The whole position was indeed for me a desperately worrying one, since I was in fact forced to make definite recommendations for dealing with a problem for which there was at the time no clear-cut satisfactory solution, and to do this without any reliable appreciation of the relevant factors for which I had constantly asked. I could not, however, evade my responsibility and when the time came for a final decision I wrote as follows on 21.6.28 to Mr. Amery as Colonial Secretary:

'. . . Nyasaland is a country which is capable of considerable further development . . . The net result of this appreciation is that, while the immediate prospects of the Bridge may be less favourable than we had thought, the need for the Bridge as a condition precedent to any real advance in Nyasaland is greater than ever.

The point which I think really requires consideration now is whether HMG as a matter of policy is prepared to take a certain amount of risk in helping a forward move in Nyasaland. If the decision to build the bridge is to be dependent on the possibility of demonstrating that, on the basis of traffic actually "in sight", the earnings will cover all charges, then I hardly think the business can be done. If, on the other hand, the question is to be decided on broader grounds of policy and HMG is prepared to take the view that, as a matter of policy, it is desirable to avoid leaving Nyasaland in a state of stagnation, then I think that the proposal has a chance of justifying itself . . . '

This letter was written from London after the return of the Hilton Young Commission. I was during this period heavily engaged in the completion of the Commission's report, but at the same time also involved in discussions with the Colonial Office about the Zambesi bridge.

The final step came for me on the 3rd July 1928 when I had a personal interview alone with Amery. I have a vivid memory of this meeting. I went over again all the relevant considerations and specially emphasised that my request for a comprehensive independent survey of the economic factors had not been satisfied. Amery said to me 'I recognise all that, but I, as Colonial Secretary, have now got to take a decision and it is on your recommendation that I must rely for my final decision.'

Faced with this challenge, I told Amery that, although none of the conditions on which I had insisted had been fulfilled, my advice was that the bridge should be built. I added of course that he should continue to do his utmost to get the Treasury to agree to provide for the service of the necessary loan during the next years of development in Nyasaland; but I did not insist on that as a necessary condition. Amery accepted my advice and continued his pressure on the Treasury. The personal letter which he then wrote (18.7.28) to Winston Churchill as Chancellor of the Exchequer is worth quoting:

'. . . (Nyasaland's) social services, particularly sanitation, education and technical services, are at a scandalously low ebb. The death rate is disgraceful. The inhabitants are migrating. Owing simply to present poverty everything in Nyasaland is below the standard of other African colonies . . . In a total revenue of less than £400,000 you charge over £50,000 interest and sinking fund for past loans besides taking a considerable bite towards the (existing) Trans-Zambesi Railway contribution. In the present circumstances this African Cinderella cannot pay for necessities let alone raise money for bridges and railways . . . '

This letter produced no result.

Since I left for India in October 1928 I had no chance to play any part in settling the practical plans for the completion of the bridge, which was built with 17,000 tons of British steel and first opened to traffic in March 1935. According to the accounts which I eventually received I formed the opinion that with more effective direction the actual cost might have been considerably reduced. It is, however, appropriate for me in reviewing my record today, half a century later, to set down certain reflections.

The first is that my advice in 1928 was right. This was the constructive line to take. I presented a challenge and created an opportunity for a comprehensive development plan for Nyasaland. The fact that there was no adequate response to the challenge and that full advantage was not taken of the opportunity created does not invalidate the decision. In support of this reflection I can refer to the official report of 1958 on the economic survey of Nyasaland (C.Fed. 152) which recognised that 'the Bridge was an essential pre-requisite to any substantial economic development' of the country.

My second reflection is on the policy of the British Government. That policy, half a century ago, as directed by the Treasury, was that the British taxpayer should not be asked to contribute anything towards the cost of measures designed to secure the economic development of the overseas territories for the administration of which Britain as an imperial power was

20. On my East African journey

responsible. It may be possible to find arguments in support of such a policy, though there is no evidence that the broad issue was ever seriously debated in Parliament.

It is not my purpose to review the possible arguments on this matter. It is, however, relevant to call attention to the changed attitudes of today when the so-called 'developed countries' of the world have come to recognise it as not only right but wise that their taxpayers should provide vast sums of money to finance measures for raising standards of living in the so-called 'under-developed' countries. The British Government today is asking the British taxpayer to provide hundreds of millions for 'Foreign Aid'. As a matter of personal experience I was impressed with this when, as Treasurer of Voluntary Service Overseas in the early days of that project, I was able to play a part in getting the British Government to provide an annual grant of £500,000 towards the cost of sending out our volunteers to a wide range of 'under-developed' countries.

CHAPTER VIII

India, 1928-1934

THE PROCESS OF TRANSITION from British rule to Indian independence, of which an important stage was covered during my years in India, has become a matter of history on which comprehensive books have been written. My purpose is only to tell a story based on my experiences and thoughts at the time, and to show what it meant to be a member of the Government of India—a Front Bench Member of the Indian Parliament—at a stage when the overall responsibility for governing India still remained with Britain and rested on a British Minister answerable to the British Parliament.

I myself felt that it was my duty as a member of the Government of India to work for Indian interests and that if at any point there was a conflict between British and Indian interests I must fight for the latter. I regarded this as my personal duty, but I also felt that it was wise as a matter of general policy. With Macaulay's well-known statement of 1833 in mind,* my view had always been that Britain envisaged the ultimate transfer of responsibility to an Indian Government and that since the Montagu Declaration of 1917 the British Government was definitely committed to practical steps for advancing towards this end. I thought that the transition must be a gradual process which would take time and which for its full success would depend on Indian confidence that the British members of the Government of India were working in the interests of India and not contrary to those interests under direction from Whitehall. This aim was all the more important in view of the increasing militancy of the nationalists, the Indian National Congress.

I recognised of course that it was legitimate for me to take account of British interests if this could be done without damaging vital Indian interests. I recognised also that the Secretary of State's advisers in Whitehall might include men of special wisdom and experience in matters of financial and economic policy, and that I ought to welcome their advice; but I felt that when I, with my close contact with conditions in India, had reached a conclusion which was supported by the Viceroy in Council, it was my responsibility to give effect to this conclusion. In short, I felt that I was a responsible member of the Government of India and not in any sense a

---

* 'The public mind of India having become instructed in European knowledge . . . may, in some future age, demand European institutions. Whether such a day will ever come I know not. But never will I attempt to avert or retard it. Whenever it comes, it will be the proudest day in English history.'

90

Whitehall Civil Servant. I might add that I felt the principle involved in the foregoing appreciation had already been accepted by the British Government in the 'Fiscal Autonomy Convention' which had been settled in 1919. I could not see why this principle should be limited to matters of customs duties.

My story begins with my first interview with the Secretary of State, then Lord Birkenhead. He started by saying that the appointment was one of first class importance—indeed he suggested of such an importance that he himself might in earlier days have considered it worthy of his own consideration. He spoke to me as though he was appointing me as a member of his own staff and went on to say 'I am afraid that I shall make your early task difficult because we have decided that we must ask the Indian Government to make a substantial increase in their contribution to the British Government under the heading of 'capitation payments'.'

The justification for this contribution was as follows. Large numbers of British troops (about 65,000 at that time) were stationed in India. The pay of these troops was provided by the Indian Government; but as they were fully trained it was considered that the Indian Government should also make a substantial contribution towards the cost which had been involved in their training in Britain. Birkenhead, in talking to me, clearly assumed that the demand for an increased contribution would be regarded as an authoritative instruction to the Government of India which must be met. I did not comment on this at our interview since I had no knowledge about the basis for the payment; but I remember being very clear in my mind at the time that it would be my duty as Finance Member of the Viceroy's Council to ensure that the justification of the claim should be fully examined.

As this was in fact a most important early incident in the story of my work in India I will jump forward and record what eventually happened. The demand from the British Government came before the Viceroy's Council at a meeting in December 1928—a meeting held in Calcutta since in those days it was the practice of the Viceroy to stay in Calcutta during the Christmas period. I, as Finance Member, expressed the view that the justification for this demand must be established and that it was the duty of the Government of India to ask for a full investigation by an independent tribunal. This view was accepted by the Viceroy's Council and after long discussions and delays the Secretary of State agreed to the appointment in 1932 of a judicial tribunal under the Chairmanship of an Australian, Sir Robert Garran, and including two British Lords of Appeal and two Indian Judges. I got my old Oxford friend, Gavin Simonds, later Lord Chancellor, to argue the Indian case. The hearing lasted several days and the tribunal decided that the claim by the India Office was totally unjustified and that the annual 'capitation payment' contribution from India, instead of being increased, should be reduced by two crores of rupees (£1½ million).

My time in India was one of exceptional financial problems. It included the years (1929-33) of 'the economic blizzard', years of critical financial and economic problems for every country in the world. This would in any case have been a very difficult period for the Finance Minister of India, but my task was made more difficult by the controversy about the rupee/sterling ratio.

It is important here to understand the historical background. The Indian rupee currency had been a silver standard currency until 1893, at which date it was in effect put on a gold standard basis by being linked with sterling at a rupee value of 1/4d. It remained on this basis until conditions in the 1914-18 war forced the Government to allow the rupee/sterling exchange rate to rise much higher—at one period above 2/-d. After the war there was much confusion for some years and various unsuccessful attempts were made to stabilise the rupee at levels higher than 1/4d. Eventually a Royal Commission on Indian Currency and Finance was appointed in 1924 which produced a report in 1926 containing two main recommendations:

1   Stabilisation of the rupee at 1/6d.
2   Creation of a Reserve Bank to operate as the currency authority for India independent of the Government.

The leading Indian member of the Commission, Sir Purshotamdas Thakurdas, wrote a well argued dissenting report recommending reversion to the pre-war rupee exchange rate of 1/4d. which had remained steady for twenty-one years. Eventually in 1927 my predecessor, Sir Basil Blackett, succeeded in getting the Indian Assembly to pass legislation fixing the rupee exchange rate at 1/6d., but failed to get approval for the establishment of a Reserve Bank.

The Commission's proposal for fixing the rupee ratio above the established pre-war level was from the beginning resented in India, especially by the commercial community who regarded the 1/6d. ratio as working to the advantage of British interests (e.g. British business organisations operating in India or exporting British products to India) and contrary to Indian interests. This resentment was of great political significance and had an important influence in ranging the Indian commercial community on the side of the Civil Disobedience movement organised in 1930 by Mr. Gandhi and the Indian National Congress.

My wife and I travelled out together in October 1928, and our days on a P. & O. gave me the first chance to concentrate my thoughts on my task in India and to realise what an amateur outsider I was, or at least would appear to be, to the very professional Indian Civil Servants in comparison with my predecessors, in particular my immediate predecessor, Sir Basil Blackett, who had come out as a top official from the British Treasury. Landing at Bombay one passed through 'The Gateway to India' and realised the immense scale of the Government's responsibility. After going through the necessary formalities we were conducted to the private saloon reserved exclusively for the Finance Member. (Each Member of the Council had, at the time, his own private saloon.) After a long hot and dusty journey we left the train at Delhi and were met by one of the Viceroy's ADC's who took us to a guest-house in the Viceroy's grounds. (The Viceroy still lived at Old Delhi although all the Government personnel had moved to New Delhi.)

My wife and I spent a quiet evening alone together, and my thoughts dwelt on this new setting for our life. It all seemed rather menacing— 'strange unhallowed ground'—and I reflected sadly on the contrast with the intimate friendly atmosphere of the small Sudan Government establishment in Khartoum. Then suddenly my whole mood was changed. At 10 o'clock Lord and Lady Irwin walked quietly in on their way back from a dinner engagement. Somehow or other I felt at once in a friendly atmosphere. Irwin said to me 'Your first job will be to come out hunting with me tomorrow morning. I have got a good horse for you to ride and I will send a car to pick you up at 5 a.m.' That was the beginning of a relationship of immense significance to me, including many intimate talks on serious matters as we rode together in the early dawn with the Delhi Hounds.

As I reflect on my time in India I look back specially on my personal relationship with the two Viceroys of the period—Irwin and Willingdon. They were very different characters, but with both of them I could have close human understanding. In Irwin's case the family atmosphere of his household was specially warming, and in his 'family' I include not only his children who often stayed with him, but also his ADC's. During the centuries of British rule in India there have been individuals among the rulers whose character, creed of life, and personal conduct have impressed Indian opinion and created an image of British mores which has had an influence on the relations between the two nations and the value of which may perhaps, even now, not have entirely disappeared. Irwin stands out as one of these individuals.

Among my first impressions that I recollect was the impact of the gigantic scale of New Delhi. The Finance Member's room in the Government offices was large enough to hold a meeting of a hundred. To 'cross the road' to call on the Council member opposite to me involved a walk of nearly half a mile, bridging two large waterways.

The Finance Member had a wide range of responsibilities. In addition to carrying out the normal duties of a Chancellor of the Exchequer, he was also the currency authority. In the Finance Department the senior officers in my time were all British members of the ICS, highly formal and professional, but the Department relied largely on the work of the Indian staff. I was impressed by the quality of this staff and especially by that of the Budget Officer, a small frail Madrasi called Shankar Rau. His capacity for work and his meticulous accuracy were of enormous value.

It was a heavy task to get an appreciation of the whole range of work and there were several immediate problems to be tackled. In my first months a good deal of time was also needed for discussions with members of the Simon Commission which had been appointed in late 1927 to review the working of the 1919 Act which had considerably increased Indian participation in government. The failure to appoint an Indian to the Commission led

21. The Viceroy, Lord Irwin (fourth from right), and his Council at Simla 1930. Author on far right

94

to its boycott by most of the nationalists and the political atmosphere when I arrived in India was thus already highly charged.

Much time was also required for attendance at the meetings of the Indian Assembly (the Indian parliament). All Members of the Council as Front Bench Members were normally expected to sit through all the sessions; but this expectation applied specially to the Finance Member. I saw it as a most important part of my task to establish friendly relations with the Indian Members, especially Front Bench Members of the Opposition. The figure which stands out most clearly in my memory is that of Motilal Nehru. In my first year he was a regular guest at our house and was always ready to talk with frankness on constitutional issues. I specially recall one remark of his, when my wife had asked him what he would have done if the recommendations of what was known as the 'Nehru Sapru Report'* had been accepted. His reply was, 'The first thing that I would have done would have been to go down on my knees to every British Member of the Indian Civil Service and beg him to stay on under an Indian Government.' In that first year Motilal used to talk frankly to me about his son Jawaharlal to whom he referred affectionately as 'the boy'—implying that he admired his enthusiasm but did not share all his extreme political views.

The preparation of the Budget to be presented on 28th February 1929 was my first important practical task. On reviewing the general financial prospects it was clear to me that in the next years there would be a need both for drastic control of expenditure and also for increased tax revenue; but I formed the view that for the next 12 months the accounts could probably be balanced without any increase in taxation. I thought it would be prudent to make provision for a moderate surplus and for this purpose I included in my budget proposals an increase in the import duty on cotton piece goods from 11 per cent to 12½ per cent. This seemed to me to stand out as an obvious first step. The duty on imports had become a major factor in Indian government finance, imposed for revenue not protective purposes. The standard rate at the time was 15 per cent, but on cotton piece goods was only 11 per cent—an arrangement which had obviously been made in the interests of the British textile industry.

My Budget proposals, after consideration by the Viceroy in Council, were, according to normal practice, submitted for consideration by the India Office and on this occasion they elicited a passionate appeal from the Secretary of State, then Lord Peel, for a withdrawal of the proposal for the increase in the import duty on cotton piece goods. He represented that the Lancashire cotton industry was going through a time of desperate difficulty and that any increased duty which would have an adverse effect on British imports to India would, just at this time, be disastrous. This raised for me a question of principle, and, when the matter came up for discussion in the

---

* Report prepared for the All Parties Conference Committee of India in 1928 which recommended in effect a Dominion Status constitution.

Viceroy's Council, I took the line that, taking account of British interests, I would be ready to take the chance of doing without any increase in taxation, but that I would not agree to propose any alternative form of taxation because I felt that, in view of the Indian position as a whole, an increase in the revenue import duty on cotton piece goods was the one step which I ought, at this stage, to recommend. My view was approved by the Viceroy in Council. This was the first incident in the story of the cotton piece goods conflict with which I was concerned. I felt sure at the time that it would not be the last.

In my Budget speech for 1929, I felt that, as the new Finance Member, I must take the occasion to review the general financial position. It seemed to me impossible to avoid making some reference to the rupee/sterling ratio because Indian opposition to this was already having some adverse effects on the general financial position. I took the line that whatever criticisms India might have about the decision taken in 1927, the position had now been firmly established and that to seek improvement in the general financial situation by a depreciation of the established exchange value of the rupee would distract attention from basic problems which were of fundamental importance. Comparing my position with that of a doctor responsible for the health of the Indian economy, I ventured to refer to the Oath of Hippocrates and continued as follows: 'Sir, I would willingly accept no less binding vows, but, if I were to listen to those who advocate inflation and depreciation of the currency as a remedy for the present state of this country, I should be untrue to such an oath. Then, indeed, should I be administering a deadly drug.' My speech on the Budget was well received and, after I had finished, Motilal Nehru, accompanied by some other leading Opposition Members, came across the Floor and said 'I liked the tone of your speech.'

The Assembly debates on the Budget were always tedious affairs, lasting several days. I had no Financial Secretary to support me and my uninterrupted attendance was essential. If I left my seat even for a few minutes, some Member of the Indian Opposition would rise to move that a protest about the absence of the Finance Member should be recorded in the official report. To get me through the weary hours I adopted the practice of bringing in a sketch book and sketching Members of the Opposition. This habit of mine eventually became known and G. D. Birla, a leading member of the commercial community and a great personal friend of Mr. Gandhi, started making sketches of me.

One of the difficulties with which we had to contend in handling government business in the Assembly was that the President (the Speaker) Vithalbhai Patel was always seeking, with great ingenuity, to find opportunities for embarrassing the Government. A significant opportunity for this came during the next weeks. The Home Member had introduced legislation concerned with measures for public safety. At the same time an important case concerned with threats to public safety, known as the 'Meerut

Conspiracy Case', was being heard. Patel had taken an early opportunity to warn the Home Member that he was considering whether he could allow the proposed legislation to be discussed in the Assembly because this would inevitably involve discussion on issues which must be regarded as being 'sub judice' in the hearing of the Meerut Conspiracy case. I had felt that this might create an extremely embarrassing position and I had expressed strong views that we ought to be ready with an effective plan of action if Patel were to take this line. The Home Member, however, had felt that this was unnecessary and that he must proceed with the introduction of the legislation. I vividly recall my feelings on the day of the debate during which I felt sure that a critical point of conflict with the President would come. I remember praying that something would prevent it. Then suddenly I heard an object fall on the steps of the gangway running down beside my seat. Perhaps something was happening which might interrupt the proceedings? A second later a bomb was thrown down from the visitors' gallery and exploded just at the right of my seat. Something had indeed happened! As I wrote to Arthur Villiers:

'. . . I feel very guilty for having caused everyone anxiety, because I was only scratched. But the journalists were all on the look-out for headlines and the bomb did so little damage that they were hard up. I only got a small piece in the back of my arm which made a neat deep cut about an inch long, but caused me practically no pain or trouble. I was amazingly lucky because the bomb (which from fragments picked up was a sort of heavy edition of a Mills bomb) burst within 2 feet of me. But the side and back of the seat protected me and as it fell in the narrow gangway the whole force of the burst seemed to be directed upwards. It brought down quite a lot of chunks from the ceiling. The second bomb was much more powerful and destroyed two whole benches, but everyone had cleared out after the first. These heavy teakwood benches with high backs and fronts act like a series of trenches and gave great protection, as both bombs burst right on the floor. My own chief feeling was relief because I thought, on the course that we were set, that the Govt. was heading straight for disaster. I still believe it was and since then I have been largely instrumental in getting the course altered. But that is another and very long story. . . . Simon got a good front seat view of the bombing. I dined alone with him last night before he left. He told me he left India with his mind in greater confusion than when he started. I told him it was no use his thinking of wonderful constitutions; what he had got to do was to stage the whole business so that for the next 5 years the British Government in India could work together with Jinnah and Malaviya—taking them as representing the moderates. There is very little more in it than that . . . '

The bomb-thrower, Bhagat Singh, had been quickly apprehended but with great confusion throughout the building there was no thought of the Assembly meeting again that day.

22. In court dress

In the afternoon we had a special Council meeting at the Viceroy's house in Old Delhi to consider how to handle the problem. I suggested that we could not charge the President with misinterpreting the rules of procedure. On the other hand it was essential in the public interest to have legislation on the lines proposed in the Government bill. Accordingly it was clear that the only practicable course in the public interest would be to change the wording of the rules. This could be effected by an Ordinance issued by the Viceroy under his reserved powers. This line of action was eventually agreed and the Viceroy arranged to attend a special meeting of the Assembly to explain his action. This he did admirably, and the result was accepted as a 'fait accompli'.

The story about the public safety legislation which I have told in the preceding paragraphs provides a significant illustration of how British/Indian relations worked out in the proceedings of the Indian Assembly. My own impression is that on the whole these proceedings provided useful opportunities for discussing issues of public policy and that they only led to a worsening of British/Indian relations when we, as members of the Government of India, were forced by the British Government to introduce measures which were clearly designed to further British interests. Thus the Viceroy's use of his emergency powers to make it possible for the Assembly to discuss legislation designed in the interests of the public safety was accepted without serious criticism while the proposals (to which I shall refer in a later paragraph) designed in the interests of the Lancashire cotton industry had a permanently damaging effect on British/Indian relations.

Before, however, coming to this part of my story, I must refer to another event in 1929 which in my view had a decisive influence on the whole course of subsequent political discussions.

On October 31st 1929 Lord Irwin made his public statement defining Britain's purpose as the establishment of Dominion Status for India. The story of the discussions on the British side which preceded and followed this statement is a complex one which has been fully told in several historical books, notably *The Crisis of Indian Unity* by R. J. Moore (1974). I had no knowledge of these discussions, but I note from my records that Irwin consulted me about the form of his proposed statement and, when it was published, he wrote:

' . . . Wednesday night.

My dear Schuster, How very nice of you, Thank you so much. I'm glad you thought the balance about right. You helped much to get it as it was.

It will be interesting now to see the different categories of scream let loose here and at home! . . . '

The statement itself had initially a remarkable effect on Indian political opinion. If it had been confirmed as indicating the true British purpose, it might have led to a cooperation and an agreed advance towards practical independence, but the bitter criticism of Lord Irwin made by leading Conservative politicians and by the Conservative press in Britain had the disastrous contrary effect of convincing Indian opinion as a whole that they would make no significant political progress in the foreseeable future without fighting for it. I am convinced that this was largely responsible for the wide support, including support from the commercial community, given in India to the Civil Disobedence campaign of 1930. I see it also as having been a determining factor in deciding 'elder statesmen' among the Indian nationalists to associate themselves with the violent younger movement. Among these 'elder statesmen' I think chiefly of Motilal Nehru. The Motilal with whom I had had intimate talks in the first months of 1929 was not the Motilal who in 1930 courted arrest and imprisonment. On that I look back as one of the great tragedies of my years in India.

During my visit to London at the end of 1929 the head of the India Office staff, Sir Arthur Hirzel, invited me to dinner. Lord Birkenhead was present and in the course of the discussion after dinner he made a most violent attack on Lord Irwin as Viceroy for his gross folly in making his Dominion Status speech. This of course was very painful to me and eventually I could stand it no longer, and I had the temerity to ask Lord Birkenhead by what authority he claimed justification for accusing the Viceroy for misunderstanding the Indian situation. To this he replied, 'Authority? Do you think I must be a sundried bureaucrat to understand the Indian situation?' I then intervened and put to him a further question, 'How do you reconcile your criticism of Lord Irwin with your own statement in one of your public speeches to the effect that you looked forward to the day when the Indians would take over the responsibility for their own government?' To this he replied, 'I did say that, but you have left out the most important words of my speech. I said "in the fullness of time" and for me the fullness of time meant a 100 years or 500 years, and anyhow it was the most damned stupid speech that I ever made and it was Sir Arthur Hirzel here who forced me to make it.'

For my task as Finance Member the last months of 1929 were affected by worries about the maintenance of the rupee/sterling ratio—worries, the cloud of which hung over all my first years in India. I was under constant pressure from the India Office to enforce a tough financial policy, raising the Bank rate to high levels, etc., all the methods which have become familiar in recent years for Finance Ministers faced with the task of attempting to maintain what has in effect become an unjustifiably high exchange rage for their country's currency. I resisted this pressure because I thought that the methods proposed would be ineffective in the conditions of the Indian money market and would merely increase Indian hostility to British policy.

A special problem occurred in the last months of 1929. It became necessary to raise additional sterling funds and the India Office proposed

23. Relaxing at our camp at Naldera

that for this purpose we should issue a long term Indian Government Sterling Loan in London on a 7 per cent basis. Since Government securities in India were running on a 4 per cent basis, I felt that this would be a shock to public opinion in India which might have serious effects not only on Indian business but also on the political situation. I eventually got agreement from the Viceroy and from Whitehall that I should pay a personal visit to London to discuss the position. In London I sought independent advice from Sir Otto Niemeyer, who had recently moved from the Treasury to the Bank of England as chief adviser to the Governor. I also asked Sir Henry Strakosch to join our discussion. I found both these experienced men very ready to appreciate my difficulties and in the event, with support from the Bank of England, I got the India Office to agree to postpone the issue of a long term loan and to meet the immediate need by placing Six Months India Bills for £6,000,000. This incident provides a futher illustration of the difficulty of my relations with the India Office about financial policy.

The world economic crisis, of which the Wall Street collapse in the USA at the end of 1929 had been an important symptom, was having its inevitable effect in India both in the field of private business and also of Government revenue receipts. In preparing my Budget proposals for 1930-31 it was clear that drastic measures both for cutting Government expenditure and for increasing tax revenue would be necessary.

For increasing tax revenue the obvious first move, as I saw it (and had seen it in 1929), must be to increase the revenue import duty on cotton piece goods from the exceptionally low rate of 11 per cent to the standard rate of 15 per cent. As might have been expected in the light of what had happened in 1929, the inclusion of this measure in my Budget proposals produced a violently hostile reaction from Whitehall, but one which on this occasion took the form not of a mere personal appeal from the Secretary of State, but of a formal representation from the whole British Cabinet—a very exceptional move.

So far as I was concerned as Finance Member, I could not agree to abandon my proposal since, taking account of Indian interests and Indian conditions, the raising of the import duty on cotton piece goods to the standard level was obviously the right first step in any programme for increased taxation. I had been ready in 1929 to take the risk of doing without any increase in taxation and accordingly to abandon my proposal for the smaller increase of 1½ per cent. Conditions, however, had entirely changed in 1930.

The Viceroy's Council supported my attitude but felt that they could not entirely ignore an appeal from the whole Cabinet. At this point the Commerce Member, Sir George Rainy, proposed a line of action which fell within the sphere of his responsibility. This was that, as a step which might help to meet the British Government's objection, the occasion might be taken to introduce a form of Imperial Preference and that, while the general level of the import duty on cotton piece goods should be raised to 15 per cent, a surcharge of a further 5 per cent should be levied on imports from all countries other than Britain, a measure directed largely against Japan. This proposal was approved by the Viceroy in Council and eventually agreed by the Secretary of State.

This particular attempt to help the Lancashire cotton industry had serious effects—long range effects in strengthening what I have described as the Indian reactions to the British criticisms of Lord Irwin's Dominion Status statement, and short range effects in helping to secure support from the Indian commercial community for the Civil Disobedience movement of 1930.

In the political field 1930 must be seen as the year of Civil Disobedience.

The general policy of the Government of India as decided in the first stages of the Civil Disobedience movement had been to arrest all the main leaders of the Congress campaign for any illegal conduct, but to defer the actual arrest of Mr. Gandhi—a policy which I personally felt to be right at the time and which I believe was proved by subsequent experience to have been right.

After the Council meeting in which this policy had been approved, I myself went on a tour of the North Western Frontier in April, during which time I was completely out of contact with current news from headquarters. I emerged from this period of isolation at a critical moment. Having reached the penultimate stage of my tour I had planned to end with a visit to Peshawar. When the military commander with whom I was staying telephoned to arrange for this visit, he got a reply from the Governor

24. On the North West Frontier

appealing for me not to come. I said that I must visit Peshawar because the Viceroy had specially asked me to do so. The reply received was 'If Sir George Schuster insists on coming to Peshawar I cannot stop him, but I shall have to send out a column of tanks to bring him in.' I could only decide that I must give up Peshawar and return to the Government at Simla.

As I motored alone on the long drive through North India I remember feeling very lonely—what a tiny element we British were in the vast area of India and how precarious was our position if serious disaffection spread right up to the North West Frontier. In my current letter to my wife I wrote about my arrival, 'It was a lovely morning—fresh after the rain and I got back all my feeling of the first approach to Simla—the soft haze over the hills—fresh air, scents from the pines and flowering shrubs—a world whose beauty made me forget for a moment the trouble of politics.' I had expected to go on to the final terminus in Simla and find my own rickshaw waiting for me; but I was surprised on arrival at the preliminary Summer Hill station to find a messenger from the Viceroy asking me to go immediately to a Council meeting and bringing a pony for me to ride up. 'So I cantered up the paths in the first sunlight and plunged again into political troubles round the Viceroy's table.' They were waiting to get first-hand news from me about conditions in Peshawar and were disappointed to find that I had been unable to visit it. I had thought that they would have received their own direct information, but I found that they had none.

The Council did not reach any final conclusion at this meeting because there were many practical arrangements to make, particularly with reference to the Peshawar situation. Two days later Lord Irwin asked me to dine and have a private talk with him after dinner. As I wrote to my wife:

'. . . The evening ended amusingly. Lady Irwin had come up to sit in his study while we continued our conversation. Suddenly there was a most appalling noise of rowdy shouting in the drive outside. The Viceroy said "What on earth is that?" She said "Oh, that's Azam and Muzam (I haven't got their names right but they were the two sons of the Nizam of Hyderabad). They came to see you dressed up as Gandhi and one of the Ali brothers. You must come down and see them." (These two boys were staying there but had been dining out.) So we went down to the Hall expecting to see two figures enter. Then the doors opened and the most appalling motley crowd came in. First these two, then Geoff Alexander and half a dozen more, quite naked except for sheets, Gandhi caps and socks and sock suspenders, C. O. Harvey as the last British policeman in India and finally George Cunningham as Mr. Patel with a yak's tail (an enormous white thing) as his beard. In the distance he was amazingly like the old devil. They really were funny—not merely silly and we were all kept laughing for ten minutes. And so to bed.'

I have included this letter to illustrate the spirit of the Viceroy's household in Lord Irwin's day. The fact that the problem was considered with a sense of humour certainly does not imply that it was not taken as desperately serious. Irwin's personal staff realised what a burden of responsibility he was carrying and felt, quite rightly, that a good laugh would do him good.

The final decision in Council was taken at the next day's meeting to proceed with the arrest of Gandhi. Since during this period there had been a good deal of criticism in the British Press of Irwin's supposed weakness I think it worthwhile to record my own judgment at the time as explained in my contemporary letter to my wife.

'. . . It is still too early to say what the full effects of G's arrest will be, but at present my feeling is that we have done it just at the right time. I am annoyed with most of the English papers which "fear that Lord Irwin has acted too late" etc. etc. They have not taken the trouble to appreciate what our policy has been. Except for the personal case of Gandhi (or the case where poor Bolton let things get out of hand in Peshawar) very strong and prompt action has been taken. All the important leaders from Jawaharlal Nehru downwards have been picked up and put into gaol at once. Now I myself think that this has entirely upset their plans. They expected Gandhi's arrest to come first and that that would be a signal for a concerted movement all over India for which they had been long preparing. Now by our leaving Gandhi alone they have missed their dramatic climax. "Zero hour" never struck and their "set piece" has fired up first in one place and then in another, but no combined effort, and in each place once fired it has fizzled out. Now that G's arrest has come all the brainy leaders have been put quietly into gaol and I think the country may be getting a bit tired of sporadic desultory disturbances which don't seem to lead anywhere. It is true that in the meanwhile we have lost something by allowing G to remain at large. He has certainly been able to do a good deal of harm to Government prestige in Gujerat; but the effect of all that has been very local. G is no longer the mainspring brain and focal centre of the movement and on the whole the effect of his 2 months' run has been to create rather an aimless impression. I have always felt myself that G arrested and in prison would be a much more significant factor in the Indian situation than G at large parading without much aim in Gujerat. And I still believe that the view was right provided that in the meanwhile strong and effective action was taken everywhere else. Now that was being done far more promptly and vigorously than in the last trouble in 1919-22 etc. and the arrests were combined with a number of ordinances to strengthen the Government's hands. But I always recognised that there was a limit to the length to which G would be allowed to remain at large and in my view the Peshawar incident made it quite essential to review the situation. If there was any risk of the Army being got at or—in a lesser degree—of the North West Frontier tribes being aroused, then we could afford to have no chink in our armour and to allow nothing to go which could be construed as a sign of fear or weakening . . . '

I myself left for England at the end of September 1930 as a representative of the Government of India, together with Harry Haig then Secretary of the Home Department, in order to advise the British delegation on the occasion of the first Round Table Conference, held in London to plan the long-term future of the sub-continent.

My voyage home proved to be of some significance because I had, as fellow passengers, a delegation from the Indian States led by Sir Akbar Hydari, the Chief Minister of Hyderabad. On our first days he started conversations with me about certain plans which he intended to put forward on behalf of the Indian Princes—plans for an All-India Federation in which the Princes would be included. These ideas seemed to me of such significance that I took the occasion of our normal stop at Aden to telephone to the Viceroy. He agreed with me about the importance of this new initiative and asked me to send him a full report and also to get Hydari to produce a written statement of his general plan. I managed to get a letter to the Viceroy posted in Aden and wrote more fully on my arrival in London. Another fellow passenger on the voyage was Edward Benthall, a leading member of the commercial community in Calcutta with whom I also had confidential discussions and whom I also found extremely interested in the possibility of an All-India Federation including the Princely States.

105

On our arrival in London our initial discussions were with Lord Sankey, the Lord Chancellor, to whom had been given the duty of conducting preliminary enquiries on behalf of the Labour Government. I can record that Haig and I were profoundly shocked at his ignorance of even the most elementary facts about India. He came to our meetings with a small excercise book in which he recorded simple notes and indeed he said to us at the end of one of our meetings with touching frankness, 'It is disturbing to think that in a few days we shall be starting on a Conference to discuss questions of major political importance for the whole of the British Empire and that we on our side have given no preliminary consideration to the issues involved.'

I myself was so disturbed about this general situation that I took the risk of making a personal approach to Ramsay MacDonald. I had a feeling that six years previously when I had been involved with him in discussions about the Sudan political crisis of 1924, I had in some way gained his confidence. Accordingly on one Saturday evening a few days before the opening of the Conference I telephoned Chequers. My call was answered by Ishbel MacDonald who said, 'Hold on, I will go and ask father.' She came back in a few minutes and said, 'Father would much like to see you and asks you to come over tomorrow morning and stay to lunch.'

My letter to Lord Irwin of 21st November gives my account of this meeting and of subsequent developments:

> ' . . . The keynote of the past week is the growth of the idea that the Conference will turn out to be a reality and the agreement on all sides to treat the Federation of All-India as the overriding practical issue. This idea, which I first wrote to you about as embodied in Hydari's scheme has, of course, completely altered the atmosphere. It is indeed remarkable that everyone grasps at it as something which creates a new situation and enables them to get away from embarrassing declarations of the past. I must confess that I feel great doubts whether all will find in a Federal scheme a realisation of the interpretation which at present attracts them to it—whether, for example, 'political' British India will accept that 'safe' form of constitution which attracts conservatives here to the idea, or whether the Princes, when it comes to examining the actual subjects in regard to which adhesion to a Federation will involve sacrifice of each State's liberty, will be ready to give practical embodiment to the principles which they have in a general way applauded.
>
> For the time, however, the idea, as of course you will have realised, is playing a great part. It has already furnished the peg on which to hang the general discussion and thus helped to frustrate any awkward effort to challenge the Government on Dominion Status in the first round.
>
> Another great thing which it has done is to enable everyone (including our Liberals and Conservatives) to say that the Simon

Report and the Government of India despatch are both already out of date because a new situation has been created since they were written. I should not be surprised to find the Conservatives riding off on this excuse and in the end committing themselves to a policy considerably more advanced than that which they have condemned so bitterly when put forward by you. This is all to the good and it is a great advantage that the All-India Federal idea has come up here in a manner which makes the Conference regard it as its own creation. It would indeed in a sense have been a real misfortune if the Government of India despatch had itself made a main feature of this idea. Geoffrey Dawson, who criticised the despatch for its omissions, admitted to me that he thought it was in practice advantageous and indeed he took the view that the despatch had served its purpose very well, for everybody, while criticising it, was pleased to be able to do so. It had put Simon in a good temper as affording no rival to his document as a best seller; it had relieved Reading, etc. etc. while at the same time it could provide most valuable material when they got down to hard facts on committees.

As regards my personal views and interviews I will not bother you with any long account. The most interesting thing from my standpoint was that I was able to spend three hours with Ramsay MacDonald at Chequers last Sunday. I was greatly relieved at this interview, mainly because I found that he was personally going to take charge of the Conference and really give his time to it. He had been spending the whole morning on India and he at once took all the points so that I felt I had got further with him in half-an-hour than in all the weeks with the others. He certainly is a "class" horse compared to the rest of his Government. We talked from twelve till lunch, again after lunch—listened to a Bach cantata on the wireless—and I didn't get away till half past three. I daresay you will be amused and possibly shocked at my "butting in" in this way—but it was all for the sake of preaching your doctrines so I hope you will regard it as a good action!

As to the Conference itself—the opening day was on the whole very good. Sapru's speech helpful and well received—Ramsay's general handling of the meeting quite admirable. He has exactly the right manner, said exactly the right things, and is complete master of the gathering, which is not easy. He really could not have been better. The next day saw a lowering of the tone, for which I am afraid I regard Peel's speech as responsible. He made the mistake of taking up debating points from the earlier speeches and of complaining that the past record of British Government in India had not been properly appreciated, trotting out all the well-known points about what we had done for the country in the way of irrigation, economic development, etc. This really changed the tone of the whole subsequent debate, as it gave everybody an excuse for bringing up the well known charges of how we had tried to strangle the Indian cotton industry to help

Lancashire, how our financial and currency policy in the last years had damaged Indian interests, etc. etc.—all the things we know "ad nauseam" in Delhi. Ramsay this evening after two days of this said humorously that as regards future speakers he proposed to rule that "Lord Peel had now been sufficently answered." Of course one can sympathise with Peel's decision to put the Conservative case, but that should have been as to the future. It seems to me a great mistake for us to go patting ourselves on the back for what we have done in the past.

Other notable points have been the Princes' solid stand for immediate federation—coupled with the running refrain of "hands off the internal affairs of the States" and a suggestion that entry into a federation would rid their backs of the load of our paramountcy doctrine—Sastri's conversion to federation—Reading's acceptance of "Dominion Status" as the natural issue of our previous declaration—and—a thing which would have pleased you—that the most genuine feeling shown at any point of the Conference has been the applause which has greeted every reference to your name and to the fact that but for you the situation in India today would have been infinitely worse.

I have just been breakfasting with Philip Kerr and the other members of the Liberal delegation (except Reading). I was astounded to find how advanced a view they are now taking. They at least are thinking in terms of some far-reaching declaration which will satisfy the delegates here, and bring Congress in—relying on the long period which the working out of a federal constitution for the Centre will necessarily take, to give the time for a more responsible opinion to develop in India (as a result of the working of the new provincial Governments) and for the preliminary conditions as regards Finance, etc. to be carried out. In fact, they are really thinking on the lines of my "postdated" cheque idea. I asked Philip Kerr what line Reading would take, and he confessed that he did not know—that indeed they none of them really knew what Reading intended to commit himself to in his speech yesterday, beyond the agreed statement that Dominion Status *is* the natural issue of past pledges. But at least he was clear that Reading had moved a great deal. This all bears out what I said earlier in this letter, that the British delegates are likely when themselves brought in contact with Indians to go infinitely further than any of the ideas which they have condemned in you. In fact, at times even I feel really apprehensive lest the Conference in its own atmosphere detached from realities in India may take the bit in its teeth and run away with the situation. But there is a long way to go yet, and it is a great thing to have started in a good atmosphere.

I have been finishing this letter at the Conference and Ramsay has just wound up with a really great speech.'

I can add that Ramsay MacDonald continued while he was still Prime Minister of a Labour Government to get his Ministers to give careful consideration to points which I made to him. He arranged two special meetings in his room at the House of Commons with members of his Cabinet at which I was present. The Ministers attending were Arthur Henderson, Jim Thomas, Wedgwood Benn and Lees Smith. At the first meeting on November 19th he put before them a detailed note about the constitutional implications of Federation based on one which I had prepared for him after our meeting at Chequers. The second meeting on November 25th was from my point of view specially interesting because it was concerned with the possible reactions in the financial field, especially as regards currency policy, of creating the impression that responsibility would be transferred in the foreseeable future to an Indian Government. I had taken the view that public opinion would assume that an Indian Government would immediately revert to a rupee/sterling ration of 1/4d. and that it would be necessary to guard against the possibility of immediate reactions. No definite action was agreed except that the whole issue should be discussed with the Governor of the Bank of England, but from my point of view the record was important because it included a statement by Sir Malcolm Hailey to the effect that the Indian demand for the return to the 1/4d. ratio 'had passed far beyond the Bombay agitation and went right through the country with the strength of a religious belief'.

What I have written up to this point gives an eye-witness account of what happened in the opening stage of the Round Table Conference. I cannot carry this further because, after 1930, I took no active part in the proceedings, mainly because the Viceroy found my presence in India essential for dealing with current financial problems. Looking back today after nearly fifty years and having read again what I wrote at the time to Lord Irwin about my first talks with Ramsay MacDonald and his handling of the opening session of the Conference, I am impressed with the thought that, if there had been no British political crisis in 1931 and if Ramsay MacDonald had retained not only his authority as Prime Minister of a Labour Government but also his full intellectual powers, the broad conception of an All-India Federation (as outlined by Sir Akbar Hydari) might have been treated as one deserving serious study by the British Government and not allowed to get lost in ineffective local discussions. If that had been done, it is at least conceivable that the partition of 1947 with all its evils might have been avoided.

In the political field 1931 can be seen as a year of peace, the year of the Irwin-Gandhi pact and of Gandhi's attendance at a session of the Round Table Conference. In the economic and financial field it was a year of crisis with sterling 'going off gold'. Finally, on the personal side, it was the year when Lord Irwin was succeeded as Viceroy by Lord Willingdon.

I have been glad to note that Philip Mason, in his fascinating record of how British rule in India really worked, has written that he saw Irwin's meetings with Gandhi in March 1931 not as an act of weakness but of wisdom and courage.* Despite opposition from both sides the two men spent several days in intensive discussion and eventually reached a compromise under which Gandhi agreed to call off the Civil Disobedience campaign and the boycott of British goods while Irwin undertook to relax the emergency security measures, and to make several token concessions sufficient to encourage Congress to take part in the next session of the Round Table Conference.

The whole experience had its humorous aspect, as indeed had many experiences with Gandhi. I see the picture of the little man, half-naked, arriving at the vast building of the Viceroy's house in New Delhi and finding a crowd of over 700 Indians waiting to greet him, thinking they represented crowds from New Delhi and not realising that they were no more than the Viceroy's household staff. I think of Irwin and Gandhi talking together and Irwin, when any point of serious difficulty was reached, suggesting to Gandhi that he should walk up and down the corridor outside for a few minutes seeking spiritual guidance—a process which he told me was generally successful.

I set out below a copy of Irwin's letter to me after the conclusion of the Pact.

6.3.31.

'My dear Schuster,

Thank you so much for your note. I don't really think that any great credit is due to me, personally—for I believe that the broad influences were on the side of peace, and that the stars were fighting in that cause. But if personal efforts had a part to play, a very large share of the contribution on that side was made as I told you by Emerson.

And you have all helped me immensely by your readiness to trust your negotiators and to strengthen my hands.

What the future may hold, we cannot say. But it has, as you say, opened a door. I have just had the Turkish Ambassador at Kabul lunching, and he has been developing his belief that it will have a very tranquillising influence on potential Amanullah-Russian intrigues. I hope it may.

Thank you again. I trust it may also indirectly contribute to the relief of your own particular financial troubles.

Yours ever,
I.'

I myself had to play a small part in the discussions because Gandhi wanted to get a token concession in connection with the tax on salt. Scattered about India there were some villages in the neighbourhood of which it was possible to recover small quantities of salt, and Gandhi wanted

---

* *The Men Who Ruled India* Vol. II p. 245 by 'Philip Woodruff' (Philip Mason).

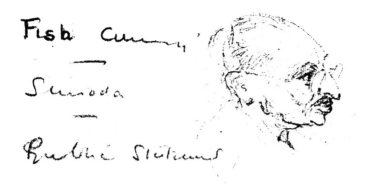

Fish Curry,

Suroda

Public Statement

25. Contemporary sketch of Gandhi from my notepad

the Government to give special licence to the people in such villages to collect salt for their own consumption but not for sale. I had no difficulty in agreeing to this concession which gave him great satisfaction. I have preserved a note that I made immediately after our meeting:

'Mr. G. arrived punctually shown in by an ADC in uniform. Mr. G. well wrapped up in homespun cotton. Bare legs of course and he took his sandals off when he sat down to talk. He looked very fresh and healthy—surprisingly so—and his whole appearance was much more attractive than I had expected. Pleasant manners—a very friendly smile, etc.

We sat down at a desk together. I said I was honoured to meet him.

He said "I have thought of you in the last 10 months. 10 months ago Miss Slade had a letter from Horace Alexander in which he sent a special message from your mother to me. She had said that she had heard that I had said that you were the greatest thief in the world and she wanted to know whether I had said it and why I would not meet you because she was sure that if I had met her son I could not say such a thing of him. I meant to speak to Horace Alexander about it when he saw me. But I forgot. Now I want you to send a message to your mother that I never said such a thing about anybody—certainly not about you."

I said I was glad and would tell my mother. I then went on that as he had started in a personal way I should like him to understand my outlook on economic questions, for even if I was not a thief, I would like him to know that I agreed in many ways with what I understood to be his outlook about money and its place in life.' (Private Note 3.3.31.)

In the financial and economic field the year 1931 must be seen as a year in which the problems for India created by the world economic slump came to a head. In my Budget proposals for the year I had to include some increases in taxation and I was very specially concerned with measures for achieving economy in expenditure. These proposals were all accepted by the Indian Assembly but as we passed on to the current business of the year we found it affected by growing depression in the field of international commerce. These conditions, during the next months, caused us special anxiety about our Indian currency position with increasing signs of lack of confidence in the Government's power to maintain the exchange value of the rupee. I myself was constantly oppressed by a feeling of impending danger.

The actual shock came without warning on the morning of Monday, September 21st. I had spent the weekend until Sunday evening at our tented camp at Naldera, one hour's run in a rickshaw from Simla. Having got back late on Sunday evening, I only came down to breakfast on Monday morning at 8 a.m. instead of, as usual, having an hour's work before breakfast. I found Denning, the head of my Currency Department, waiting for me in the hall. He said, 'Have you seen the Reuter telegram this morning?' I said, 'No. Why?' He said, 'Sterling has gone off gold.'

We got on at once to the Cipher Office attached to the Foreign Department and asked whether any cable had come in, to which they replied 'Yes. A long cable in five parts began coming in at 5 a.m. and we are still deciphering it.' This faced us with a critical problem on which we had to take immediate action. The first necessity was to stop the opening of the Government Currency Offices in Calcutta and Bombay due at 9 a.m. If they had opened when the London news was known but without any instructions from us about the basis on which they could do business, there would have been a mass of public applications with which they would not have known how to deal. The immediate practical need, therefore, was to keep the Currency Offices closed until we could settle Government policy. This closure required the authority of an Ordinance by the Viceroy. We telephoned to the Legal Secretary asking him to go up at once in his rickshaw to the Viceregal Lodge and get the Viceroy to authorise the issue of an Ordinance ordering the closure of the Currency Office for three days. I still do not know how he managed the task in the few minutes available, but it was done.

Having settled this immediate action, I turned to ask Denning the vital question—What course did he advise? He replied without hesitation, 'Take this occasion to break the rupee link with sterling.' He adhered strongly to this view throughout our subsequent discussions.

Our next step was to study the long cable from the India Office when it was eventually deciphered. It contained a carefully reasoned argument for continuing the link of the rupee with sterling at the current level of 1/6d. and it explained that the senior officer of my Finance Department, Sir George MacWatters, together with the assistant director of the Currency

112

26. In an official rickshaw at Simla

Office, Mr. Taylor, who happened both to be on leave in London, had been brought in to the discussions and supported the India Office's view.

At this stage it is appropriate to record some reflections on the way in which the India Office handled their relations with the Government of India. Our impression at the time was that they had merely shown incompetence in failing to appreciate that our time in India was five hours in advance of London, so that a cable despatched at midnight on Sunday would only start coming in to our headquarters after 5 a.m. on Monday and that a very long cable received without preliminary warning during night duty hours could not be expected to be deciphered in time to receive the attention of the Government until normal business hours on Monday—long after the morning newspapers had appeared.

That was our impression at the time; but, on subsequent reflection, I am convinced that it was the deliberate purpose of the Secretary of State to confront the Government of India with a 'fait accompli' which we should be forced to accept without any opportunity for argument. From my point of view it is satisfactory to reflect that we had the ability to defeat that particular purpose. What we achieved in effect was to give ourselves a period of three days, while the Currency Offices were closed, during which we could reflect on the issues involved and argue the matter with Whitehall.

These three days proved an unforgettable experience. In our discussions on the Viceroy's Council I myself, greatly influenced by the strong opinion of the head of my Currency Department, felt bound to urge that the change in the position of sterling created entirely new conditions which gave us a legitimate opportunity to escape from what had proved to be a most damaging commitment to the 1/6d. ratio. It so happened that Sir Malcolm Hailey, one of the wisest statesmen in the whole history of British rule in India, was in Simla at the time and joined all our discussions. He, with his unique knowledge of Indian conditions, strongly supported my views.

During these three days I also took some independent personal action. The Assembly was in session and I thought it wise to arrange frank confidential talks with four Indian members who held leading positions in the commercial community. I found that these men, who had all been violent and uncompromising critics of the Government's currency policy, when confronted with the responsibility of advising on practical action, behaved very differently. In fact they gave me no help at all and were quite clearly themselves in doubt about what would be the right course in the new conditions. This had some influence on my own ultimate attitude.

The result of our deliberations was that the Viceroy and all members of the Council supported my view and the Viceroy informed the Secretary of State that they would all resign with me if my advice was not accepted.

The response was a personal appeal to Lord Willingdon from the Secretary of State, Sir Samuel Hoare, on behalf of MacDonald, Baldwin and the entire Cabinet:

'The political situation with which the Government of India and His Majesty's Government are faced is probably more serious that any that has so far occurred in the relations between India and this country. Anything like resignations upon the scale which you indicate as possible would present the appearance of an open conflict of interest between India on the one hand and Great Britain on the other. In reality this is not so. We and you are solely concerned with the interests of India but unfortunately we take divergent views as to the best means of serving these interests . . . We say with great seriousness that any concerted resignations by your colleagues would be comparable to the resignation of a general staff in the face of the enemy . . . You have given a lifetime of service to the Empire in many fields and we are sure we can count on you to stand by us now in the greatest Imperial emergency since the war.'

This appeal had, of course, to be taken very seriously and threw a heavy personal responsibility on me. I had been much moved by the fact that the Viceroy and all my colleagues on his Council had shown such confidence in my personal judgement; but the responsibility for provoking a major political crisis could not be taken lightly, and I felt it necessary to reflect again on the basic issues involved.

The legitimate objection to the existing arrangements had been not that the rupee had been linked with sterling, but that the currency policy of the British authorities for maintaining the link of sterling with gold had in fact resulted in an over-valuation of sterling and consequently of the rupee, which had been very damaging to the Indian economy and had been leading recently to a most embarrassing 'flight from the rupee'. On my experience of the past years I was convinced that in Indian interests it was essential to break the link with sterling if the policy of the British currency authorities for sterling was to continue unchanged. On the other hand the fact that Britain had been forced to abandon the gold standard for sterling had opened the possibility for a change in British currency policy, and I had to recognise that it was not unreasonable that this possibility should be given a trial.

In the end, after getting most valued personal advice from Sir Malcolm Hailey, I decided that I would agree to carry on as Finance Member, supporting the old rupee sterling link, but subject to the condition that if future experience showed that, in spite of the fact that the link of sterling with gold had been broken, British currency policy for sterling resulted in the continuance of pressure on the rupee, I would feel myself justified in tendering my personal resignation. What this in effect meant was that I could not agree to accept an immutable commitment to support the maintenance of the existing link with sterling regardless of the way in which the British authorities operated their own policy for sterling. This attitude I felt (and still feel) was fully justified.

In the actual result there was no need to avail myself of my 'escape clause', since British currency policy was in fact changed. Two significant developments affected the immediate position. First, the British Government's new currency policy resulted in effect in a devaluation of sterling of about 25 per cent on its former gold standard value. This brought about a devaluation of the rupee more than double that demanded by the advocates of a 1/4d. exchange rate. Secondly, the consequent rise in the rupee value of gold induced private individuals in India to sell large quantities of their gold ornaments, amounting in total to a value of about £99 million sterling—an amount large enough in effect to give substantial help to the British Government in dealing with its own international currency problem. It was incidentally rather sad in going round the currency offices to see great piles of gold ornaments, some of them of considerable artistic value, lying in heaps in the corner having been sold just for their gold value.

In this way the immediate controversy with Whitehall over currency policy was settled, but it was not the end of our disagreements with the Secretary of State about the handling of our general financial problem. I was faced with the need to prepare emergency Budget proposals for immediate presentation to the Legislative Assembly. This course, taking account of the devaluation of sterling and the world economic conditions which had made it inevitable, had been considered necessary for Britain, and we agreed that it ought to be followed in India.

I felt that if anything was to be done it must be done quickly—in fact in a few days. This task, following on the controversy about currency policy, involved a great personal strain for me. It is in times of strain and practical emergency like this that the value of support from colleagues is most vividly felt and engraved in the memory. In taking the decision about the Emergency Budget, I was much strengthened by Sir Malcolm Hailey and I have always remembered, and on some later occasions been guided by, one of his sayings. This, as I recall it, was: 'If you have to ask a meeting to consider taking unpleasant measures to deal with a difficult situation, do not seek to minimise the difficulties, but rather make the most of them. In fact, overwhelm them with a "load of beastliness". Then any subsequent development will look like a change for the better.'

When it came to working out actual proposals I decided that the only practical course within the time available was to rely mainly on two simple lines of action: First, to increase tax revenue by imposing a percentage surcharge on all existing taxes. (This policy, incidentally, earned me the popular nickname of 'Sur-Charge' Schuster.) Secondly, to achieve economies mainly by an all round 10 per cent cut in pay.

The proposal for the cut in pay was simple but drastic. I felt that it would be intrinsically wrong to impose such a cut without explaining the whole position to members of the ICS. I look back with feelings of the deepest gratitude for the response from the British members of the ICS—in particular to Bob Emerson who arranged a large meeting of specially appointed British representatives. To many of these men with family commitments a 10 per cent cut in pay meant serious hardship, but they accepted the position in the public interest and no suggestion of criticism was ever made.

In the result, my Emergency Budget plan was approved by the Assembly, but in the meanwhile we had become involved in another acute quarrel with the Secretary of State. The cut in the pay of the British members of the ICS could not be imposed without the approval of the British Parliament, and the Secretary of State took the line that he could not possibly introduce parliamentary legislation. On this point there could be no yielding by the

27. Lady Schuster and Mr. Gandhi at tea

Viceroy's Council and in the end the Secretary of State had to give way. We had, indeed, been profoundly shocked that Sir Samuel Hoare should have considered it possible that we, as the Government of India, should ask Indian opinion to approve a course of action which would give British members of ICS a specially privileged position as distinct from all Indian Government servants, including Indian members of the ICS itself.

Apart from the strain of dealing with the currency crisis and the Emergency Budget, the year 1931 was a time of some happy experiences. My two sons, who were at New College, Oxford, came out during the Long Vac to stay with us at Simla under the tutelage of John Maud, then a young don at University College. It was a time of political peace, with the Congress leaders all out of prison. During such periods I was always able to maintain friendly relations with leading politicians such as Mr. Gandhi and Jawaharlal Nehru. Mr. Gandhi invited John Maud and my two boys to have tea with him and they had an amusing and on some points really interesting talk with him. He was preparing to go to England for the next session of the Round Table Conference and he intended to take the opportunity for a visit to Oxford. My young party asked him how Oxford University should prepare for his visit. After some thought Gandhi, with a characteristic twinkle in his eye, said, 'I think you should tell them all to live for a week on goat's milk.' In Simla I had a palatial house, Peterhof, which had been the first Viceregal Lodge and which had wonderful views across many ranges of hills to the Himalayas. Mr. Gandhi and Jawaharlal Nehru used to visit me there. Mr. Gandhi always walked—a distance of about five miles from his own camp—and all my servants would stand out along my drive to watch him arrive. There was often glaring hot sunshine at Simla, but when I offered him refreshment he would take nothing but a glass of hot water with a little salt.

Looking back to these autumn months in 1931 I think also of a visit from Jawaharlal Nehru. We talked frankly together in my study and he was in a very serious mood, obviously oppressed by the thoughts of the struggle which he saw as inevitable. At the end of our talk I told him that my two boys had greatly hoped to have a chance to meet him. I asked him to join the family party in the next room. He hesitated, but as a matter of courtesy agreed to do so. When he first came in he was obviously still oppressed by his own serious thoughts, but I have a vivid picture in my memory of the change in his face when he suddenly felt the attraction of being again in the society of young people which he himself had so greatly enjoyed in his own Cambridge days. He then joined in a general lighthearted conversation and was absolutely charming.

The year 1931 was also a notable period for me because it covered Lord Willingdon's succession to Lord Irwin as Viceroy. I have already made clear how greatly I admired Lord Irwin's character and creed of life and how much my relationship with him had meant to me. Lord Willingdon was an entirely different kind of human being, but in my view he was a very wise

28. Lord and Lady Willingdon in 1933

118

man of fine character and qualities which were well adapted to the conditions during the years following the period of Lord Irwin's influence. I found him an ideal chief—ready to talk with complete frankness on all subjects, to discuss problems seriously and realistically without losing a sense of humour and, above all, ready to trust my judgement on financial and economic issues and to give me his unqualified backing.

In the political field he had a difficult part to play. At the stage of his arrival, Lord Irwin's message had been that the British Government genuinely intended to work for the earliest possible transfer of responsibility to an Indian Government—in effect that 'The British Raj was going'. As a matter of practical reality, however, there must be some years before a new constitution could be settled, during which it was essential that the authority of government should be maintained. Willingdon was clearly influenced by these considerations and therefore he chose in effect to put across the message that 'The British Raj is still responsible for the government of India and that the time for its going has not yet come'. No man, however, could have been further than Willingdon from the view of British Conservatives like Lord Birkenhead who visualised the achievement of Indian responsibility 'in the fullness of time', which for him meant something like 500 years. Willingdon in his previous positions as Governor of Bombay and of Madras had always shown special friendship with Indians and sympathy with the Indian point of view. He had taken a lead, for example, by establishing in Bombay a social club for both nationalities, and Lady Willingdon also had set an example by establishing social relations with Indian women.

I can only speak with personal experience of the first half of Willingdon's term as Viceroy, but my impression while I was in India was that he was handling the political position in a way which was broadly appropriate to that particular stage in the long period of transition.

In 1932 I moved out of the atmosphere of constant anxiety which in the past years had oppressed me about our currency position. This relief was not due to any lessening of the economic difficulties created for India by the world economic slump, leading to dramatic falls in the price levels for its main exports. This falling tendency still continued in 1932, but the plan covered by my Emergency Budget of September 1931 was adequate to protect the Government's financial position, and in my Budget proposals for 1932-33 I had to propose no changes in taxation.

In July 1932 I attended the Imperial Economic Conference held in Ottawa as a member of the Indian delegation. Looking back over my memories, I see it as an occasion which actually produced some most valuable results and which, beyond this, might have been of decisive significance for the development of satisfactory relations between Britain and India. The tariff arrangements settled in the UK/Indian Agreement concluded at Ottawa were of substantial practical value to India. In spite of the usual criticism from Nationalist political representatives, this fact was recognised by the Indian commercial community and, even in political

119

circles, the opinion of thoughtful members was influenced by the fact that the Indian delegation at Ottawa had included a man like Shanmukam Chetty of Madras who had been the main spokesman on financial policy for the Opposition party in the Assembly. From an Indian point of view the distinctive feature was that the Indian delegation was treated as one of the group of Dominion delegations presenting its case in parity with the established Dominions and not treated as a unit under the special tutelage of the British Government. If the whole series of discussions about constitutional development of India had been conducted in this kind of atmosphere and spirit the final result might have been very different.

On this subject I think it worthwhile referring to a letter which I wrote to Stanley Baldwin, the British Prime Minister and leader of the British delegation at the Conference. In this letter of 12.12.32 I suggested that Mr. Baldwin should write a note of appreciation to Chetty, praising him for standing by the Ottawa agreement through difficult Assembly debates, and I continued as follows:

> ' . . . The attitude of the Assembly in this matter has really given me ground for encouragement. They were ready for once to study a question on its merits and to be convinced by reason. But of course the Assembly just now is not fully representative and the leading figures of Indian public life are outside. Unfortunately the whole of the Congress and Liberal Press has attacked the agreement and the old prejudice is still affecting the country. But there is hope and I see signs of division in the opposition. Particularly in commercial circles and in the Federation

29.
With Henry Strakosch on *S.S. Bremen* crossing to the Ottawa Conference 1932

of Indian Chambers of Commerce, which has hitherto unanimously supported Congress, there are signs of cleavage, and I believe that the present moment—more than any during the four years which I have been in India—offers hopes of our being able to detach an important block to the side of constructive work and cooperation.'

I myself was specially impressed by the 'spirit of Ottawa' in my work as a member of the Committee on Monetary and Financial Questions, on which Sir Henry Strakosch (of the Secretary of State's India Council) and I represented India. For me a significant feature in my work on this Committee was the difference in the attitude of Strakosch when he was playing the part of the financial expert arguing, in partnership with me, the case for India with the representatives of the British Government, as contrasted with his attitude when he was the financial expert advising the Secretary of State in Whitehall in controversial arguments with the Government of India. At the Ottawa Conference I found Strakosch supporting all my views about the basic needs of India and by implication criticising what had been the monetary policy of the British Government for sterling before its break with gold. I refer specially to the following passage from his Ottawa statement:

' . . . As originally conceived in 1930, the scope of the Conference was limited to commercial and fiscal questions. Since then, however, the outlook has undergone drastic modification as the intensity of the world-wide economic depression has deepened and its nature has been more accurately perceived. Not only has the problem of recovery assumed an importance of vital urgency, but it has come increasingly to be realised that among the factors of dominant significance is the direction of monetary policy.'

This can fairly be interpreted as implying a recognition that there had been in the past justification not only for Indian criticism but also for my own views.

These discussions on monetary policy, however, were regarded at the time as no more than a minor background feature of the Ottawa Conference, which in its work for the encouragement of trade within the British Empire can be seen today as having been a really great occasion which actually produced results of considerable value. I myself was specially impressed with the part played by Neville Chamberlain and by the efficiency shown by Horace Wilson in directing the practical arrangements. I was brought into close consultation by these men and, as a result, formed a high personal regard for both of them which had a definite influence on me in a later chapter of my life.

Shortly after the conclusion of the 1933 Budget debates, I had to attend the World Monetary and Economic Conference held in London in June of that year. At this Conference Sir Henry Strakosch and I worked together as the representatives of the Government of India on the same lines as we had done at Ottawa. The paramount need was to raise the general level of prices for the products on which the prosperity of mainly agricultural countries like India depended, and accordingly the purpose of the Conference, as we saw it, was to consider how monetary policy could be worked to meet this need. Seen in this way, the London Conference was a complete failure. It was attended by an unmanageably large group of countries and the agenda had not been adequately prepared. As a 'world' conference it was inadequate because the USA was not represented. The only practical result which came out of the London discussions was an agreement about silver between India and China. In the conclusion of this agreement I had an interesting series of discussions with the Chinese Finance Minister T. V. Soong, whose sister was the wife of Chiang Kai-shek. China, whose currency was still on a silver standard, had a much greater interest than India in avoiding a collapse in the world price level of silver, but on behalf of India we felt justified in agreeing to certain steps which might be helpful for this purpose.

When the business of the World Economic Conference was completed, our attention had to be concentrated on an Indian issue of great importance. In preparing for the great step forward towards a self-governing Indian federation I was involved in lengthy discussions about the nature of the financial safeguards that should accompany the political advance involved in the 1935 Government of India Act. In the course of 1933, discussions between the India Office and the Government of India had been reopened about practical steps to give effect to the second recommendation of the Royal Commission on Currency for India of 1926, i.e. the recommendation for the establishment of a Reserve Bank to be the currency authority for India, independent of the Government. I have already referred to this recommendation and to the fact that my predecessor, Sir Basil Blackett, had been unable to get the approval of the Indian Assembly for the necessary legislation. I myself had always regarded this as a desirable objective, and my colleagues on the Viceroy's Council were in full agreement.

In telling the story of what then happened, I must confess that I found some humour as well as personal satisfaction in the situation which now arose. The Secretary of State, Sam Hoare,(who, incidentally, had been an exact contemporary of mine at the same College in Oxford), had made no secret of his bitter personal hostility to me and of his desire to find some way for eliminating 'this pestilent fellow' from the Viceroy's Council. He now, however, found himself advised that the only chance for getting the Reserve Bank proposals approved by the Indian Legislative Assembly was that I should be in charge of the proceedings. He accordingly found it necessary to ask me to extend my original five year appointment by a further six months until April 1934. This meant that I would have to be responsible not only for the Reserve Bank legislation but also for a sixth Annual Budget for 1934-35. I was ready to agree, largely because I felt that my plan for the 1934 Budget was necessary to round off my whole work as Finance Member.

After this extension of my appointment had been arranged, I took immediate steps to prepare for the presentation of a Bill for the establishment of a Reserve Bank for India. The debates were fully reported in the Indian Press and got much public attention.

I finally got the legislation approved in the third week of December. The reports in the Indian Press were most favourable, for example, a long article in the *Star of India* (Calcutta) with the headline 'A TRIUMPH FOR SIR GEORGE SCHUSTER'. I also got the following personal letter from the Viceroy which gave me great pleasure.

> *Viceroy's Camp*
> *India*
> 22.12.33

My dear Schuster,

My warmest congratulations. If I may say so, you have achieved a great personal triumph and I am very grateful to you for surmounting all difficulties and piloting the Bill into port.

I am a lucky man to have such colleagues to help me; my one real regret is that I am going to lose you so soon.

The Budget is yr. next fence but that you'll get over it I haven't the smallest doubt, and then you will feel when you leave us that you have pulled India through the most difficult time she has ever faced and have served the Empire well in the most trying job that I expect you have ever undertaken.

We shan't allow you two to rest idle at home for long and if you want any help at any time you know you've only got to ask me for it. Bless you both and again my warmest thanks,

Yrs. sincerely,

Willingdon

Having completed my Reserve Bank task I was able to turn to working out proposals for the 1934 Budget and simultaneously to consider constructive action to help the Provincial Governments and to improve the general economic position of the whole country, with special emphasis on the needs of the vast agricultural population. This involved much discussion leading to conferences with representatives of all the Provincial Governments to review the whole economic field and to work out lines on which the Central and Provincial Governments could cooperate in a joint effort. I believe that I can claim that this was the first occasion on which such Conferences had been convened by the Central Government. The discussions covered a wide range of subjects and, in terms of practical results, were concerned mainly with methods for improving marketing procedure for agricultural products. Some definite action was agreed including, for example, the appointment of an experienced officer to work out plans for the agricultural credit department of the Reserve Bank.

These discussions influenced me in framing my proposals in my Budget for 1934-35. I made a practical start to help Provincial Governments by the proposal to hand over half the proceeds of the jute export duty to the Governments of the impoverished jute-growing provinces, and in order to fill the resulting gap in Government revenue I proposed a new tax—an excise duty on matches.

The task of preparing my final Budget speech inevitably forced me to reflect on the whole record of my service in India and it is of course natural for me to do the same, now that more than 50 years later I come to write the story of my life. Looking back over the past in this way, I feel that one of my main purposes in India was (as it had also been in the Sudan) to make all my colleagues in the Government appreciate that to maintain the financial viability of the country was not the exclusive responsibility of the Finance Member but needed the cooperation of all members of the Government and that the financial allocation to each Department must be settled according to an order of priorities agreed by the Government as a whole.

At this point I must pay a special tribute to the cooperation which throughout my years of office I received from all sides, especially from the Army, the service responsible for the greater part of Central Government expenditure. As to this I can quote some figures which I gave at the Ottawa Conference of 1932 in my general review of the Indian financial position. When I took over my appointment, Indian annual military expenditure was running at 55 crores of rupees (£41½ million sterling). By 1932/33 this had been reduced to 46½ crores (£34½ million sterling)—a reduction of over 15 per cent achieved by cooperative efforts without the need for cuts recommended by an outside 'Economy Committee'.* I was very fortunate in my time in having to deal as Commander-in-Chief with Sir Philip Chetwode who was not only a first-class soldier but a broadminded statesman.

Reviewing the whole record, I feel that we in the Government of India fought a good fight against our economic difficulties. I could have done nothing without the help of my colleagues; but I had the responsibility for settling the practical plan of action.

It is interesting to reflect on the methods according to which I thought it right to fight against financial difficulties more than 50 years ago in the primitive days of what might be described as 'bow and arrow' methods of economic warfare. These may be seen as childishly elementary by those who work according to the sophisticated methods of today following on the Keynesian revolution. Possibly they were primitive, though I can interject that at the time I was constantly in personal contact with Keynes and had his unqualified support in my controversy with the India Office about monetary policy. At any rate, according to the principles of the time I tried to do what was right and can claim some success. This was generally recognised by the press in India and Britain and it may be a fitting ending to what I have to write about my work in India to quote the following passage from the leading article in *The Times* after the presentation of my sixth and final Budget:

> 'In view of the peculiar difficulties which have been imposed on India by the world-wide trade depression, the strength displayed by the finances of the Central Government during the past four or five years reflects the greatest credit upon the skill and firmness of the Finance Member. And, though the burden of the fresh taxation imposed has undoubtedly been heavy, the people of India have every reason to view with satisfaction the stringent reductions which have been effected in Government expenditure which has fallen since 1930 from 93 crores of rupees to 76 crores. In claiming that India's financial position challenges comparisons with that of any country in the world, Sir George Schuster was guilty of no exaggeration. His record during his six years of office is one of which he may be justly proud.'

This, however, as my subsequent narrative will record, in no way marked the end of my connection with India.

---

* Further reduced by 2 crores by the award of the Garran Tribunal of 1933 (see p. 91 above).

CHAPTER IX

Business and Politics, 1934-1945

WHEN I RETURNED from India in April 1934 I was 53, but I still regarded myself as a young man who had a personal career to make. I recognised that I could not make this in Whitehall. I was by nature too independent-minded and accordingly, quite justifiably, had become regarded in Whitehall as a 'rebel'. I therefore had to find scope for soul-satisfying activity (supported by the means for earning a living) in the private financial world. For this I anticipated no difficulty, since my work in the Sudan and in India had earned me a good reputation in the City.

I did not regard this as involving any reduction of my interest in public policy and I felt that my past experiences had given me ideas which deserved public attention.

My first main idea was that Britain now had a special role to play in the world, not as an 'Imperial Power' but as a trustee for the peoples of the territories of the British Empire with the duty to help develop local self-government on lines which would provide for social and economic welfare.

My second main idea was that there was a basic need for Britain to work out social and economic policies to provide for the true welfare of her own people. I saw this as involving problems of special difficulty for all countries whose economy depended on modern methods of industrial production and I thought (and still think) that Britain might give a lead to the world in finding a solution.

I felt that public attention ought now to be concentrated on working out practical plans to give effect to these two main ideas; but in 1934 I had to recognise that the whole future was overshadowed by the threat of conflict with Hitler's Germany. This made me appreciate the vital importance of Britain's relations with the rest of the world, especially with North America. Accordingly, before getting committed to business responsibilities I arranged a tour in Canada and the United States. This was for me a rewarding educational experience. I had talks with leading personalities and also took part in discussions at some large public meetings.

On my return from this tour I was appointed to the boards of several important companies such as the Westminster Bank (as it then was), the Commercial Union, the English Scottish and Australian Bank, and the London Board of the Bank of New Zealand. I found, however, that to be an ordinary board member of such companies, while extremely interesting, did not absorb me totally, and I wanted something to 'get my teeth into'.

126

An opportunity for this came when, early in 1935, I was asked by Lord Kindersley, on behalf of Unilever, to undertake the Chairmanship of Allied Suppliers, which was then responsible for the largest retailing group in Britain for groceries and provisions (including Home & Colonial Stores, Maypole Dairies, Liptons, Pearks Stores, etc.). These companies had got into serious difficulties and drastic changes were necessary in the central direction and in the practical working of the small shops. To achieve such changes was a normal task of business reorganisation, and it is sufficient to record that the results of our reorganisation were fully successful so that, when the outbreak of war disrupted normal business conditions, a profitable basis of operation had been established.

When I reflect on my work during these years, I see two experiences which have a key significance for my personal story.

In the first place my work brought me into close contact with Unilever, which company, as holding a large interest in Allied Suppliers, had taken the leading responsibility for the reorganisation. I see D'Arcy Cooper, the chairman, as an example of the truly valuable type of business leader who combined practical efficiency in running his company with a recognition that private enterprise must also take account of public interests. He was indeed one of the finest characters that I have ever met. I was able during the war years, as a Member of Parliament, to bring him into contact with Ernest Bevin, as a result of which he did extremely valuable work for the British Government, especially in contacts with the United States. I see his premature death from cancer during the war as a national tragedy.

My second experience which deserves special mention is concerned with relations between management and labour. In the first stages of my talks about reorganisation with the executive officers of Allied Suppliers, a moment came when they told me that they had a complaint about wages from the secretary of the trade union concerned and that they had asked for postponement of any reply until I, as their new Chairman, had been able to review the position. I then asked for a full statement about the rate of wages which we were paying to our distributive staff. When I got the figures my immediate reaction was that the existing level of wages was indefensibly low and that I thought it essential that I should have an early meeting with the trade union secretary. At that time there were two trade union organisations for 'distributive' workers. The Allied Suppliers employees were members of the Shop Assistants Union whose Secretary was Maurice Hann.

I accordingly arranged an interview with Hann at which I told him that I could not defend our present wage levels, but that I must ask him to give me time for further consideration. To this he readily agreed. I had two reasons for asking for this delay. I definitely needed more time to study what improvement would be immediately practicable; but there was also another factor. I had found that there was a general feeling on the management side of distributive organisations against the idea of having anything like a formal agreement about wage levels with a trade union. It was thought that, with their distributive staff scattered in small groups over hundreds of branches all over the country, it would be impossible to maintain adequate discipline if the trade union authority was recognised.

It is surprising today to realise that, as late as 1935, such an attitude was possible. I strongly disagreed with it, but I felt that I ought at least to give it consideration. In order to provide for further discussion I got in touch with my great friend Jimmy Mallen who was at that time the Warden of Toynbee Hall. He, I knew, was a close personal friend of Sir Frederick Marquis (later Lord Woolton) who was then, as Chairman of the Lewis Stores group, an important figure in the distributive trades. I asked them both to dine with me for a full discussion. I then found that Frederick Marquis had very strong feelings on the subject. He told me that if I were to enter into any formal agreement with the Shop Assistants Union I would be 'letting the whole side down'. We discussed the issue at great length, but my final reply was that I felt that satisfactory human relations in industry, based on frank and understanding relations between wage-earners and management, were absolutely essential and that I considered it impossible to achieve this without formal contacts with the trade union concerned. Frederick Marquis strongly disagreed with me, and our personal discussions ended on this note. After our meeting, however, he must have reconsidered his position. Perhaps he felt that the battle which he wanted to fight had been lost or, as I prefer to think, I had persuaded him that my view was right. At any rate, only two weeks later, there appeared a press report of a Lewis Stores meeting in Birmingham which included a photograph of Frederick Marquis, as Chairman, with my friend Maurice Hann sitting as the honoured guest at his right hand. Frederick Marquis had obviously wanted to 'get in first' in establishing good relations with the Shop Assistants Union.

In due course, after these preliminary discussions, I arranged for a meeting with Hann at which I was able to propose some immediate improvements in the general wage levels for our distributive staff. Hann accepted these proposals as an adequate first step, and it is satisfactory for me to record that this meeting marked the beginning of a continuous relationship of constructive cooperation between Maurice Hann and myself.*

I have referred to these two experiences as having a key significance for my personal story. This is because they are relevant to what I have described as 'the basic need for Britain to work out social and economic policies to provide for the true welfare of our people'. In all my later life I have come to recognise that a key problem for us (and indeed for all the 'developed' countries of the world) is the problem of how to organise the processes of economic production in such a way as to provide not only a basis for a satisfactory standard of living for the whole country but also an opportunity for the working population to find a satisfying form of activity in salaried

---

* When, 40 years later, I came to the task of writing this record of my life, I received a friendly telephone call from Hann on the occasion of my 95th birthday.

or wage-earning employment. To solve this problem requires a concerted national effort and it is an essential part of my own belief that this cannot be achieved by Government action alone. It must be supported by voluntary cooperative efforts. Those responsible for directing private economic enterprises must recognise their duty to take account of the public interest and also secure the understanding cooperation of those who are working in their employ.

My work as Chairman of Allied Suppliers involved visits to the United States in connection with the Lipton business in that country. I was able, as in 1934, to contact leading personalities (this time including President Roosevelt) and I was also asked to address several large meetings, including one held at the Commonwealth Club in San Francisco. My main purpose in addressing meetings in the United States was to create a true understanding of the British position and to dispel American prejudice against Britain as a colonialist power. In all these efforts I had great encouragement from our Ambassador in Washington, Sir Ronald Lindsay. As I have already recorded, I had, at the Ottawa Conference, got to know Neville Chamberlain and I now started a practice of calling to see him to report on my visits to the United States.

During the years from 1935 to 1938 I was asked to speak at public meetings in Britain such as those organised by the Royal Empire Society (as it was then called) and also to take part in more private discussions at Chatham House. On these occasion I took as my main theme the distinction between 'Welfare States' and 'Power States' and urged that the basic role for Britain and other countries of the British Empire must be that of welfare states though we might now be forced to concentrate on building up our military strength in order to counter the threat from Germany as a power state.

It was in this setting that I was asked in August 1938 to allow my name to be proposed as the Liberal National candidate at the forthcoming by-election in Walsall. (A convention had been made between the Conservative and Liberal National organisations in that constituency that the two parties, as the anti-Labour parties, should support alternate candidates, and on this occasion it was the turn of the Liberal National party.)

I felt able to accept this invitation. I regarded myself as a 'Liberal' in general outlook, but most definitely not as a party politician. I saw the Liberal National group as having, of all political groups, the least distinctive party colour. I was concerned only to have an opportunity to express my personal views on issues of public policy. Before finally committing myself I consulted and got approval from D'Arcy Cooper as Chairman of Unilever to whom I felt a responsibility in connection with my duties as Chairman of Allied Suppliers.

I was in due course officially adopted as candidate, a short time before Chamberlain's notorious Munich meetings with Hitler. Chamberlain's policy and conduct therefore inevitably became a central issue at the

31. Election Meeting in Walsall, November 1938

by-election. I definitely supported his purposes in arranging these meetings, though I had been disturbed by his unrealistic optimism in reporting their results. In subsequent discussions Horace Wilson emphasized to me that Chamberlain's power to take action had been constantly frustrated by the refusal of the French Government to give any support despite that government's direct obligations to Czechoslovakia. The current reaction in Walsall is worth recording, since it illustrates the general reaction in one important part of the country at the time. In my excitement about the news, which I felt must be shared by public opinion in Walsall, I telephoned the Liberal National Party Chairman, Cliff Tibbets, to ask what was the general feeling in the constituency. His reply was that there was no special reaction or excitement. 'You must understand, Sir George' he said 'that we are not very temperamental up here.' That remark provides a good prelude to my story about the Walsall election which has some historical significance.

In my election campaign the general line which I took was that the country must continue to support Chamberlain's efforts to work for peace; but that these efforts could only succeed if made from a position of military strength. We must therefore intensify the effort to build up our strength for war and to achieve this while at the same time continuing constructive social policies. This would require a united national effort.

This general line of policy was well received at all my public meetings, but what for me was more significant was the impression of prevailing opinion which I gained in my personal contacts which included many visits to factories where I discussed the position frankly with individual workers. My broad impression was that the great body of people in this constituency had not yet appreciated the reality of the danger of another war. They were still in a sense living in a 'post-war atmosphere'. Their attention was concentrated on internal social and economic problems. It would have seemed to them a preposterous idea that we should again get involved in the horrors of war for the sake of protecting the interests of the people of an unknown small country like Czechoslovakia. It was only at the very end of my campaign that in a talk with one factory worker I got an expression of strong resentment against the idea of 'Hitler getting away with it'.

The poll was held on 17th November 1938 and I got 28,720 votes, giving me a majority of 7,156. This was a notable success. The most optimistic forecast had been a majority of two to three thousand. The result seemed to confirm that my appreciation of the general public feeling in this Midland industrial area had been correct. I still feel that this was justified. I must of course recognise that the result of Vernon Bartlett's campaign against the Government in Bridgwater on the following day seemed to support a directly opposite conclusion. Bridgwater, however, was a rural area and in no way representative of industrial England, and I still maintain the opinion that in 1938 the country as a whole was not yet ready to respond to an heroic appeal on Churchill's lines.

Whatever truth there may be in this appreciation, the practical question for me after taking my seat was what line I should take on the issues with which Parliament would, during the next months, be concerned. Behind all of these lay the growing issue of whether the time had come to replace Chamberlain by Churchill. On my very first day in the House I was approached by Duncan Sandys as a possible ally and later had talks with Leo Amery and Harold Macmillan in which I was pressed to join the Conservative rebels.

My personal decision on this question requires some explanation. In standing for Parliament I had no idea of making a political career leading to ministerial office. I was satisfied with the position which I had established for myself in the world of private business and had no wish to sacrifice this for the uncertainty of a political career. Also, as I have already noted, I did not regard myself as a 'Party man'. I recognised that to make our Parliamentary system workable there must be a broad division between political parties; but I felt that at all times, and especially in times of national crisis, it would be valuable to have a group of members, whom I called a 'suicide squad', who felt themselves free to express individual opinions. On the two dominant figures of the day I had already formed a decided view.

For Chamberlain I had always felt special respect as a political leader who was essentially concerned with doing his ministerial work efficiently, rather than with the advancement of his personal political career. I had been

32. Arrival at the House of Commons with my mother and my wife

specially impressed by one incident in his past life when he had decided to complete his task at the old Ministry of Local Government rather than accept promotion as Chancellor of the Exchequer. I felt that this was the kind of man who was specially needed in our political system.

About Churchill, on the other hand, my broad feeling was that on important issues in the past his judgement had always been wrong. I had specially in mind his action as Chancellor of the Exchequer in returning Britain to the Gold Standard, his violent opposition to political advancement in India, the line which he took on the 'Abdication' issue and, to come to a matter with which I myself had been closely concerned, his attempts to organise with British support a White Russian campaign to defeat the Red Revolution. I felt indeed that Churchill's effort had been a decisive factor in uniting the Russian people behind the Bolshevik Party.

Reflecting on these differences in the political records of the two men, I saw a fundamental difference in their conception of the purposes of British policy. Churchill was thinking essentially of the greatness of Britain as a world imperial power. Chamberlain's thoughts were concentrated on the lives of the ordinary men and women of the Midlands industrial area which he knew so well. I myself had, and still have, a vision of a great role in the world for Britain as giving a lead in working out a solution for the essential social and economic problems of our time, but not as a world imperial power. I felt that we must not abandon the Chamberlain conception but that we were now tragically forced to concentrate immediate efforts on building up our fighting strength to counter the threats from Hitler's Germany as a Power State. I recognised that if we were forced to fight there must eventually be a change of leadership. Influenced by my appreciation of public opinion in Walsall and also by the fact that Chamberlain had recently strengthened his Government by the inclusion of Sir John Anderson and Sir Frederick Marquis I felt that the time had not come for this.

My final conclusion for my own conduct was that the most useful contribution which I could make in Parliament at this stage would be to concentrate on practical proposals for improving the effectiveness of the national plans for increasing the country's strength for war, with special emphasis on ways in which private business organisations could cooperate with Government departments. I felt strongly on this last point and took it as the main theme for my maiden speech which I made on 20 December 1938.

At the same time I thought it necessary to look beyond the impending war to consider the problems with which we in Europe in general and in Britain in particular would be faced. For a satisfactory solution I felt that cooperation with the United States was essential, and here I was able to make use of the contacts I had established in recent years.

In October 1939 I sent J. M. Keynes a paper on 'British War Aims and Cooperation with the USA' concluding:

> ' . . . I want to see an approach to the USA made on the following lines:
> "We do not want to drag you into war—to the extent of sending your citizens to be killed with ours; but we do want you to collaborate with us and France to 'hold the ring' for an ordered, healthy and materially beneficial international economic regime when the war is over so that victory for the 'Welfare States' may mean the chance to promote real welfare. We want you to work with us (a) in planning for such a regime now, (b) in avoiding the distortions of the world's economic channels by the war tides and strains, thus making easier the shift from war to peace and economy, as well as (c) helping us economically in securing victory for the Welfare States" . . . '

Conversations with Keynes and Halifax followed and, as a result, in the spring of 1940 I was involved in arranging with Sumner Welles, the U.S. Under Secretary of State, for the establishment of an Anglo-American group for the study of post-war economic problems.

In my speeches in Parliament during the next months my main purpose was to continue on this constructive line without committing myself as a supporter of either side in the main political controversy. As a result I can claim that my speeches were taken seriously on all sides.

I did, however, eventually on one occasion relinquish this independent attitude. On February 1st 1940 Herbert Morrison, on behalf of the Labour Party, tabled a motion proposing the inclusion in the War Cabinet of a Minister specially charged with the responsibility for general economic planning. This of course was intended as a criticism of the efficiency of the Government—part of the campaign to get rid of Chamberlain. I, however, was concerned that the actual proposal, which involved abolishing the overall responsibility of the Treasury, was dangerously wrong. I was most anxious to get a chance to express this view in the debate, but I found that my only chance to get called would be for me to agree to second the Government amendment to Herbert Morrison's Motion. I did, in fact, make an effective speech which received much comment in the subsequent debate. One of the later speakers was Harold Macmillan and his comment was that for the Government to have got positive support from the Honourable Member for Walsall was a 'real scoop'.

Three months after this came the crucial debate which led to the change of Government. This took place on an Opposition Motion criticising the Government's action to counter the German invasion of Norway, for which indeed Churchill himself as First Lord of the Admiralty bore a large part of the responsibility.

My only purpose now is to give an explanatory record of my own personal conduct. I recognised that the time had come when we must have a National Government which would only be possible under Churchill. I also felt certain at the end of the debate that the voting on the division would make this change inevitable. This made me regard my own vote as of no more than personal significance. I was being got at by both sides; but what finally decided me was an approach by a member of my own party who urged me that for the sake of my own career I must vote with the critics of the Government as otherwise I should have no chance of getting appointments under a Churchill administration. That settled me. On the one hand I could not allow myself to be influenced by thought of my personal career, while on the other hand I wanted to give expression to the ideas which had, as I have already explained, influenced my support for Chamberlain.

The result of the Division was decisive since the Government majority dropped from over 200 to 81 and as a result Chamberlain resigned and Churchill was appointed Prime Minister. In the whole of our history there has been no more striking example of the differences in human fortune as that between Churchill, who was offered the supreme opportunity to be the 'man of the hour' in 1940, and Chamberlain, whose great qualities were not the ones most needed in the crisis of the war.

I wrote to Chamberlain a few months later to express my sympathy with him on his final retirement from the Government on grounds of health and I received a personal reply which may be of some interest.

Highfield Park
Heckfield, Basingstoke
26th October 1940

My dear Schuster,

I was very much touched by your letter which was one of those which have given me particular pleasure.

You have put into words what happily for me I believe to be true, namely that though peace could not be maintained the three things that were gained—a united Country and Empire, the moral support of the decent part of the world, and time for preparation—constitute a sufficient sum of achievement to satisfy one's mind.

Let me take this opportunity of thanking you for the help and support that you have personally given me in the past. I am proud to think that I may have been instrumental in bringing you into political life.

Yours very sincerely,

Neville Chamberlain.

Returning to my narrative, the important point to note is that concurrently with the change of Government there was a complete change in the significance of Parliamentary proceedings. Churchill's assumption of a dictatorship of the war effort would alone have made this inevitable, but even more important was the fact that we now had to face the reality of an attempted invasion by Germany. For myself I felt that I must be doing more that just attending Parliamentary Debates. Although I now became an enthusiastic supporter of the new Prime Minister I realised that after my vote in the crucial division I could have no hope of being offered any executive post in the direction of the war effort. I therefore decided that I must try to get some direct military work and with this in mind I wrote to General Haining who was then GOC Western Command and with whom I had been in contact in the 1914 War. He replied that he wanted an officer to supervise and organise the development in the Western Command area of the Home Guard (known at that time as Local Defence Volunteers). He told me that he would like me to wear uniform and I therefore took up my rank as Lieutenant Colonel on which I had retired at the end of 1919. Haining was soon moved to London as a deputy CIGS and the new GOC Western Command was my very close friend, General Sir Henry Jackson, for whom I had worked in North Russia and also got to know intimately when he had a command in India during my years in the Indian Government. He had been called back from retirement to this post and was tackling his task with immense energy. After ten hectic days with him going round all possible landing points for German aircraft, we had the great disappointment of getting a telephone message to tell us that Jackson's post had only been temporary and that General Gordon Finlayson had been appointed to the Command.

I then had a very wearing task during the next few months. I had to report on the whole area of the Western Command which extended from Cumberland to the Bristol Channel and I had the special responsibility of organising practical activities in the area lying between Carlisle and Birmingham. I found great enthusiasm everywhere and felt that we had organised quite effective local defence arrangements. One of our keynotes was 'Every Factory a Fortress' and I got valuable cooperation, expecially from ICI works in the area.

In the last quarter of the year, however, when the intensive bombing of London began, I felt that my responsibility as Chairman of Allied Suppliers became of paramount importance, and since the Home Guard organisation was well established I decided that the right course for me was to resign from my post in Western Command and resume regular work at the City office of Allied Suppliers, combined with attendance at the House of Commons. For the next years my main work in Parliament was as a member of the Committee on National Expenditure and as Chairman of its Sub-Committee on Weapons of War. This involved a wide range of visits to factories with special attention to plans for tank production.

In this period there also began my friendship with Stafford Cripps which became a significant factor in my subsequent life. In his responsibility as Minister of Aircraft Production he asked me to undertake investigations into some of the important aircraft production companies, notably Short Brothers and Boulton & Paul. The essential problems to be considered were those affecting companies which had been organised to work on a small scale and which were now confronted with the task of large-scale production. I found working with Stafford Cripps a most satisfactory experience. He had an immediate grasp of the essential issues in each case and was notably sympathetic in handling personal problems—for example, when it became necessary to replace a man who had been a suitable leader for a small family business by one of greater experience in directing large-scale operations.

During the following years in Parliament until the General Election in 1945, I spoke on many subjects and took special interest in measures concerned with social policies for the future, such as the Butler Education Bill, and the 'Beveridge Plan'—in the universal praise for which I did not join because I regarded as totally inadequate Beveridge's conception of 'welfare' defined in exclusively material terms.

In particular I continued my active interest in India. I spoke in all the Parliamentary debates on Indian policy and I collaborated with my friend Guy Wint in writing a book which was published under the title of *India and Democracy*. It is a fair summary of this book to say that the general conclusion of the first part written by Wint was that democracy would not survive in India, while I in the part which I wrote expressed a contrary view. I sent a copy of this book to Jawaharlal Nehru who at the time was in prison in India and received from him the following reply:

District Jail
Dehra Dun, India.
2nd December 1941

Dear Schuster,

Your letter of the 23rd September reached me three days ago. I have not yet received your book. It was good of you to write to me in the friendly way you have done and may I say that I shall always appreciate letters from you even though I may not agree with all you say. So do write to me when you feel that way.

As for your book I shall certainly read it carefully and let you have my reactions. But I must say that sometimes I feel, when writing to friends in England about the Indian problem, that our approaches are so different that we do not really meet intellectually even though that meeting may lead to a difference of opinion. Much less do we meet emotionally or psychologically and that is far more important. And yet when we discuss some other subject, political, economic or cultural, where India is not in the centre of the picture, we meet easily enough. Why is that so? The fault may lie with individuals on either side but I think it is due to essentially deeper causes. It lies in the unnatural relation of England and India and I feel that till this goes even the best of us will be at cross purposes.

I think you are wrong in imagining that you have particularly irritated me on any occasion. I had completely forgotten the Chatham House episode till your letter reminded me of it. Not that my memory is not good, but I had attached no importance to it. Probably I felt a momentary irritation and, having had my say, it passed. But I did feel something deeper than irritation (not about you) when I read the full report in Hansard of the Indian debate in the House of Commons last August. It brought home to me the wide gulf that separated us and, as I think, the utterly unreal and often perverted way in which India was looked upon by Britishers in Parliament. Perhaps fundamentally this is due to a mental revolt against sermons from others, sermons which are seldom disinterested, and at the compulsion we have to face at every turn. That is the natural reaction of every Indian, in varying degrees, to whatever group or party he may belong. But there is something more than that.

I remember well and with pleasure my visit to Peterhof ten years ago. I was happy to meet your wife and sons and I think it must have been the presence of the boys, bright and fresh from Oxford, that took me out of the political shell that usually surrounds me and made me feel at home. I was distressed to learn that one of them is no more. What an infinity of human misery has decended upon this world because of this war! It would be a tragedy greater even than that of this war if all of us cannot sweep away trivialities and reach down to the fundamentals and find a way to a better world.

I try to be sincere with myself and with the world, in so far as I can, and I try to believe in the sincerity of those who differ from me. But all of us are tied up in so many ways and are creatures of our environment and have to function with the human material that surrounds us. Even so it should be possible for humanity to behave with some reason if only to escape self-destruction or complete degradation. Perhaps this terrible war is meant to teach us that lesson, but at what a cost!

Yours sincerely,

Jawaharlal Nehru

Looking back over my years in Parliament I feel it to have been of great value to have had this experience as a chapter in my life. There is something unique about the House of Commons—an underlying spirit of comradeship in spite of Party differences. Perhaps this was specially strong in the war years of national crisis. I certainly felt it very strongly since I had great friends in all quarters outside my own Party.

As to my position in the House, I can claim that I was always listened to with attention and general approval (except possibly from my own small Party) and I can record with satisfaction that the Independent Liberal group led by Archibald Sinclair was always trying to get me to join them. At one point, I was actually invited by Quintin Hogg, later Lord Hailsham, to join the 'Young Conservative Group', which he was then forming with Peter Thorneycroft, a request I had to decline because I was not a Conservative. With several members of the Labour Party I had really intimate friendships.

I made many long speeches (too many, perhaps—too long, certainly). I felt it very important to keep in touch with my constituency and I accordingly had reprints made of what I regarded as important speeches, of which I circulated hundreds of copies among my constituents. Altogether in my seven years in Parliament I made 47 speeches of which I circulated copies in this way.

Certain incidents stand out in my memory. In a Debate on the Butler Education Bill, for example, I recall that in one of my speeches I told the story of my own unsuccessful effort after the First World War to become a teacher in a 'Continuation School' as proposed by H. A. L. Fisher. Chuter Ede, the Under Secretary for Education, later in this Debate referred to my story and said that the possibility of my being caught as a school teacher reminded him of the Fisherman's Prayer:

'Pray God that I might catch a fish
So large that even I
In boasting of it afterwards
Shall have no need to lie.'

All through my years in Parliament I had kept in close touch with my Walsall constituents, not only by circulating copies of my speeches, but by many personal visits. I felt that I had established a safe position there and it was with this feeling that I started in 1945 my election campaign. During the campaign I got an enthusiastic reception at all my public meetings. This was particularly marked at my final large meeting in the Town Hall and I recall that Arthur Salter, who had come down as a Member of the Government to speak for me, turned to me after the end and said 'Well, at any rate *you* seem safe to get back.'

The final result came as a great shock. I got 24,197 votes as against 28,324 for the Labour candidate. The general explanation was that the postal votes from the members of the fighting services overseas had swung the balance; but subsequent evidence has convinced me that the true explanation was that the local leader of the Liberal National Group had allied himself with the Labour Party and taken his followers with him.

The fact remained that I was out of Parliament and had to seek new opportunities to work for national interests in other ways.

CHAPTER X

Human Relations in Industry, 1945-1952

AFTER 1945 I PASSED into the final and, as I have come to see it, most significant phase of my long life. I continued my chief executive responsibility as
Chairman of Allied Suppliers until 1946 when, at the age of 65, I retired;
but, after that, although I held several directorships, (notably the
Westminster Bank and the London Board of the Bank of New Zealand, of
which I was Chairman for some years), I devoted myself mainly to voluntary work for causes of public importance. This, as my story will show, has
involved a wide range of work: special tasks for the Government, service on
public bodies such as a Regional Hospital Board, on a County Council,
together with work for many private organisations. I have emphasised this
last phase of my life, because I see it as a matter of the highest public importance that people with practical experience when they come to the age of
relinquishing daily executive responsibilities should not pass into private
retirement but be ready to give their services for public purposes.

After the defeat of Germany as a Power State the essential need, as I saw
it, was for a combined national effort to work out social and economic
policies which would make Britain a true 'Welfare State', for which I
regarded the Beveridge Plan (with its emphasis on material welfare) as totally inadequate. I wanted to play a part in this national effort.

My first important task in this final phase in my life came to me when in
October 1945 Stafford Cripps asked me to act as Chairman of a working
party on the Cotton Industry, 'to report as to the steps which should be
adopted in the national interest to strengthen the industry and render it
more stable and more capable of meeting competition in the home and
foreign markets' *Board of Trade: Working Party Reports—Cotton*
(HMSO 1946). Writing in 1978 and considering the problems and con-
troversies with which the country is faced today I look back on Cripps'
ideas for Working Parties in a number of leading British industries as
having shown wise and imaginative foresight. As an alternative to nationalisation Cripps' idea was that plans for certain important industries should
be worked out in discussions between representatives of management and
labour in each industry together with a group qualified to appreciate what
was required in the national interest—men with experience in public
administration, industrial management and economics.

I saw the case of the Cotton Industry as one of key importance, and
wanted our Working Party to give a lead in producing an early business-like

report. I got the Working Party to divide the task and, after six months, in April 1946 I drafted a comprehensive report based on the findings and recommendations of four sub-committees. The general conclusion was that there was a 'need for interaction between the Government and the industry by some method that will ensure that the industry's activities fit in with the national interest without hampering the initiative and incentive of individual enterprise'. It was agreed by all members that the industry should rely on fewer and better mills but then, at the last moment, I was told that a Dissenting Report was being drafted. Six members, led by Professor John Jewkes, fearing the extension of government control, rejected six out of the Report's thirty-four recommendations and in particular those recommending compulsory amalgamation and a re-equipment levy. The main object of this Dissenting Report was obviously to make the whole Working Party Recommendations ineffective. I personally felt that we had worked out a valuable set of proposals which would help to avoid many troubles and difficulties for the Cotton Industry in the post-war period. When the Dissenting Report was submitted the trade union members felt it necessary to make some response and they submitted an Explanatory Memorandum on their attitude. This was an able document which makes interesting reading today. What they said in conclusion was:

'We believe that the working of industry should be regulated in accordance with the national interest and it has been our feeling that this can best be achieved by a policy of nationalisation. We have, however, been ready to cooperate in discussions on the Working Party with employers' representatives in the hope of devising a plan for the handling of the Cotton Textile Industry in the national interest in the face of the difficulties of post-war conditions. The introduction, however, of the Dissenting Report signed by representatives of the employers shows that they are not ready to cooperate, which leaves us no alternative except to press for nationalisation.'

A major cause of the objections to our Report by the Cotton Industry employers concerned Raymond Streat's position as Chief Executive Officer of the Cotton Council. Stafford Cripps had made it clear to me in personal discussion that he would not accept any plan which left Raymond Streat in control. I personally felt that Raymond Streat was playing an invaluable part and in framing the recommendations I wanted to put up a plan which would leave him in his position but which would be acceptable to Stafford Cripps. It was for that reason that I devised the proposal for setting up a superior authority called the Re-Equipment Board which would have supervisory powers over the Cotton Council.

What actually happened shows how easily one's personal motives can be misunderstood. I was actually accused of having made the proposal for the Re-Equipment Board with the idea of securing its Chairmanship as an office for myself. Nothing could possibly have been further from my intentions than to take on a post which would have involved living in Manchester.

In spite of the difficulty caused by the disagreement on the Working Party I had looked forward to the possibility of achieving a practical result with the support of Stafford Cripps and at this point I met my second and much more serious difficulty. Cripps' health had completely broken down after a visit to India and his deputy secretary at the Board of Trade, John Belcher, was a man of no substance or authority, who in fact shortly afterwards had to resign from his office and from Parliament. The responsibility for settling what action could be taken on the recommendations of our Working Party Report passed entirely into the hands of the civil servants who were determined to leave all arrangements affecting the position in Lancashire and the cotton textile industry exactly as they were.

After completing my task on the Cotton Working Party I got absorbed in a wide range of activities in London. My resignation from the Executive Chairmanship of Allied Suppliers did not involve an entire break of my work in connection with the distributive trades. I remained for some years as an adviser to Allied Suppliers and continued active work as Chairman of the Multiple Shops Federation, a post which I held from 1939-52. It had been our special effort to make a reality of this Federation so that the very able leaders of the most important multiple shops companies might have an opportunity to give constructive advice on Government economic policy. This was consistent with my general idea that private enterprise, while primarily concerned with running its own business profitably and efficiently, should also take account of national interests.

In addition to this I was closely concerned with activities in the field of education. On my return from India I had been appointed a member of the Governing Body of Charterhouse and in 1939 had become Deputy Chairman. According to our statutes the Chairman was the Archbishop of Canterbury and my position as Deputy Chairman involved me in close contacts with a succession of Archbishops: Cosmo Lang, William Temple and Geoffrey Fisher. With William Temple and Geoffrey Fisher I had specially close friendships, and with the latter after the war I played a part in the formation of the Governing Bodies Association to consider the post-war prospects and problems of the independent public schools. I also promoted an organisation called the Public Schools Appointments Bureau, which was concerned with finding openings for 18 year old school leavers in business. I had personally always felt that for a great number of young people it would be better for them to go into some form of practical work after leaving school instead of going straight to a university. Another project in which I took an active part was the establishment of the William Temple College.

I also got involved in work on various Government Committees, one of which deserves special mention. This was the Newson Smith Committee, which was appointed by Ernest Bevin as Minister of Labour to consider the possibilities of business training for demobilised men thought capable of filling higher managerial or administrative positions. In my work on such Committees I always found my chief task was to get the Committee to have a clear conception of its purposes and of what practical steps could be taken to fulfil them. As to my work with the Newson Smith Committee I am tempted to quote from what has been written by Charles Tennyson, in his book *Stars and Markets*. Tennyson was a representative of the FBI on the Newson Smith Committee and he wrote about its work as follows:

' . . . I do not believe it would ever have agreed on a recommendation had it not been for the vision and energy of Sir George Schuster that tireless worker for the public good . . . Calm and indefatigably persuasive, when once he saw the way to a solution of our problem Schuster grudged no expenditure of time or words in its exposition. While the rest of us were dithering and drifting, he practically drafted the report and, by determined lobbying, converted even the most sceptical members of the Committee to his views. As a result there emerged a scheme for a three months' theoretical business course to be given in technical colleges up and down the country, followed by courses of from nine months to two years or more in the factories or offices of firms who put up approved schemes for the purpose. The firm was not under any obligation to take on the trainee at the end of the course and the government assisted trainees with substantial grants of money. As a result over a thousand firms provided specialised courses and over 7,000 trainees passed through the scheme during the two years of its existence, almost all of them finding employment in due course.

The success of the Newson Smith scheme undoubtedly did a great deal to convince industrialists of the truth of Pete Ryland's claim that "extreme youth and long years of drudgery are not essential for the production of an efficient business man", and materially helped the FBI Committee in its campaign to interest industry in the possibilities of the Arts Graduate and the Public and Grammar school boy. The solution of the latter problem was again largely due to Sir George Schuster.'

Looking back on the memories of my life I see in the post-war years I was mainly concerned with the need to create satisfactory human relations in industry as a foundation for cooperation between management and labour. I wrote letters to *The Times* on this subject and took an active part in discussions at conferences of the Glacier Metal Company which, under the imaginative Chairmanship of my friend Wilfred Brown (later Lord Brown), had inaugurated an effective procedure for joint consultation. Under the influence of Ernest Bevin, Stafford Cripps and Herbert Morrison the Government had been giving much thought to these issues and at the end of 1947 decided to set up under the Chairmanship of Sir Henry Tizard a Committee on Industrial Productivity with the work divided among four panels on:

Technology, Imports Substitution, Human Factors and Technical Information Services.

I accepted appointment as Chairman of the Panel on Human Factors.

This provided a great opportunity. The problem was how to exploit it in a way which would produce valuable practical results. To solve that problem required full support and cooperation from the members of the Panel, especially from those representing management and labour. I did in fact get this support from the labour representatives, among whom were Jock Tanner of the Amalgamated Engineering Union (as it then was) and Tom Williamson of the Municipal and General Workers' Union, but, on the management side, the representatives selected by the FBI were men who made it quite clear that they regarded the general purposes of the Panel as visionary and unrealistic. If the attitude of the FBI representatives had been fully cooperative we could have had valuable discussions on the Panel, but in the circumstances I could do no more than get the Panel to agree to sponsor a number of research projects to study questions affecting industrial productivity. This led eventually to the publication of over 30 reports of which the most important were:

The Foreman; Status, Selection and Training
Joint Consultation in British Industry
Problems of Work Load and of Human Ageing
Factors affecting the adjustment of young people
    to work and to society.

One of the more important researches promoted by the Human Factors panel was that involving the Glacier Metal Company Ltd. and The Tavistock Institute of Human Relations which took place over three years. When the research grants came to an end the company continued the project which was under the guidance of Dr. Elliot Jaques. The rather extraordinary fact is that this project continues today nearly thirty years after its initiation by the Human Factors Panel. It has led to the emergence of a wealth of conceptualised ideas concerning organisation and participation. The results have been written up and commented upon in more than twenty books published in many languages.

The research projects which we had undertaken involved expenditure and the Government had to find a recognised heading through which money could be allocated. It was decided that the Medical Research Council would be appropriate for this purpose and that I accordingly should be appointed a member. This move was not very well received by the Council and I found myself rather an unwelcome 'cuckoo in the nest'. The orthodox members of the Council were suspicious of any attempt to involve them in discussing the practical applications of our research, particularly as they did not consider sociological research as truly scientific. In spite of this feeling of hostility among some members I found the experience of attending meetings of the Medical Research Council extremely interesting. I was eventually appointed

33. One of many factory visits in the 1940's

Treasurer and was able to establish some stimulating friendships, in particular with Sir Harold Himsworth who became Secretary to the Council in 1949.

The basic fact, however, remained that the studies to be undertaken by the Committee on Industrial Productivity could not be regarded as scientific research and this affected the attitude of Sir Henry Tizard, the Chairman, who had done such brilliant work in the field of scientific research and its application during the war years. He had never been really in sympathy with the general purposes of the Committee on Industrial Productivity and eventually recommended its dissolution. Herbert Morrison, on behalf of the Labour Government, accepted this recommendation, but was specially anxious that the work of the Human Factors Panel should continue, as to which he wrote to Sir Henry Tizard as follows:

' . . . I hope therefore that the Medical Research Council and the Department of Scientific and Industrial Research will jointly be able to devise machinery by which this need will be met . . . Sir George Schuster has given much time and has made a valuable contribution in this field which I hope to see continued under the new arrangements.'

While this matter was under consideration there was a change of Government and the responsibility for taking a decision on this particular issue rested with Lord Woolton who wrote to me as follows:

Privy Council Office
Whitehall, SW1
27th February 1952

Dear Sir George,

Following our talk I think I should write to place on record the thanks of Her Majesty's Government for all the help and advice which you have given in connection with your activities as Chairman of the Panel on Human Factors of the Committee on Industrial Productivity.

In addition to promoting research on the human background of the problem of increasing industrial activity, you have also done much by speaking at conferences of employers and employed, by broadcasting and in other ways to impress upon industry and upon the nation the greater attention to human relations in industry. Every advance in this direction is an important gain, both in our economic and our social development, and following their joint appraisal of your Panel's work the Medical Research Council and the Department of Scientific and Industrial Research have, as you know, submitted to me a scheme for following up these problems in concert in their respective fields.

I have been glad to give my approval to these proposals and thus to ensure that there will be continuing activity, by the research organisations principally concerned, in the field in which you have pioneered.

Sincerely yours,

Woolton.

In spite of this warm appreciation, in the new arrangements which he approved for continuing studies in the field which had been covered by the Human Factors Panel, he found no place for my inclusion.

As I write my story in 1978 and consider the economic and social problems which face our country today, I look back on the years of the post-war Labour Government as a period of great opportunity which was lost because the leaders of British industry did not cooperate. Ernest Bevin and Stafford Cripps, working with trade union leaders like Walter Citrine, were able to get the whole trade union movement to understand the realities of the national economic problems and, by exercising restraint on demands for wage increases, to cooperate in a constructive national economic policy. Stafford Cripps and Herbert Morrison with the plans for Working Parties and the Committee on Industrial Productivity tried to stimulate a cooperative effort. My own experience on the Cotton Working Party and Committee on Industrial Productivity provides clear illustrations of the negative and uncooperative attitude of the leaders of the British industry. If the reports of the Committee on Industrial Productivity had been taken seriously by the FBI as representing the management side in industry and used as a basis for realistic discussion with representatives of the trade unions they might have led to a really effective movement of cooperation between the two sides. In fact, however, the only serious attention which it received was from the left wing side of the labour movement, as evidence of which it is worth quoting the following extract from an article by Ian Mikardo in the *Tribune* (24.8.51):

'. . . When Herbert Morrison was Lord President of the Council, one of his bright ideas was to set up a Committee on Industrial Productivity. It was a high-powered affair, subdivided into four specialised panels; but nobody was very clear about its functions, so it wound itself up. Departing, however, it has left one footprint in the sands of time. The best of the Committee's four panels was the Human Factors Panel under the Chairmanship of that lively youngster, Sir George Schuster. The panel initiated a number of important studies . . . that are must-reading for every industrial manager and every trade union leader in the country.'

I have quoted this passage because it seems to me highly significant that an extreme left wing member of the Labour Party like Ian Mikardo should have written like this in 1951.

Although as explained above I ceased to hold a position in any Government organisation, I continued my personal efforts to stimulate thought and practical action which would be helpful in creating satisfactory human relations in industry. I collaborated with a number of people who were equally concerned with this objective and got invitations to speak at many meetings organised by industrial companies, including a memorable conference on labour relations organised in 1951 by the Corning Glass Company in the United States to celebrate their centenary.

In 1951 also I was asked to give the Beckley Lecture at the annual Methodist Conference and I chose as a subject for this *Christianity and Human Relations in Industry*. This lecture in an extended form was published by the Epworth Press under the same title later in the year. This gave me the opportunity to develop at greater length the ideas which had governed my approach during these years. I emphasised that it was possible to combine the efficient conduct of industry with the fulfilment of Christian principles but that this required intellectual effort and practical efficiency as well as good intentions. Above all, the greatest need of modern industrial society was to make industrial employment something which would be seen as an essential part of a satisfactory human life and not as a cause of conflict or an evil burden to be escaped from as quickly as possible.

The following extracts from my book make clear my line of thought.

'If I, as a "manager", am to "love my neighbour as myself", my primary aim must surely be to do all that lies in my power, within the sphere of his activities that I can affect, to enable him to achieve for himself the sort of worldly life and opportunities of self-realisation which, according to my own belief, I regard as a good life or "happiness" in the highest sense, and which I accordingly seek for myself. Thus the essential question for me is how to make each worker's time within the factory something which fits in with a good life or happiness properly interpreted.' (p.22)

'The objective to be aimed at is a form of community cooperation (within each factory, but backed by trade unions) in which all ranks can feel that they have an interest in improving production results and an opportunity to contribute to such improvement and can satisfy themselves that the proceeds are fairly divided.' (p.66)

'The whole industrial field is bedevilled with suspicions based on past memories. As a result even the most honest attempts to improve human relations tend to be viewed with mistrust—either as dodges to get something extra out of a temporary mood "produced by force of circumstances rather than by a change of heart". The only way to overcome these suspicions is for management to pursue with complete honesty methods of communication and joint consultation in such a way that the purposes are really understood.' (p.75)

Education had a vital role:

'I want to stress the importance of ensuring that education is so handled as to help people to get full value from their work, whatever form that work may take. I want to protest against the conception of education as a process which does no more than prepare the soul for the enjoyment of leisure when practical needs have been satisfied. It should be a preparation for getting the best self-realisation out of all life's activities. We can have no healthy industrial society if our system of education is one which makes those whom it influences able to find happiness only in escape from their breadwinning work . . . It is important to have close contact and collaboration between the world of education and the world of industry. Industrialists (and here I include trade unionists as well as "management") should interest themselves in the study of how our educational system is working. Beyond this industrial employers have themselves a definite educational responsibility. And that means much more than giving facilities for part-time education to their young employees. It means handling the work of young entrants in an educational way.' (pp.81-82)

Reviewers of the book were particularly interested in my view that nationalisation was irrelevant to the basic problem:

'We have got to face the fact that in this country (and this is true of the whole human race, except in a few undeveloped parts of the world) we have brought ourselves into a position in which we cannot earn our daily bread except on the basis of factory production in which large numbers have to work together in organised fashion, using equipment which they cannot themselves supply, working for pay, subject to some measure of discipline and leadership and some form of central direction and guidance. This is a condition which creates problems in the relationships of men with each other and men with their work which cannot be evaded. Certainly the transfer of industry to State ownership will not eliminate them. All the problems which I have discussed must arise, and all the measures which I have advocated will be required, whether the industries are owned by the State or by private citizens. And it is these things—the things which determine whether daily bread-winning work in industry can provide the foundation for a good human life—which really matter when one is considering the application of Christian principles to human relations in industry.' (pp. 97-98)

The book was widely reviewed and demand was sufficient to cause the publishers to reprint it the following year. In addition to the usual notices the book was discussed in leading articles in *Nature* and in *The Manchester Guardian*. Particularly gratifying among the favourable comments that the book received was the review by Seebohm Rowntree who concluded:

'Speaking as one who worked in a factory for 50 years, during a large part of which I was responsible for labour relations and all negotiations with trade unions, I can testify to the wisdom and importance of all that Sir George has written. I should like to see hundreds of thousands of employers, workers and trade unionists read the book. If they did so, not only would many of them find greater satisfaction in their work, but the effect on productivity might well be startling.'
(*Spectator* 10.8.51)

If anything, the problems of which I wrote and the need for solutions along the lines I suggested have become only more urgent in the past 25 years.

As I look back on the record of all my efforts to promote good human relations in industry I think specially of all that my friendship with Stafford Cripps meant to me, and of the part which he played in the public life of our country. His health broke down in 1951, and when he finally died in Switzerland in 1952 I was asked by the Royal Society to write a special memoir for inclusion in their published records. This gave me an opportunity to write of his life and character, and also of the force of his example. I mentioned his conception of work as service to God with 'men working together as a great cooperating social unit for the development of human civilisation and the achievement of the Kingdom of God on earth', devoting themselves to their material tasks as part of a worthy human life, but not becoming obsessed with material values.

CHAPTER XI

A Variety of Tasks, 1951-1963

(i) The Oxford Regional Hospital Board

I HAVE TOLD THE story of my work in the first post-war years as a member of Government Committees chiefly concerned with industrial productivity and human relations in industry. At the same time my close and sympathetic relations with members of the post-war Labour Government led to my being asked to undertake two specific tasks which have become a significant part in my life's story. One of these tasks was the Chairmanship of the Oxford Regional Hospital Board.

In 1951 it was mentioned to Aneurin Bevan that I might be available to take on this post. After the retirement of the first Chairman Nye Bevan had in fact made an appointment, but when he heard that I was available he decided that he must inform his original nominee that the appointment had only been a provisional stop-gap one to be held for six months and at the end of this period I was to take over. (Nye Bevan had in fact during my years with him in the House of Commons always shown special friendship to me.)

I look back on the 12 years of my Chairmanship of the Oxford Regional Hospital Board as a specially rewarding period of my life. I had the supreme satisfaction of working in harmony with a band of comrades on tasks of great human interest and national importance. My dominating purpose was to make the hospital organisation in our Region a truly human one inspired by a spirit of service. The effective accomplishment of my purpose depended on the quality of the headquarters staff, the work of the Hospital Management Committees (of which there were 15 in the Oxford Region) and, most important of all, the spirit of the doctors and nursing staff working in the hospitals. It was also necessary to collaborate closely with the Local Authority Health Services and with the work of general practitioners distributed over the Regional Area which covered the whole of Oxfordshire, the greater part of Northamptonshire, Berkshire, Wiltshire and Gloucestershire.

In handling headquarters work I was fortunate in having an able and sympathetic Board, among whose members I must specially mention my Deputy Chairman, Colonel Krabbé of Reading, my old friend Sir Frederick Puckle, whom I had known in my Indian days as the Finance Member of his

Provincial Government, and, among the medical members, Sir John Stallworthy, whose lively mind and broad vision always added interest to our Board discussions. For the day-to-day work I had an able and devoted group of officials which for the greater part of my time consisted of Dr. J. A. Oddie as Senior Administrative Medical Officer, George Watts as Secretary, C. R. Poole as Treasurer and W. J. Jobson as Architect. In all my varied experiences I have never worked with a better group of staff officers and with all of them I have retained personal friendships throughout the remaining years of my life.

For handling the current business I followed the example of Stafford Cripps who, as Minister of Aircraft Production, had established a practice of holding daily meetings (which came to be called 'Morning Prayers') to be attended by heads of all departments so that every section of the Ministry should know what was happening on the whole front. I arranged weekly meetings of this kind with my chief staff officers and other members of the Headquarters Staff and these were of most significant practical value in helping to create effective collaboration and a common spirit of service.

Relations with the Government authority were also of importance. During the years of my service the Government authority for the Hospital Services was a separate organisation detached from the Ministry of Health. Accordingly it tended to be regarded rather as a backwater by Ministers and Civil Servants, and it is worth noting that during my 12 years as Chairman I had to deal with eight different Ministers. All of these, with one exception, saw their posts as a very low rung on the ladder of a ministerial career from which they wished to step up at the earliest possible opportunity. The one exception was Enoch Powell and he in his own special way made a considerable contribution to the general efficiency of the Headquarters organisation, though this would have been more valuable if he had ever been ready to listen to anybody else's ideas. It was customary for Chairmen of the Regional Hospital Boards to have periodical meetings with the Minister, at all of which I tended to take a lead in asking awkward questions. In general, however, as I look back at my record, I feel that we in the Oxford Region did in effect receive satisfactory support from the Ministry, largely owing to the influence of Sir George Godber who, as Chief Medical Officer, showed understanding and sympathy with all that I was trying to do.

While efficient performance of the Headquarter function was essential, the results in terms of service in the hospital depended on the quality of the Hospital Management Committees and I regarded the selection of good Chairmen of my 15 Hospital Management Committees as my most important responsibility. I was on the whole very fortunate in securing the services of first-class men and women and I can claim that broadly speaking the members of our Hospital Management Committees really cared for their hospitals. We resisted all demands for anything like party political representation and the membership of our Management Committees covered a wide social spread, with the Chairmanship ranging from the Duchess of

34. With the Minister of Health, Enoch Powell, at Nether Worton, May 1961

Marlborough at the Nuffield Orthopaedic Centre in Oxford to a railway guard at Aylesbury.

Our essential aim was to ensure efficiency in action inspired by a sense of common purpose. My Board Secretary and friend George Watts has written:

> 'All these memories, however, I see against a background where everyone connected with the Board—members, officers and staff—knew exactly where they were going and what was to be done to get there; knew what problems they were likely to meet on the way and

how they might best be surmounted; and did their level best to see that we got there. The record of those years speaks for itself.'

As to efficiency, I note that we in the Oxford Region took a lead in developing methods of operational research and work study, in which we were greatly helped by the ICI organisation. For promoting a spirit of common purpose we not only kept in close touch with the medical and nursing services in the hospitals but also with those working in supporting services such as almoners (now known as medical social workers), the physiotherapists and hospital chaplains. We held joint conferences with all of these which were valuable to us and, I believe, encouraging to them.

When, however, I look back over the whole record of my years with the Hospital Board the picture which stands out most vividly is of the two Services of Dedication which we organised at the University Church of St. Mary the Virgin in Oxford, at each of which I gave the Address. On both occasions every level of hospital service was represented, from chairmen to cleaners, about 950 being present on the first occasion and about 1,150 on the second. I still feel vividly my emotions as I gazed from the pulpit on the vast congregation with the nurses in all their different coloured uniforms. In retrospect I feel that my experience in working in the hospital organisation was of special value because the essential purpose of the work was personal service. In the whole range of human activity there is no line of work in which this matters more than in that covered by physicians, surgeons and nursing staff. Workers in this field can in a very special way earn the blessings of their fellow men and women. As examples three figures stand out in my memory, but there were many more.

The first is Dr. Ludwig Guttmann, who was in charge of the Paraplegic Section of Stoke Mandeville Hospital, which the Oxford Regional Board took over from the Ministry of Health during my term of office. During his years at Stoke Mandeville Guttmann gave new courage to face life to thousands of people, who, as a result of accidents or otherwise, had become partially paralysed. He taught them to become active and even skilled athletes in wheelchairs, and eventually established a second kind of Olympic Games for paraplegic players.

For my second example I take John Stallworthy, who in his work as a practising obstetrician and gynaecologist earned the blessings of countless women and their husbands.

The third image which stands out specially in my memory is that of Winifred Aldwinckle, who was Matron for many years of the Reading General Hospital. I see her as my ideal Hospital Matron, carrying the burden of a great administrative task, giving personal attention to all patients, and having to see some 400 deaths every year. Thousands who passed through Reading Hospital blessed her name.

Writing in 1978 as I look back on my own experiences I am concerned with the complete change in the administrative system for the hospitals

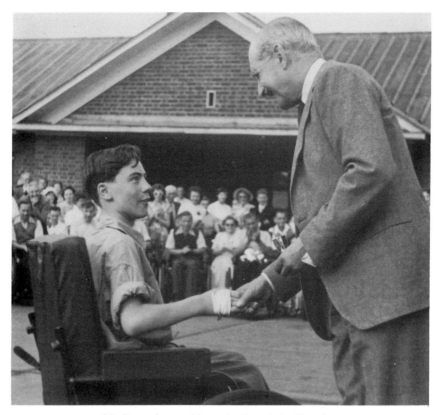

35. Presenting trophies at the Paraplegic Olympics

which has taken place in recent years. All the Regional Hospital Boards and Hospital Management Committees have been abolished and the whole administration is now directed by civil servants. As evidence of the increased expenditure involved in the present system I note the following changes. In 1963 our headquarters staff was accommodated in three small houses in Banbury Road, Oxford, and our total staff was 140. In 1975 accommodation was provided in an enormous range of buildings on Headington Hill and the total staff was 362. While the overhead administrative cost was thus enormously increased, the spirit of the front line service in the hospitals has apparently deteriorated. Many members of the medical services and the workers in the hospitals are still doing devoted work, but the general spirit of service seems to have changed, and we tend to hear more about the rights of the workers than the service given to patients.

I had indeed during my years as Chairman of the Hospital Board been concerned about the whole system for the direction and organisation of national services of this kind. I was at the time Chairman of a research organisation—The Acton Society Trust—financed by one of the Rowntree Trusts, and under my direction the Trust had prepared a series of pamphlets

154

tracing the growth of the National Hospital Service. I myself had written the final pamphlet in this series under the title of *Creative Leadership in a State Service*, as a preface to which I had quoted the following extract from Mill's *Essay on Liberty*:

> 'To determine the point at which evils, so formidable to human freedom and advancement, begin, or rather at which they begin to predominate over the benefits attending the collective application of the force of society . . . to secure as much of the advantages of centralised powers and intelligence as can be had without turning into Government channels too great a proportion of the general activity—is one of the most difficult and complicated questions in the art of Government . . . But I believe that the practical principle in which safety resides, the ideal to be kept in view, the standard by which to test all arrangements intended for overcoming the difficulty, may be conveyed by these words: the greatest dissemination of power consistent with efficiency; but the greatest possible centralisation of information and diffusion of it from the centre.'

In considering the problems which are facing our country today Mill's words seem to me to give inspiring guidance.

As I look back on the experience of my own long life I find myself obsessed with concern about what has been happening to our country in the last 15 years. There can be no more vivid illustration of this process of change than the story of the National Hospital Services. On the one hand the work has been de-humanised and made less efficient and more costly. On the other hand great numbers of public-spirited men and women such as those who served on my Board, on Management Committees and on House Committees of hospitals, have been deprived of the opportunity to give voluntary personal service.

(ii)   Malta and Dom Mintoff

The second important task in which I became involved at the request of the post-1945 Labour Government was concerned with Malta.

In November 1947 a Labour Government under Dr. Boffa had obtained a majority in the Maltese Parliament, and in 1949 they were pressing the British Government to make regular contributions to provide funds for current administration and future economic development. In response to this request the British Government decided to appoint a Financial and Economic Adviser to report on current and future prospects. Early in 1950 Mr. Creech Jones, as Colonial Secretary, asked me to undertake this task and agreed to provide me with the services of one of the Colonial Officials as a Secretary. I accepted on condition that my wife should accompany me.

On our arrival at Malta Airport the Governor and Prime Minister were there to welcome us and we got off to a good start. As I felt sure that I should have to preach economy to the Maltese Government I thought it wise to set an example by practising it myself. I had therefore arranged to book rooms at an inexpensive small hotel in a suburb instead of at the expensive first-class Hotel Phoenicia in the centre of the town. After a short time it became clear that this arrangement was inconvenient since members of the Maltese Government wanted to be able to keep in constant touch with me. As a result Dr. Boffa urged me to change my base and occupy a suite at the Hotel Phoenicia, which I agreed to do. This experience tended to create very good relations between us and I found no difficulty in getting the necessary information as to the relevant facts and reaching a conclusion. Dr. Boffa and the members of his Government were men of moderate left wing views and did not include Dom Mintoff. He had in fact resigned from the Government shortly before my arrival and I made no contact with him on the occasion of this first visit. My final decision was that it was justifiable for Malta to ask for financial assistance from the British Government and I recommended a sum of £1½ million to cover the next five years. In my discussions about this with the Maltese Ministers I emphasised that the British Government would be more likely to agree to give financial assistance if they were satisfied that the Maltese Government were raising sufficient income from local taxation, and I specially urged the inclusion of a direct tax of incomes. They found difficulty in agreeing to this, but on the morning of my departure the Finance Minister came to see me personally to tell me that he had reconsidered the position and decided to introduce proposals for income tax on the lines that I had recommended. In the event this had no result, since in the debate in the Maltese Parliament on the following day Dr. Boffa's Government was defeated and resigned from office. For the Finance Minister himself this marked the end of his political career since he decided to become a monk and retire into a Capucin Monastery.

On my return to London I completed a full report and asked for an early interview with Stafford Cripps as Chancellor of the Exchequer. On my way up the stairs to his room in the House of Commons I met Hugh Dalton coming down who on hearing my business, instead of showing any interest in what my conclusions about Malta might be, kept me for nearly a quarter of an hour explaining the Maltese position to me. When I was able finally to extricate myself from Dalton I went on to Stafford's room. From him I had a very different reception. He listened to my story which I was able to tell in about five minutes and gave an immediate reply that he would have no difficulty in recommending a grant of £1½ million spread over five years to be met from the Colonial Development Fund. A statement summarising my report and recommendations was in due course submitted by Herbert Morrison to the House of Commons and approved.

To complete the record of my first visit to Malta I must write something about the prevailing social atmosphere at that time. Although after the war internal self-government in Malta had been established under the dyarchal constitution of 1947, as recommended by Sir Harold MacMichael, the general social atmosphere in Malta was still essentially British. On the British side the dominating social figure was neither the Civil Governor nor the Commander-in-Chief Mediterranean but Lord Mountbatten, who had only a subordinate naval command. For my personal story the presence of Lord and Lady Mountbatten in Malta was of interest since it marked the beginning of my friendship with them. I was a frequent guest at their house at a time when Princess Elizabeth and Prince Philip were staying with them a few months before the birth of Princess Anne.

The years following my visit marked a period of great change in the Maltese political position. Before I had set off for the island Lord Alanbrooke had told me that its strategic significance was rapidly dwindling. It was now quickly becoming clear that the decline of the naval dockyard would severely increase the unemployment problem unless some alternative industry was rapidly developed. Dr. Boffa and some of the moderate Labour ministers whom I had seen had retired from public life and a vigorous left wing Labour Party had been established under the leadership of Dom Mintoff. Whenever his Party were in power he initiated active social and economic development policies and steadily increasing demands were being made for financial assistance from the British Government. I found myself asked occasionally to give advice to the Colonial Office and I was brought into regular consultation by Alan Lennox Boyd (Lord Boyd of Merton) when he became Colonial Secretary in 1954. During these years Dom Mintoff came to London for personal talks with the Colonial Secretary at some of which I was present and in this way I started a personal connection with him.

Dom Mintoff had undertaken vigorous plans for social and economic development in Malta for the fulfilment of which he was demanding financial assistance from the British Government on a scale to which it was found difficult to agree. This led him to take an entirely different line of approach by proposing that Malta should be integrated into the United Kingdom with representation in Parliament at Westminster. This new proposal led to many discussions in London and I have a vivid memory of one of these discussions for which an opportunity was found at a party given by Lennox Boyd in the garden of his house in Belgravia. My host asked me to go into his house for a private talk with him and I strongly urged him to give serious consideration to this new proposal from Mintoff. I said to him, 'It would be an intolerable position for the British Government to be shooting people in Cyprus because they want to get out of British control and to be in conflict with the Maltese because they want to come in.' In the event the British Government agreed to take Mintoff's proposal seriously and a Round Table Conference published its agreement that 'the people of Malta are entitled to a special road to political equality and that that road should be, if they so choose, representation at Westminster.' Lennox Boyd warmly accepted these recommendations but it was not long before Mintoff again raised the stakes and insisted on general financial support which would ensure full

157

36. With Dom Mintoff in Malta, 1956

'economic equivalence' for the people of Malta in the sense that their standard of living should be raised rapidly to the same level as that of the people of the United Kingdom.

I was not associated in any way with the proceedings of the Round Table Conference or with the financial discussions which followed on its breakdown. In August 1956, however, while my wife and I were staying for a night in Durham on our way up to our annual stalking holiday in Scotland, I was called to the telephone by Lennox Boyd who said to me 'George, will you go out to Malta this autumn to advise on British Government financial assistance.' This I agreed to do. I then found that after the breakdown of the political integration proposals considered by the Round Table Conference, discussions between the Colonial Office and Malta had been resumed about the scale of financial assistance to be given by HMG to Malta over the next two years, and the Colonial Secretary decided to appoint a special Commission, under Sir William Scott (former Financial Secretary in Northern Ireland) to undertake this task. Mintoff, however, had insisted that I should be brought in as a senior member of the Commission to which, subject to my concurrence, Lennox Boyd had agreed.

I went out with William Scott at the end of September and spent the month of October investigating the position. The conditions which I then found were strikingly different from those which I had seen on my first visit. Mintoff had created a new spirit of life in every field of national activity— education, hospital administration and economic development. I felt strongly that this must be encouraged not only by financial help but also by provision of sound practical advice in many fields. Obviously the scale of financial assistance which was needed and justified was very different from that which I had found on my first visit.

We produced an interim report at the end of October advocating a wide measure of support from the British Government and in our final report we recommended a substantial annual British grant-in-aid, the amount of which for 1957-58 we put at £5,877,000. In further negotiations Mintoff was able to extract another £200,000 from HMG.

It would be inappropriate for me in telling my personal story to give any detailed account of the way in which the political relations between Malta and United Kingdom developed over the next years. My broad impression is that power alternated between the intensely active Labour Government of Mintoff and the completely inactive government of Borg Olivier. I kept in constant personal touch with Mintoff and was also frequently consulted by Lennox Boyd as Colonial Secretary. In all these contacts my effort was to persuade Mintoff to be reasonable in his demands and to get Lennox Boyd and his successors to appreciate the value of Mintoff's creative qualities. Also until 1963 I had a formal position as a member of the Industrial Advisory Committee for Malta which had been set up largely on my recommendation in order to encourage the development of manufacturing undertakings on the island. This Committee during the active years of its work was under the Chairmanship first of Lord Hives and later of Sir George Dowty, a specially valuable member, who himself, on behalf of his own business undertaking, had set up a small manufacturing unit on the new industrial estate at Valetta.

The end of the Industrial Advisory Committee came in 1963 as a result of a decision taken by Borg Olivier. This marked the termination of my official connection with Malta; but in the years which followed I have continued to keep in personal contact with Mintoff. He has turned to me for advice on certain matters, especially in connection wih the development of medical services in Malta, and on my recommendation Dr. Oddie, my former Chief Medical Administrative Officer on the Oxford Regional Hospital Board, has paid frequent visits to the island. Just as I have been writing these words in 1978 I have at Mintoff's request received a visit from a medical officer in Malta bringing me good wishes and a case of Maltese wine.

Looking back over my connections with Malta I must record some general impressions. In the first place it was clear to me that Britain had an undoubted responsibility to give the island financial support. For strategic reasons an economy had been developed based on the British naval presence; the Imperial government could not honourably withdraw without helping to develop some alternative means of livelihood. Turning to individuals, Alan Lennox Boyd as a Colonial Secretary in a very special way took a personal human interest in the vast range of problems with which he had to deal during his years in office. He was always approachable, always ready to talk frankly, and indeed handled all his many problems in a spirit very different from that of his Colonial Office officials.

In Mintoff I see a man of quite exceptional intelligence and force of character. His father had worked in the gardens of the Admiralty House in Valetta. He had won a Rhodes Scholarship to Oxford and had married an English wife of a distinguished aristocratic family. On getting into office he had completely transformed the spirit of the Maltese Government and vitalised all sections of the Government Services. He had to fight against the bitter hostility of the Roman Catholic Archbishop and the whole Catholic community in Malta, as well as against the ordinary lethargy of the Maltese people. Power, however, has gone to his head and of all the statesmen with whom I have dealt I can think of no-one whose record more clearly demonstrates the truth of Lord Acton's dictum about the corrupting nature of high office. Yet in spite of this I myself look upon him as a friend for whom I feel personal affection.

(iii)   India Again

Three years after my first visit to give financial advice to Malta I was again involved in thinking about the economic development of India.

Early in 1953 I was asked by the Federation of the Indian Chambers of Commerce, the organisation representing private business enterprises in India, to pay a visit to the country to study current financial and economic conditions and give them advice on future policy. The President for that year of the Federation of Indian Chambers of Commerce was G. D. Birla who, in spite of his political opposition, had been a close personal friend of mine during the years when I was a member of the Viceroy's Council. I accepted the invitation on condition that my wife should accompany me.

We flew out to New Delhi and then had an extremely interesting tour around India including districts which I had been unable to visit during my years of office as Finance Member—in the south beyond Madras and in the north to the University of Pilani founded by G. D. Birla and to his own village home from which in his early days he had had to ride 40 miles on a camel before getting a railway connection with Calcutta.

I found my task an extremely difficult one. In the end, although I believe that I made a useful contribution to current thought, I am afraid that I failed to fulfil the expectations of my hosts. They clearly wanted me to complete a detailed appreciation of Indian economic and financial conditions and to make practical recommendations about the lines of Government financial and monetary policy. I on my side felt that I had no useful practical

37. With Moraji Desai, then Chief Minister of Bombay State, in India in 1953

recommendations to make in this field, but that on the other hand I had views on fundamental general issues affecting the future prosperity of India.

I concentrated on two main points. The first was that 'private enterprise in India was on trial for its life', by which I meant that private enterprise in India could only expect to survive and prosper if it were able to demonstrate that in all its operations it was taking full account of the public interest. My second point was that the basic foundation for the prosperity of India must be found in the development of agricultural production and in the life and work of the rural community, rather than in large scale industry and great urban concentrations. I made a special plea that the leaders in India's financial and manufacturing activities should take a personal interest in the development of village communities and that a special effort should be made to encourage the best qualified young people of India to look for

161

careers in the development of village communities rather than all flocking together into white collar jobs in the main urban concentrations.

My visit also gave me opportunities for personal talks with Jawaharlal Nehru who asked me on several occasions to lunch at his house. He would often come back very late after stormy meetings in the Indian Parliament and while we were waiting for him we were entertained by his daughter Indira who in those days seemed to me a very young girl. I certainly got no picture of the Indira Gandhi of recent years attempting to exercise a dictatorship which her father would never have contemplated.

Looking back over my memory of this visit to India two impressions stand out. The first is of the genuine welcome which I and my wife received in all parts of India. It was indeed a heartwarming experience that an Englishman could receive such a welcome from the people of an independent India. My second general impression was that Jawaharlal Nehru in practice had not the capacity to give the true leadership which he had envisaged in the days when he was a rebel against the British Government. I felt that he was being overwhelmed by his task and in particular that he was failing to support the development of the rural communities in India on which I myself felt that the true prosperity of the Indian people really depended.

(iv) Oxfordshire County Council

As the years went by I was increasingly involved in local affairs. In April 1952 I was asked to stand for election to the Oxfordshire County Council as representative of the Deddington Division in order to fill the vacancy created by the appointment of my friend Mrs. Lionel Hichens as an Alderman. I was duly elected and continued as a member of the County Council until its reorganisation in 1974, having had on several occasions to fight a contested election, always standing as an 'Independent'. I see my years as a Councillor as a rewarding experience which helped me to understand what is involved in securing for the community the efficient performance of the social services which are the responsibility of the Local Authorities and affect the daily lives of everyone.

My general impression of the County Council during my years of membership is that it consisted of a body of people who were sincerely interested in securing the best possible results regardless of political party or social distinctions. At the quarterly meetings of the County Council there were genuine discussions of important issues of policy based on the Reports of the various Committees. It can further be said that the Committees themselves did really good work in meeting current social needs and problems. The Education Committee, for example, conducted some most successful experiments which attracted the interest of other authorities, and achieved the transition from secondary modern and grammar schools to a comprehensive system without upsetting parents or teachers, or disturbing

38. Meeting of the Heythrop Hounds at Nether Worton

the education of the children. As a general result it can be said that members of the teaching profession invariably welcomed an opportunity to serve in Oxfordshire schools. The Health Committee was also active and progressive and ready to work in close co-operation with the Hospital Service, and with General Practitioners. As one practical result it can be noted that Oxfordshire took a lead in the establishment of local Health Centres. Outstanding work was also done by the Children's Care Committee. The work of this Committee raised a policy issue which I myself felt needed the special attention of the Council. In terms of cost per head of the population, the expenditure of the Oxfordshire Children's Care Committee was almost twice as high as the national average for all Counties. The point which I made in the Council discussions was not that this high cost was necessarily wrong, but that it put upon the Council a special duty to investigate the working of the service and to satisfy itself that the relatively high cost was justifiable.

My chief effort as a member of the Council was to devise procedure which would ensure effective financial control and it is fair to claim that, in the last years of the working of the County Council in its old form, really efficient procedure had been established. In my work for this purpose I got constant support from the County Clerk, Gerald Burkitt, who became a great personal friend, while the final success of my efforts depended entirely on the exceptional ability of Robert Weir as Chairman of the Budgetary Committee. (He eventually became Deputy Chairman, and then Chairman, of the County Council.)

163

The reorganisation of Local Government in 1974 completely changed the picture for Oxfordshire. What has been gained? Certainly there is, so far, no indication that the new Councils, County or District, are more efficient than their predecessors, whilst inevitably they are more costly to run and more remote from their ratepayers. My personal impression is that there was a feeling of identification in the old Oxfordshire County Council which produced a spirit of voluntary service, and avoided the pitfalls of corruption and self-interest to be found where power politics existed.

What concerns me is that service in the traditional sense has begun to fade away, and indeed that there is now the very real danger that membership of a local authority will become a profession and public service sacrificed to self-interest. Certainly now that fees are payable for attendance at Council and Committee meetings and for other duties, it is possible for anybody, regardless of qualifications, to gain enough to live on by becoming a 'full-time' member, whilst having no real contribution to make to the work of the local authority. Again, I can only record my sadness that in this field, as in others, we have moved so far away from the traditions of the last hundred years of service to the community freely given.

(v) Voluntary Service Overseas

In 1961 I entered a new field of interest. In response to a letter to *The Times* from Lord Amory which stated his need for help in the development of the VSO project, I called on him to offer my services. At that time the purpose of the project was to send out 18 year old school leavers as volunteers to help in work of various kinds (education, agricultural development, etc.) in countries of the so-called 'Third World'. The original inspiration for the project had come from the imaginative genius of Alec Dickson; but difficulties for its future development had arisen. Alec Dickson was an inspired individual and his method of working did not fit in with the orderly administration of a project for which businesslike organisation was necessary. Alec Dickson was in the habit of taking files to his own home and did not keep other workers informed about his movements. It was clear that if the project were to expand, as it showed signs of doing, an efficient organisation was essential. Just at this moment a new problem presented itself because Lord Amory had accepted appointment as High Commissioner to Canada and had to leave while the future was still unsettled.

I found myself forced into undertaking some responsibility for the future. After discussions with my old friend Robert Birley, who at the time was still Headmaster of Eton, we arranged a meeting of the leading personalities who had been interested in the project. There I put forward the proposal that a formal Council should be appointed and I appealed to Alan Lennox Boyd to undertake the Chairmanship of the Council. With some reluctance he responded to this appeal and all who were interested in the project owe him a great debt of gratitude for his services for the next two years. I myself agreed to accept the post of Hon. Treasurer, and it then became necessary to consider how the central office was to be operated. This presented us with a most difficult personal problem and I appealed for help to my friend Sir Paul Sinker who at that time was Director-General of the British Council. In response to this appeal he proposed that Duncan Mackintosh, who had been working for the British Council, should take over the business direction of VSO. I look back on this as one of the key factors in the eventual success of the whole project. His first task was to organise an adequate office and to find an efficient general manager. His choice of a man for this post (Douglas Whiting) was another notable success.

My own responsibility as Hon. Treasurer was a difficult one. The project had to rely entirely on voluntary charitable donations and in commenting on this I must record a special debt of gratitude to Christian Aid who for the next years provided the project with an annual contribution of over £50,000. Taking into account, however, the volume of applications from volunteers and of the demands for their services in 'Third World' countries, the full potential growth of the project could not be financed by private charitable donations alone.

At this stage the British Government was embarking on a policy of 'Foreign Aid' to 'Third World' countries and a small office had been established in Carlton House Terrace under Dennis Vosper as Minister. Duncan Mackintosh and I made an application to this office and in response to this received a first grant of £17,000. There were rapid developments after this and it is sufficient to record that at the end of two years VSO was receiving an annual grant of £500,000 from British funds under the heading of 'Foreign Aid'.

I cannot here give a full account of subsequent developments of the VSO project and am only concerned to give an impression of what it has meant in my own life. My first contacts with the whole project made me optimistic about the character of the rising generation of today. I was profoundly impressed by the quality and spirit of adventure shown by the 18 year old school leavers who were the main volunteers in the early days. Looking back to the conditions of my own youth I felt that this spirit of the young people of today justified some faith in the future of our country. I also felt that in starting this service Britain had given a lead to the world. The work of the USA Peace Corps and of similar services in other countries was stimulated by the British example. Beyond this, my connection with VSO has been of great value in my life as providing an opportunity for making a number of new friends. Among these I think specially of Derrick Amory (who, after his return from Canada in 1964, directed the whole project on continually expanding lines), of Alan Lennox Boyd and of Duncan Mackintosh. Among others who have taken a leading part there are many notable characters whose comradeship and friendship have meant much in

165

my life. Amongst these I have specially in mind Sir Paul Sinker, Launcelot Fleming (at that time Bishop of Norwich and later Dean of Windsor) and Field Marshal Sir Gerald Templar whom I saw as a man with all the distinctively valuable qualities of a first-class soldier.

CHAPTER XII

The Atlantic College

LOOKING BACK ON my whole long record I see my years of work for the Atlantic College as the most rewarding experience of what I can describe as my personal working life. It brought me into contact with a great human being, Kurt Hahn, and offered the chance to work as one of a band of comrades for a creative purpose. Above all it has had for me two special values. First, in my very old age it has given me a continued interest in life. Secondly, at a time of gloom in the world's conditions it has shone a bright gleam of hope for the future.

Towards the end of 1962, at the suggestion of my friend John Marsh of the British Institute of Management, I called to see Kurt Hahn at the Kipling Room in Brown's Hotel. Kurt described his hopes for the project. A College had been opened that September in the magnificent setting of St. Donat's Castle on the coast of South Wales. It was a residential Sixth Form College, its first fifty-six students drawn from twelve countries. He explained his basic ideas about the purposes of the College under three headings:

First, it was to be an international college with students drawn from a number of different countries in order to make education an instrument for creating understanding between the peoples of different countries. (Kurt had been immensely impressed by the value of the courses of instruction for NATO officers which had been held in Paris under the presidency of Air Marshal Sir Lawrance Darvall.)

Secondly, it was to be an all-sixth form college for students of the ages of 16-19, i.e. of students at a particularly impressionable age when idealism was strong and the pressures of a specialised university course and a career were not yet dominant.

Thirdly, the education provided should be a combination of high-grade academic instruction with activities requiring qualities of courage and resourcefulness and a sense of social responsibility and human sympathy. (I was always specially impressed with Kurt's emphasis on the need for compassion.)

Kurt further told me that £65,000 for the cost of St. Donat's Castle and estate had been provided by a Frenchman, M. Antonin Besse (who was convinced that a College of this kind could only be successfully started in Britain), and that substantial funds for the development of the College had been raised as a result of a well-attended inaugural dinner.

167

My own energies at the time of my first meeting with Kurt were fully committed (as Honorary Treasurer) to securing the success of VSO, and my general impression was that he was not expecting me to play an important part in this new educational project. I told him that I would be greatly interested to remain in touch with him and that I would make an initial financial contribution. He on his side told me that he had set up a Council to undertake the practical development of the project which would work with two Committees—an Executive Committee and a Finance Committee. He asked me to become a member of this Council and its two Committees, which I agreed to do.

During the next months I found my feelings about the project changing in two ways. On the one hand I came to see more clearly the value and significance of its purpose. On the other, I became increasingly concerned about the inadequacy of the funds which had already been raised and the magnitude of the effort required to create a structure of financial viability. I became convinced that the Council discussions were entirely unrealistic and I therefore started a practice of direct consultation with Admiral Hoare, the Headmaster, Robert Blackburn, the Director of Studies at the College, and Michael Schweitzer, Secretary to the Appeal and formerly Kurt Hahn's private secretary.

On the financial side a critical point was reached early in 1964. The Bankers for the project, Glyn Mills and Co., gave formal notice that they could not continue our overdraft facilities and they asked Sir Spencer Summers, Chairman of the Finance Committee, to meet them to discuss the position. He invited me to join him in this discussion. We made the point that there was in fact adequate security for the overdraft in the form of donations promised to the College in seven year covenants. The Bank's reply was that these seven year covenants provided no security because, if the project collapsed, the covenants would become ineffective. It then fell to me to find practical ways for dealing with this dilemma. I took two lines of action. In the first place I sought an interview with the Governor of the Bank of England, Lord Cromer. In my early days in the Sudan and in India I had had many meetings with Montagu Norman as Governor of the Bank of England and, basing myself on his interpretation of his role, I looked upon the Governor as having a general responsibility for the good name of the City. I told Lord Cromer that the good names not only of the City but of the country were involved because approaches for support of the Atlantic College had been made to different Governments through British Ambassadors. I asked Lord Cromer to make representations to Glyn Mills. He gave me a friendly and sympathetic hearing, but I do not know whether my approach to him had any effect on the position. What I can record is that my second line of action proved effective. This was to make personal approaches to those who had undertaken to support the project by donations in the form of seven year covenants to make interest-free advances to the College against the security of their own covenants. Nearly all our seven year covenanters agreed to do this, which meant an immediate substantial reduction in our overdraft. At the same time we got financial support in another way. The Secretary of the Municipal and General Workers' Union, Jack Cooper (later Lord Cooper), who had from the beginning been an active member of the Council and its Committees, agreed that his Union would make an interest-free loan of £50,000 to the College. This offer—although we did not need to make use of the loan facility at the time—gave us most valuable moral support and, as I shall record later in my narrative, support for the project from the Trades Union side has from the earliest days been an element of special significance and value.

All this led to a change in my own position. Kurt Hahn in effect said to me: 'George, we must accept the fact that you have taken on the general financial responsibility for the project. You cannot go on doing this from the sidelines.' It was agreed that a small Action Committee should be appointed under my Chairmanship. It was to prove a heavy and challenging responsibility.

There were two needs. First, to raise the capital to provide accommodation for enough students to make it possible to balance income and expenditure at an acceptable level of fees per student; secondly, to meet the operating deficits incurred during the period until adequate accommodation had been provided. In 1964 we had ninety-eight students at £500 per annum each. The operating costs were £1,189 per student, giving a total deficit for 1963/64 of £67,522. The situation was clearly a menacing one.

As I look back over the story of how the financial problem was solved I see it as a record of hard slogging appeal work producing a steady flow of substantial donations from Charitable Trusts, from the business world and from private individuals, interspersed by flashes of what I came to regard as miracles without which we could not have survived.

Two outstanding miracles in 1964 were the support secured from the British Government and the promise of a six-figure donation from the Dulverton Trust. First, our approach to the British Government. A valuable friend of the College in the early years was Robert Cecil, Head of the Cultural Relations Department of the Foreign Office. He had always taken the view that the Foreign Office ought to be directly interested in our project and had advised that it would be worthwhile to make an approach to the Foreign Secretary for a financial grant. A General Election was imminent and we felt it of vital importance that an approach should be made to the Conservative Government in its last days of office. Through his son-in-law, Lord Brabourne, a member of our Council, we asked Lord Mountbatten to write personal letters to R. A. Butler as Foreign Secretary and Reginald Maudling as Chancellor of the Exchequer. Lord Mountbatten readily agreed and wrote two letters, one addressed to 'Dear Rab', the other to 'Dear Reggie'. He concluded the second letter: 'Do not let this get into the hands of your Financial Secretary as he is sure to turn it down.' The financial support we asked for was a total grant of £100,000, to be paid in three annual instalments of £50,000, £30,000 and £20,000 for the purpose of covering operating deficits during those three years. This approach was successful and in due course led to a reception by Sir John Nicholls at the Foreign Office. It was left to me to expound our case. After this meeting the first instalment of £50,000 was duly paid.

In the following year, 1965, it became necessary to get approval for the second grant of £30,000. By that time the Labour Government was in power and Jim Callaghan was Chancellor of the Exchequer. It was obvious that there might be difficulties in getting a Labour Government to continue to implement an undertaking given by their political opponents. Once again I had to appeal for help to Lord Mountbatten. He readily agreed and again wrote a personal letter to the Chancellor. We were then asked to send a second deputation to the Foreign Office in which it again fell to me to explain the financial position of the College and make good the case that the contribution towards meeting our operating deficits in the next two years would be adequate. We were able to satisfy the Foreign Office on this point and the next two contributions were also paid.

I turn now to what I have noted above as the second of the 1964 miracles: the promise of major support from the Dulverton Trust which became possible through my friendship with my nearest neighbour in the country, David Wills. After full consideration the Trust decided to give to our project the largest contribution which they had ever made to a single cause. This in the end amounted to a total of £365,000. At the same time David Wills from his own personal Trust funds made extremely generous donations for which he insisted at the time on anonymity.

Further important contributions were received in 1964 from the Federal German Government and from the Drapers' Company, enabling among other things the building of a second dormitory block. The extension of dormitory accommodation was also made possible by a substantial personal donation from Sir James Whitaker and this has special significance for my story since friendship and collaboration with James Whitaker have been of outstanding value in this last chapter of my own life. Also, as the years have passed, he has become a most important worker for the practical success of the College.

Our progress during 1964 was immensely encouraging, but, looking to the future, I also felt it necessary to create a sense of interest and confidence in the project among British financial and industrial organisations. In this area I found that a great effort was necessary. Opinion in the City was worryingly sceptical. At this stage Kurt Hahn introduced me to Sir Siegmund Warburg, who gave a lead by securing major capital grants from Shell and Unilever. At the same time I myself, as a director of the Westminster Bank, was able to initiate approaches to the Big Five Banks (as they then were), and eventually secured an agreement for each of these to give the College a substantial donation in the form of seven year covenants. This support had an important influence on general opinion in the City.

The year 1966 included a fresh miracle which has proved to be of paramount importance for the success of the College. The Headmaster, Desmond Hoare, perpetrated a calculated indiscretion. In an interview with *The Observer* he stated that his aim was for the College to become a co-educational institution and that if anybody would give a donation of £40,000 he would at once start building a dormitory block for girls. This statement, which was taken up by other national newspapers, came as a shock to members of the Governing Body since the idea of a co-educational policy had never been formally discussed. It evoked infuriated hostility from one member, Sir John Masterman, who was totally opposed to the introduction of girls. It was clearly necessary to call an immediate meeting of the Governing Body, and I got to work at once to fix a date. While I was engaged on this, the Manager of the London Branch of an American Bank telephoned the College that a Mr. Maresi, an American citizen living in a villa on Lake Como, had instructed the Bank to pay £40,000 to the College as a response to Admiral Hoare's statement as reported in the William Hickey column of the *Daily Express*.

This stands out in my memory as the most dramatic incident in my whole story about the College. At the emergency meeting of the Governing Body the general view was that Mr. Maresi's money must be returned immediately, since, even if we eventually went co-educational, there must be a long delay before the money could be used. I strongly opposed this negative line of action and in the end I got the Governing Body to agree that Kurt Hahn should pay a personal visit to Mr. and Mrs. Maresi to have a frank discussion with them about the whole position. This proved to be a most successful move. Mr. and Mrs. Maresi were specially interested in education and were deeply impressed by a visit from the great educational leader. It was agreed that the donation of £40,000 should be retained by the College pending further development of its educational programme and that discussions with them should continue.

The next step was that two months later I and my wife paid them a personal visit. This we were able to arrange in August 1966 by motoring from a clinic in the south of Switzerland where I was receiving treatment for arthritis. This visit stands out in my memory as one of the great occasions of my life, for it meant the beginning of a personal friendship with Sonny and Phebe Maresi which has been of inspiring value to me during all of my last years. It also marked the beginning of a long term interest by Mr. and Mrs. Maresi in the Atlantic College which has led to their making it the main recipient of their charitable donations and providing financial support on a scale which has become a dominating factor in the progress of the College.

In the year 1967 the hard, slogging fund raising work still continued with substantial results, and the record of this year also included an event of major financial significance—the beginning of support on a large scale from the Bernard Sunley Foundation, totalling over the years more than a quarter of a million pounds. I have a specially vivid recollection of my

171

39. Laying the foundation stone of the Schuster Science Building. From left to right:
Desmond Hoare, Sir Lawrance Darvall, the author, Kurt Hahn, Lady Schuster

meeting with Bill Shapland, the Administrator of the Foundation, on his
first visit to St. Donat's. His personal friendship has meant a great deal to
me and his interest in the College has made him a most valuable member of
the Governing Body and its Finance and General Purposes Committee.

Looking back over my memories I can record that by 1967 I felt that we
had in effect gained control of the financial problem. We had converted an
annually worsening situation into a steadily improving one and could with
some justification feel that we were on the path towards ultimate financial
viability, based on a continuing and increasing flow of financial support
from many quarters. I realise now, however, that the justification for this
optimistic appreciation depended entirely on what had been happening at
the College itself. It had always been my own view that the long-term future
of the College would depend on gaining the support from government
bodies worldwide. The annual flow of scholarships, so essential to the conception of the College, had depended on the continuing readiness of local
authorities and national governments (as well as of private individuals,
public companies, trades unions and trust funds) to show faith in the
relevance of our educational experiment. My early responsibilities for the
College were dominated by financial considerations, but the success I have

described above would have been wholly impossible had not the College itself, its staff and students, carried so much conviction with all who travelled to see them.

I had from the earliest days of my connection with the project paid regular visits to the College. My outstanding impression was that, in contrast to the work of the General Council, the running of the College was being handled with efficiency, wide vision and confidence in the future. It was quite clear that Desmond Hoare was displaying the great powers of imagination, innovation and personal leadership which had marked him out for the most senior responsibilities on the engineering side of H.M. Navy. By 1967 the College had 141 students from 31 countries. Some 65 per cent were attending on scholarships awarded by National Committees operating within their own countries. Despite the gloomy prophecies of many experienced educationalists, and the difficulties faced by students who were taking their university entry examinations under new teachers and a new system, in a foreign language and away from home, the academic success of the College was such that over 90 per cent of leavers each year were gaining entry to highly competitive universities round the world. The College's name too for its Community Services stood high—many lives had already been saved by the seagoing and cliff rescue services which had been developed to a high pitch of effectiveness under Admiral Hoare's expert guidance; and the Royal National Lifeboat Institution was about to introduce into service on many of its stations the Atlantic Class inshore life boat which had been designed by Desmond Hoare and built and tested by the College students themselves in the rigorous conditions of the Bristol Channel.

After I had been given direct responsibility as Chairman of the Action Committee in 1964 it had fallen to me to consider formal administrative arrangements. An obvious need was to appoint a Governing Body for the College, the first meeting of which was held on 27th April 1965. I myself took on the Chairmanship and after a number of preliminary meetings, Sir James Whitaker and Sir Paul Sinker were elected as Deputy Chairmen. At this point I must record a special tribute to Sir Paul Sinker. I had got to know him well during my work for VSO when he was Chairman of the British Council and I had been greatly impressed by his efficiency. He was a man who never wasted a word and concentrated attention on matters of practical importance. His death in 1976 meant a great loss to the College and also personally to me. I must also record a special tribute to Sir Eric Berthoud since his work from the earliest days in securing scholarship support from European countries has been a factor of decisive importance in securing the success of the College.

Looking back over my memories I see other members of the Governing Body in its early days who deserve special mention. As the first of these I note Les Cannon, the Secretary of the Electrical Trades Union, who was a man of high intelligence and great personal courage. He took a deep interest in the College and provided many valuable contacts with leading figures in the industrial world. I look upon his premature death in 1970 from lung cancer as a great loss to us and, more than this, as a national tragedy. I must also refer specially to Launcelot Fleming, former Bishop of Norwich and Dean of Windsor, whose influence has had a profound effect on the whole spirit of the College. Among other members who made a distinctive contribution were Sir Robert Birley, my old friend from Charterhouse days, Robin Hankey (Lord Hankey) who gave valuable support to Sir Eric Berthoud's work in securing scholarship entries from overseas countries, Alec Peterson who played the leading part in the development of the International Baccalaureate, and Lola Hahn (Kurt's sister-in-law) who has given dedicated personal service to the project and has had a special value in keeping alive the memory of Kurt Hahn in discussions on the College following his death after a long period of illness and inactivity. (Eric Weiss and David Atterton who have come to play such important parts in the whole project became members of the Governing Body at later dates—Eric Weiss in 1968 and David Atterton in 1969.)

As Chairman of the Governing Body my key purpose was to bring this body and its members into close contact with the teaching staff and students of the College. My own experience on the Governing Body of Charterhouse had given me the impression that Governing Bodies tended to be rather remote authorities keeping in close touch only with the Headmaster. At the Atlantic College I started the practice of annual dinners providing opportunities for discusion between members of the Governing Body and of the teaching staff. Beyond this we began appointing an individual member of the Governing Body as 'godfather' (or 'godmother') to each House. I myself made an effort on all my visits to the College to find some opportunity for informal or formal discussions with groups of students. I have specially vivid memories of my meetings with these young people at which I attempted to convey some of the thoughts and considerations which had provided the motivation for my own actions during a long and eventful life.

Turning to the international significance of the project, it was intended from the outset that Atlantic College should be the first of a series of similar schools. The original Council which had been appointed as the body responsible for the supervision of the whole project had included a large number of representatives of other countries, and it had been a practice to hold an annual meeting of the Council at the College called the International Meeting, which was widely attended by the non-British members. This annual meeting had been held under the Chairmanship of Air Marshal Sir Lawrance Darvall. For a number of reasons it was clear to me that this practice was inadequate and that the time had come for the creation of an International Council under the Chairmanship of an outstanding personality of world-wide repute. After discussion with my colleagues at the end of 1967, I approached Lord Mountbatten. After careful consideration he told me that he would accept the position. He appointed David Wills and myself

40. In discussion with staff and students, 1973

as his two Vice-Presidents, but wanted to make two points clear—first, that he would only be interested in the international development of the project, and secondly, that he could only agree to serve for a limited period. 'You must recognise, George,' he said to me, 'that I am in my 68th year and that I cannot look forward to undertaking active work after I reach the age of 70.' On the latter point I told him that he could hardly expect me to take it seriously since I myself was already in my 87th year. As to this I can, as I write these words, record with appreciation that Lord Mountbatten continued to work actively as President for a further ten years and that on 1st January 1978 he was able to render great service to the whole UWC project by getting Prince Charles to take over the post of President.

Lord Mountbatten reorganised the constitution of the Council and gave the whole project a clear public image with the new title of United World Colleges. (This incidentally meant that the title of the College at St. Donat's, initially the first Atlantic College, was changed to 'The United World College of the Atlantic'.) I recognised that his vision for international development was right, but I felt that my own personal duty was to work for the full success of the Atlantic College and to build up a sure financial foundation for its work. My view was that the Atlantic College must be the pilot model for all Colleges and that if the Atlantic College failed there was little hope that any other Colleges could succeed.

As my purpose in this chapter is merely to tell my personal story I include no account of the steps taken for the wider international development of the whole UWC project, including the establishment of further Colleges in Singapore and on Vancouver Island. I confine myself to recording my appreciation of the debt which the whole project owes to Lord Mountbatten for his leadership in this field, in which he received valuable support from his second International Vice-President, my great friend David Wills.

Looking back over my own personal relationships with the students one special incident stands out in my memory. In 1971 it happened that the annual International Council meeting was held at the Atlantic College on April 23rd, which was two days before my own 90th birthday. As usual, on the evening after the Council meeting, a large dinner party was held attended by members of the Council and the teaching staff. As the dinner was drawing to its conclusion suddenly all the lights went out and we were left in complete darkness. I thought that this was simply a failure in the electricity supply; but then there were sounds from outside and a group of 90 students, each carrying a lighted candle, came two by two into the hall and the leaders came to the corner at which I was sitting. Then all joined in singing 'Happy Birthday to You', and when that was over the two leaders approached me, made short speeches and handed over a number of presents. I was completely overwhelmed but I have been told that I made a suitable reply.

In the years which followed there were many occasions for close personal contacts with the students, and so the work continued until, in October 1974, six months after my 93rd birthday, I felt that the time had come for me to retire from the Chairmanship of the Governing Body and make way for Dr. David Atterton. At the end of the dinner held to mark that occasion, the Governing Body and the teaching staff presented me with a portrait of myself to be hung in the Staff Common Room, and a crowd of students came into the hall to hear my speech of thanks and farewell. The theme of that speech was that it was an occasion for looking to the future rather than to the past, and that if any thanks were due it was for me to express my gratitude to the Governing Body, the teaching staff and the students for giving me one of the most rewarding periods of my whole life.

In the years since my formal retirement from the Chairmanship of the Governing Body I have been able to continue some active work for the College, particularly on the fund-raising side. But before concluding my personal story I must record my appreciation of the true significance of the College and of the part played by our two Headmasters—Rear Admiral Desmond Hoare and David Sutcliffe—in its realisation.

I start with the two Headmasters. I see them as men of very different character but each admirably fitted to fulfil the responsibilities involved during his own period of office. The credit for the first crucially important steps must be given to Desmond Hoare. My conviction is that without the strength of his determination and vision, his total dedication to the success of the ideals of the founders, and the support and enthusiasm of his dynamic wife Naomi, the full vitality of the project could not have been achieved. He was sent down to St. Donat's Castle with few instructions and

41. 90th Birthday Party at St. Donat's, 1971

had alone to carry the responsibility. His drive and faith inspired confidence in the teaching staff, students and the whole body of workers concerned with the project. He found opportunities also not only to ensure the successful development of the College, but to widen the range of support for the project in the outside world, especially in the countries of South East Asia. I see him as one of the rare individuals who have true creative power, combined with the vision to see the significance of any line of activity opening up before them.

I pass now to my appreciation of our second Headmaster, David Sutcliffe. He has had the wide vision and powers of leadership required for the development of a unique form of international education, for it was under him that in 1971 Atlantic College became the first school in the world wholly to abandon a national system of education in favour of an international curriculum—but the greater academic opportunity offered by the new system, and the enhanced record of university entry, have shown the wisdom of the move. The International Baccalaureate, until recently under the leadership of one of the earliest members of the Governing Body of the College, Alec Peterson, has made the most remarkable progress and in February 1978 was the subject of an International Conference at Lancaster House in London, chaired by the British Secretary of State for Education, Mrs. Shirley Williams, and attended by Ministers of Education or their representatives from 33 countries. I see David Sutcliffe's work for the adoption by the College of the International Baccalaureate as an outstanding

177

achievement, but it would be a mistake to judge him merely by his academic vision. He has also widened the range of the non-academic activities of the students and by the expansion of the Extra Mural Services of the College he has made it a centre of great significance and importance to the local community. His faith in Kurt Hahn's original ideas, his sympathetic understanding of the aspirations and problems of the students, and his own spirit of risk-taking adventure (as evidenced by his solo crossing of the Atlantic in a small sailing boat) have been an inspiration not only to the teaching staff and students, but to all who have played any part in the administration of the College.

I turn now to my picture of the Atlantic College today. Since Atlantic College opened with 56 boys in 1962, the project has grown so that currently there are 343 boys and girls aged between 16 and 19 from more than 60 countries. All are attending on scholarships. We have had students in significant numbers from every continent and from a wide variety of religious, social and political backgrounds. We also have 15 nationalities on the teaching staff, many members of which are seconded by their own governments. 'Services to the Community' are an integral part of the United World Colleges' philosophy for promoting international understanding and social responsibility in young people and, to date, over 100 lives have been saved along that stretch of the coast for which the College Rescue Services are responsible; many handicapped, elderly and infirm in the neighbouring community have been helped in one way or another by the students. Another facility offered by Atlantic College is for groups of disadvantaged youths to spend a period of time with the students at St. Donat's Castle and to experience a complete change of environment; some of these children have come from the probation services and the inner city areas of the U.K.

In my own vision of the significance of Atlantic College I take account not only of the present numbers of its students but also of a great body of ex-students who have already gone out into the world. At the end of the academic year in 1978 there were over 1800 ex-students of the Atlantic College. I ask myself a number of questions: What are these young people doing? Are they keeping in touch with each other in their national groups? Are they maintaining their interest in the whole United World College project? Are they helping to fulfil the purposes which inspired Kurt Hahn in starting the whole project? What was the essential significance of these purposes? Reflecting on all these questions I want to record some personal views. According to my interpretation Kurt Hahn's original purpose was not to provide a form of education which would produce a high proportion of world leaders—future Prime Ministers, et cetera. His essential idea, as I interpret it and with which I profoundly agree, was to create a body of young people whose purpose in life would be to work according to a standard of 'excellence' and with the full sense of their social responsibilities as members of an international community.

178

These last years have meant much to me. I have been greatly cheered by visits from a wide range of persons playing an active part in the life of the College, members of the Governing Body such as James Whitaker, Eric Berthoud and Lola Hahn, the Headmaster, members of the teaching staff, students and, above all, my dear friends Sonny and Phebe Maresi. I have made special efforts to keep in touch with ex-students and have been elected as an honorary member of the International Ex-Student Network.

As I reflect on the full significance of the Atlantic College and its value as a pilot model for Colleges in other countries, my feeling is one of deep thankfulness that I have been able to play a part in achieving the practical realisation of this project. My own concluding thought is that, in the world as it is today, this is one of the really hopeful and constructive movements that is going on, and it is especially significant that it was started in Britain as I do not believe it could possibly have got off the ground in any other country.

42. At St. Donat's in the 1970s

Index

Aba Island, 55
Acton, Lord, 160
Acton Society Trust, 154
Advisory Committee on East African
  Loans, 58
Agenda Club, 7
Alanbrooke, Lord, 13
Aldwinckle, Winifred, 153
Alexander, Geoffrey, 104
Alexander, Horace, 111
Allenby, Lord, 42, 43, 44, 45, 52
Alexandria, 43
Allied Suppliers, 127, 129, 136, 140, 142
Amanullah, 110
Amery, Leo, 61, 62, 63, 64, 81, 87, 131
American Metal Co., 8
Amin, Idi, 65
Amory, Lord, 164, 165
Anne, Princess, 157
Anglo-Danubian Syndicate, 35, 37
Archer, Sir Geoffrey, 54, 55, 56, 57
Archangel, 16, 17, 27, 29, 32
Archipoff, 32
Aristotle, 4, 5, 7
Asquith, Arthur, 49, 50
Asquith, H. H., 44, 50
Astor, John, 38
Atbara, 42, 60
Atlantic College, xi, xiii, xvi, xvii, 168-179
Atterton, David, 174, 176
Austria, 35

Bailey, Robin, 54
Baldwin, Stanley, 114, 120
Bank of New Zealand, 126, 140
Barclays Bank, 20
Barotseland, 78
Bartlett, Vernon, xii, 131
Beckley Lecture, 147
Beira, 69, 76
Belcher, John, 142
Benthall, Edward, 105
Benn, Wedgwood (1st Lord Stansgate), 109
Benningson, Count, 25
Bernard Sunley Foundation, 171, 172
Berthoud, Sir Eric, 173, 174, 179
Bernard, Sir Edgar, 58
Besse, Antonin, 167
Bevan, Aneurin, 150
Beveridge, William, 2, 136, 140
Bevin, Ernest, 127, 142, 143, 146
Birkenhead, Lord (F. E. Smith), 91, 100, 119
Birla, G. D., 96, 160
Birley, Sir Robert, 164, 174
Blackburn, Robert, 168
Blackett, Sir Basil, 59, 92, 122
Boffa, Dr., 155, 156, 157

Bolsheviks, xii, 16, 18, 19, 23, 24, 25, 26
Bombay, 92, 161
Boulton & Paul, 136
Brabourne, Lord, 169
Brest Litovsk, 16
Bright, John, 2
British Council, 165
Brown, Haig, 2
Brown, Wilfred (Lord), 143
Burkitt, Gerald, xvi, 163

Cairo, 43, 44, 50, 57
Callaghan, James, 170
Cameron, Sir Donald, 73, 74, 75, 76
Campbell Case, 43
Cannon, Leslie, 173, 174
Cape Town, 80, 81
Cecil, Robert, 169
Chamberlain, Austen, 44
Chamberlain, Neville, 129, 130, 131, 132,
  134, 135
Chancellor, Sir John, 79
Charles, Prince, 175
Charterhouse, 2, 3, 4, 142, 174
Chatham House, 129, 137
Chelsea, 10
Chetty, Shanmukam, 120
Chetwode, Sir Philip, 13, 125
Christian Aid, 165
Chiang Kai-shek, 122
Churchill, Winston, 12, 13, 16, 22, 87,
  131, 132, 134, 135
Citrine, Walter (Lord), 146
Clarke, Peter, 60
Colonial Development Act (1929), 85
Colonial Development Fund, 156
Commercial Union, 126
Congo, 68, 69
Corning Glass Co., 147
Coryndon, Sir Robert, 71
Continuation Schools, 35, 138
Cooper, D'Arcy, 127, 129
Conservative Party, 10, 43, 138, 169
Coole Park, 5
Corsica, 10
Cooper, Jack (Lord), 169
Cotton Industry Working Party, 140-142
Committee on Industrial Productivity,
  xii, 143-147
Cripps, Alfred (Lord Parmoor), 5
Cripps, Seddon, 5
Cripps, Fred, 5
Cripps, Stafford, xii, 5, 136, 140, 141,
  142, 143, 146, 149, 151, 156
Creech Jones, Sir Arthur, 155
Cromer, 1st Lord, 40, 52

180

Cromer, 3rd Lord, 168
Cunningham, George, 104
Currie, Sir James, 38, 49
Cumberland, North, 10, 11
Cyprus, 157
Czechoslovakia, 36, 130

Dar-es-Salaam, 68, 75, 76
Darvall, Sir Lawrance, 167, 172, 174
Dalton, Hugh, 156
Daily Express, 171
Dawson, Geoffrey, 107
Deddington, 162
Desai, Moraji, 161
Delhi, 92-93
Delamere, Lord, 61, 69, 72
Dickson, Alec, 164
Dombashawa, 79
Dowty, Sir George, 159
Drapers' Company, 170
Dulverton Trust, 169, 170

Eckstein, Sir Frederick, 49, 50
Ede, Chuter, 138
Egypt, 39-46
Elizabeth R., 157
Emerson, Sir Herbert, 110, 116
Empire Cotton Growing Corporation, 38, 49, 77, 86
Empire Parliamentary Association, 42
English, Scottish and Australian Bank, 126
Entebbe, 63, 68, 75
Epworth Press, 147
Ermeloff, 19, 20

Federation of Indian Chambers of Commerce, 160
Federal German Government, 170
Finlayson, Gen. Gordon, 135
Finns, 16, 27, 29
Fisher, Archbishop Geoffrey, 142
Fisher, H. A. L., 35, 138
Fisher, Sir Warren, 82
Fleming, Bishop Launcelot, xi, xvi, 166, 174
Fleming, Val, 12
Frankfurt, 1
Frazer, Sir Drummond Drummond, 37
Fuad, King of Egypt, 50

Gaitskell, Sir Arthur, 47
Gandhi, Indira, 162
Gandhi, M. K., xii, 92, 102, 104, 105, 109, 110, 111, 116, 117
Garran, Sir Robert, 91, 125
Gezira Irrigation Project, 40, 44, 47, 48, 49, 50, 51, 54, 68
Glacier Metal Co., 143-144
Gladstone, 2
Godber, Sir George, 151
Gordon, Gen., 39
Governing Bodies Association, 142
Gowers, Sir William, 65, 75
Greenwood, Arthur, 37
Gregory, Robert, 5
Gregory, Lady, 5

Grigg, Sir Edward (later Lord Altringham) 61, 63, 66, 70, 71
Gujerat, 105
Guttman, Dr. Ludwig, 153

Hadow, W. H., 4, 5
Hahn, Kurt, xii, 167, 168, 169, 170, 171, 172, 174, 178
Hahn, Lola, 174, 179
Haig, Harry, 105, 106
Hailey, Sir Malcolm, 109, 114, 115, 116
Haining, General, 135
Halifax, Lord (see Irwin)
Hammond, Brig.-Gen., 85
Hankey, Lord Robin, 174
Hann, Maurice, 127, 128
Harrow, 2
Harvey, C. O., 104
Henderson, Neville, 44
Henderson, Arthur, 109
Hertzog, J. B. M., 80
Hewins, John, 60
Heythrop & S. Oxfordshire Hounds, 5, 37, 163
Hichens, Mrs. Lionel, 162
Hilton Young Commission, xii, 61-82, 83, 85, 87
Hilton Young, Sir Edward (later Lord Kennet) 62, 64, 65, 69, 70, 71, 74, 75, 76, 80, 81, 82
Himsworth, Sir Harold, 145
Hirzel, Sir Arthur, 100
Hitler, Adolf, 36, 126, 131
Hives, Lord, 159
Hoare, Rear Admiral D. J., 168, 171, 172, 173, 176, 177
Hoare, Naomi, 176
Hoare, Sir Samuel, 114, 117, 122
Hogg, Quintin (Lord Hailsham), 138
Hope Bros., 37
Horthy, Admiral, 36
Huddleston, General, 41, 44
Human Factors Panel (see Committee for Industrial Productivity)
Hungary, 36
Hutchinson, Tommy, 13
Huth, Frederick & Co., 36, 37
Hydari, Sir Akbar, 105, 106
Hyderabad, Nizam of, 104

ICI, 136, 153
Imperial Tobacco Company, 77, 86
India, 82, 85, 88, 90-125, 126, 135, 136, 137, 160-162, 168
Indian National Congress, 90, 92, 120
International Baccalaureate, 174, 177
Ireland, 5
Ironside, General, 16
Irwin, Lord (later Lord Halifax), 93, 94, 99, 103, 104, 106, 109, 110, 117, 119, 133

Jackson, General Sir Henry, 30, 34, 135
Jaques, Dr. Elliot, 144
Jewkes, Professor John, 141
Jinnah, M. A., 97
Jobson, W. J., 151

Johnston, Tom, 42
Joseph, H. W. P., 4

Kabaka of Uganda, 65
Karelian Regiment, 27, 28, 29
Kassala Province, 51, 54, 68
Kem, 17, 26, 27
Kenya, 61, 63, 67, 68, 69-73, 76, 77, 81, 85, 86
Kerr, Philip (Lord Lothian), 108
Keynes, J. M., xii, 125, 133
Khartoum, 39, 43, 45, 50, 54, 55, 62, 65, 68, 93
Kikuyu, 70-72
Kindersley, Sir Robert (Lord), 38, 127
Kitchener, Lord, 39
Kolchak, Admiral, 26
Kostandi, Colonel, 19, 21
Krugliakoff, Colonel, 25, 26
Kuhn, Bela, 36

Labour Party, xii, xiii, 32, 35, 38, 41, 43, 109, 138, 139, 145, 146, 147, 150, 170
Lang, Archbishop Cosmo, 142
Lansbury, George, 42
Lawrence, Geoffrey (1st Lord Oaksey), 5
League of Nations, 37
Lehtimaki, General, 23
Lennox Boyd, Alan (Lord), 157, 158, 159, 160, 164, 165
Lenin, V. I., 16, 25
Lewin, Ernest, 13, 15, 16, 18, 19, 22, 23, 34
Liberal Independents, 138
Liberal National Party, 129, 130, 139
Liberal Party, 1, 10
Lincoln's Inn, 7
Lindsay, Sir Ronald, 129
Lugard, Sir Frederick (Lord), 62, 76
Livingstone, Sir Richard, 4, 5
Livingstone, Northern Rhodesia, 78
Liwonde, 78
Lloyd, Sir George (Lord), 52, 57
Local Defence Volunteers (Home Guard), 135
London, World Monetary and Economic Conference, 121
Loos, Battle of, 12
Lowther, Christopher, 10

Macaulay, T. B., 90
MacDonald, Ramsay, 41, 42, 43, 44, 106, 107, 108, 109, 114
MacIntyre, Alexander, 49
Mackintosh, Duncan, 165
MacMichael, Sir Harold, 58, 156
Macmillan, Harold, xv, 131, 134
McWatters, Sir George, 112
Manchester Guardian, 149
Manchester University, 1
Maffey, Sir John, 54, 62
Mahdi, Said Abderahman, 55
Malaviya, 97
Mallen, J. J., 37, 128
Malta, 155-160
Mant, Sir Reginald, 62, 65, 69, 75, 81, 82
Maresi, Sonny and Phebe, 171, 179
Marlborough, Duchess of, 151

Marsh, John, 167
Marquis, Sir Fred. (Lord Woolton), 128, 133, 145-146
Masaryk, 36
Maselga, 31
Mason, Philip, 109, 110
Masterman, Sir John, 171
Maud, John, 117
Maudling, Reginald, 169
Maynard, Gen. C., 16, 18, 19, 20, 22, 27, 30
Maxwell, Sir James, 78
Meerut Conspiracy Case, 96, 97
Medical Research Council, 144, 145
Merton, Henry, R. & Co., 8, 10, 11
Mikardo, Ian, 147
Mills, Glyn (Bankers), 168
Mill, J. S., 155
Milner, Lord, 61
Mintoff, Dom, xii, 155-160
Mitchell, Philip, 73, 74
Mirghani, Sidi el, 55
Moberly, Walter, 5
Montagu Declaration, 90
Morrison, Herbert, 134, 143, 145, 146
Mountbatten, Lord, 157, 170, 174-176
Multiple Shops Federation, 142
Munich Settlement (1938), 129
Municipal & General Workers Union, 169
Murmansk, 15, 16, 17, 18, 22, 24, 26, 27, 30, 33, 34, 35

Nairobi, 61, 68, 69, 70, 71, 72
Nansen, Fridtjof, 37
Nature, 149
Nehru, Indira (later Mrs. Gandhi), 162
Nehru, Jawaharlal, xii, 95, 104, 117, 136, 138, 162
Nehru, Motilal, xii, 95, 96, 100, 163
Nether Worton, xi, xvii, 15, 152, 163, 180
Newbold, Sir Douglas, 57
New College, Oxford, 3, 4, 5, 117, 122
New Statesman, 24
Newson-Smith Committee, 142, 143
Nicholls, Sir John, 170
Niemeyer, Sir Otto, 101
Nigeria, 67, 75
Nile, River, 39, 44, 47, 50, 51, 54, 55, 62, 68, 76
Noel-Baker, Philip, 37
Norman, Montagu, 58, 168
N.W. Frontier of India, 102-103
Nubians, 53
Nyasaland, 60, 61, 68, 77, 78, 81, 85, 86, 87, 88
Nyeri, 70, 71

Oaksey, see Lawrence, Geoffrey
Observer, 171
Oddie, Dr. J. A., xvi, 151, 159
Oldham, J. H., 62, 65, 69, 75, 76, 77, 81, 82
Olivier, Borg, 159
Onega, Lake, 17, 21, 25, 30, 32
Ormsby-Gore Commission, 83
Ottawa (Imperial Economic Conference), 119-121
Oxford, xv, 3-6, 8, 137

Oxford Regional Hospital Board, xiii, xvi, 150-155, 159
Oxfordshire County Council, xvi, 162-164
Oxfordshire Yeomanry, xiii, 11, 12, 13

Parker, Gwendolen (see Schuster, Gwendolen)
Parker, Hubert (2nd Lord Parker of Waddington), 9, 10
Parker, (1st Lord Parker of Waddington) xi, 7, 8, 9, 10
Patel, Vithalbhai, 96, 97
Peel, Lord, 95, 107, 108
Peshawar, 102, 103
Perham, Dame Margery, 53
Peterhof, 117, 137
Peterson, Alec, 174, 177
Petrograd, 16, 17, 21, 26
Philip, Prince, 157
Pilani, University of, 160
Plender, Sir William (later Lord), 38
Pole, Sir Felix, 47
Port Sudan, 42, 50
Poole, C. R., xvi, 151
Powell, Enoch, 151, 152
Public Schools Appointments Bureau, 142
Puckle, Sir Frederick, 150

Rainy, Sir George, 102
Rau, Shaukar, 93
Rashdall, Hastings, 4
Rawlinson, General, 30, 31
Reading, Lord, 108
Reserve Bank of India, 122-124
Rejaf, 60
Rhodesia, Northern, 61, 77, 78, 79, 86
Rhodesia, Southern, 61, 77, 79, 80
Roosevelt, President Franklin, 129
Rothschilds, 36
Round Table, 26
Rowntree, Seebohm, 38, 149
Rowntree Trusts, 154
Royal Empire Society, 129
Royal Society, 149
Royal National Lifeboat Institution, 173
Russell, A. E., 5
Ryland, Peter, 143

St. Donat's Castle, xiii, 167, 172
Salter, Sir Arthur, 139
Sandys, Duncan, 131
Sankey, Lord, 106
Santayana, G., 52
Sapru, Sir Tej Bahadur, 95, 107
Sastri, V. S. S., 108
Schuster, Alfred, 5, 9, 12
Schuster, Arthur, 1
Schuster, Ernest, 1, 3, 9
Schuster, Felix, 1
Schuster, Gwendolen, xi, 8, 9, 10, 15, 59, 116, 132, 155, 158, 160, 171, 174, 180
Schweitzer, Michael, 168
Scott, Francis, 72
Scott, Sir William, 158, 159
Sennar Dam, 51
Shackleton, Sir Ernest, 18, 30

Shapland, Bill, 172
Shell Co., 170
Shire River, 78
Short Bros., 136
Shoucair Pasha, 45
Simla, 94, 103, 113, 117
Simon, Sir John, 10, 97
Simon Commission, 93, 106, 107
Simonds, Gavin, 91
Sinclair, Sir Archibald, 138
Singapore, 176
Sinker, Sir Paul, 165, 166, 173
Skobeltsin, General, 31
Slade, Miss, 111
Smuts, J. C., 81
Smith, Lees, 109
Soong, T.V., 122
Soroka, 17, 25
South Africa, 81
Spectator, 149
Stack, Sir Lee, 42, 43, 44, 46, 54
Stallworthy, Sir John, 150, 151, 153
Star of India, 123
Sterry, Sir Wasey, 45, 57
Stoke House, Stoke Poges, 2
Stoke Mandeville Hospital, 153
Strakosch, Henry, 101, 120, 121
Streat, Raymond, 141
Sudan, 39-60, 62, 67, 70, 71, 73, 77, 79, 86, 93, 124, 126
Sudan Plantation Syndicate, 49, 50, 54, 60
Sudan Political Service, xiii, 50, 52, 55, 57
Sutcliffe, David, xvi, 176-177
Switzerland, 2

Tanganyika, 61, 67, 68, 73, 75, 77, 78, 81, 85, 86
Tanner, Jock, 144
Tavistock Institute, 144
Templar, Sir Gerald, 13, 166
Temple, Archbishop William, xii, 142
Tennyson, Charles, 143
Thakurdas, Sir Purshotamdas, 92
The Times, 125, 143, 164
Thomas, J. H., 43, 109
Thorneycroft, Peter (Lord), 138
Tibbets, Cliff, 130
Tizard, Sir Henry, 143, 145
Toynbee Hall, 128
Trade Facilities Act (1922), 38, 40, 58
Trieste, 43
Trotsky, L., 25
Tyrell, Sir William, 42

Uganda, 54, 61, 62, 65, 66, 67, 69, 70, 71, 76, 81, 85, 86
Unilever, 127, 129, 170
United World Colleges, xii, xiii, 175

Villiers, Arthur, 8, 11, 13, 97
Voluntary Service Overseas, xii, 89, 164, 168
Vosper, Dennis, 165

Wad Medani, 60
WAFD, 40
Wagg, Arthur, 8

Index

Walsall, 129, 130, 133, 138
Warburg, Sir Siegmund, 170
Watts, George, xvi, 151, 152
Weber, Sir Hermann, 1
Weir, Robert, 163
Weiss, Eric, 174
Welles, Sumner, 133
Westminster Bank, 126, 140, 170
Whitaker, Sir James, 170, 173, 179
White Sea, 16, 17, 26
Whiting, Douglas, 165
Williams, Shirley, 177
Williamson, 144
Wilson, Sir Horace, 130
Willingdon, Lord, 93, 109, 114, 117, 118,
    119

Wills, David, 170, 174
Wint, Guy, 136

Yeats, W. B., 5
Young Conservative Group, 138
Young Kikuyu Associations, 71
Ypres (1914), 12

Zaghlul, S., 40, 42, 43, 46
Zambesi River, 59, 60, 68
Zambesi Bridge, 77, 83, 85-88
Zanzibar, 68, 73
Zusya, Rabbi, xv

43. Diamond Wedding at Nether Worton